GANGSTER FILMS

virgin film

Jim Smith

First published in Great Britain in 2004
by Virgin Books Ltd
Thames Wharf Studios
Rainville Road
London
W6 9HA

A catalogue record for this book is available from the British Library.

ISBN 0 7535 0838 9

Typeset by TW Typesetting, Plymouth, Devon
Printed and bound in Great Britain by Mackays of Chatham PLC

Dedicated to my grandparents

G G Smith and O A Smith (née Rawlins)

and the memories of

M W Lea and W E Lea (née Dockerill)

'More debt than words themselves can show'

Contents

Acknowledgements

Kirstie Addis (my editor, for seemingly infinite patience this time out), Mark Clapham, James Clive Matthews, Stephen Lavington, Kirk O'Connor, Matt Symonds and Harris Watson (useful discussion, arguments and complaints) with especial thanks to Jason Douglas for new perspectives, new material and uncanny recall and Jim Sangster and Eddie Robson – for putting up with, and perhaps acquiescing to, the Henry Hill thing. Also Mom and Dad (again, and always), my sister Louisa, Sarah McAllister, Dr Henry Potts and the staff at the British Library, the University of London Libraries and the BFI Library. This latter place, a fine institution, seems to be continually under siege, and deserves all the support it can get.

Introduction

'gangster'
(noun) a member of an organised gang of criminals

With declared subject matter that is as vast and varied (and that has such nonspecific and ill-defined boundaries) as the one I'm tackling in the book that you've got in your hands, it is obviously necessary to establish a few precepts and ground rules before we even begin. The list of pictures that comprises this history was not handed to me. I chose it myself. That said, I didn't choose it arbitrarily, but around a hundred thousand words on a topic such as this is always going to be *a* history rather than *the* history, an angle rather than exhaustive.

This is, at least partially, because what could be loosely termed the 'gangster film' (and we'll get round to debating that terminology a bit later) has been with us virtually as long as the medium itself. This means that we're dealing with something that has been a key component of cinematic culture for very nearly a century. Now, that's a long time, and it's also a lot of movies. In fact, tap 'gangster' into the keyword section of www.imdb.com (the Internet Movie Database) and see the 700-plus suggested titles you get. I'm sure you'll disagree with half a dozen suggestions on the first page (I did) but it's an indication of the significance of the genre to moviemaking, and its grasp on the filmgoing public's perception of their own personal celluloid world.

When trying to decide what a 'gangster film' is, it's perhaps easier to start with something that you're confident it isn't, and then work backwards. The problem with this is that you can decide that almost anything is, if you see it in the right way. The number of people who have suggested to me that Clint Eastwood's Harry Callahan (*Dirty Harry* (Don Siegel, 1971)) or Denzel Washington's Alonzo Harris (*Training Day* (Antoine Fuqua, 2002)) is merely 'a gangster

1

with a badge' is vast. I've also had to consider the compelling notion of 'Nazis as organised criminals'. (Is *The Sound of Music*, on some level, thus a gangster movie? Answer: Perhaps yes.) And I've needed to assess whether a crew brought together to perform a heist – as in, say, either version of *Ocean's Eleven* – counts as a 'gang' of 'gangsters' (answer: probably not, although it depends on their backing and personalities). And that's even before we get on to the notion of the sublimated gangster movie (where characters behave like gangbangers, but are on the right side of the law – such as in *G Men*, produced by Warner Bros and starring Jimmy Cagney, directed in 1935 by William Keighley – of which more later).

So – to pull an instant, instinctive definition out of a hat – the gangster movie is concerned with 'the filmic portrayal of organised, violent crime and those who perpetrate it'. If we're going to try to trace a path through the gangster films of the first hundred years of cinema we're going to have to be selective in order to get that 700-plus down to 25 or so key 'texts' or examples.

In deference to this, I'd like to point out that, unlike many books in this series (including two of my own previous three), this one isn't designed to be read piecemeal, skipping from chapter to chapter, checking out favourite movies first and leaving disliked or unseen movies forever unread. I'm doing this in order (well, mostly in order) and so I think you should too; and despite what I said earlier about quality, every picture that has a chapter devoted to it in this book is absolutely worth your time.

So, my next decision is this. The book is restricted to motion pictures made primarily in English, which pretty much means we're restricted to the cinema of the United Kingdom and, primarily, the United States; and, while we're going to hop from one side of the Atlantic ocean to the other often enough, it's going to be far less frequent than you might suspect.

This limitation is not intended to denigrate the portrayals of gangsters in the cinemas of other countries. It is simply to allow us to keep our task down to something resembling a manageable size, the genre of 'heroic bloodshed' alone demands tens of thousands of words for the most shallow discussion, while much of the work of the Japanese director Takeshi Kitano (for example) remains worthy of enormous praise. People like Kitano will become relevant to the ongoing narrative of this book only when they break through into mainstream US culture by starring in, or making, a Hollywood picture (in Kitano's case, *Brother* (2000), an excellent picture we'll come to in due course).

It is also worth bearing in mind that, historically, in both Britain and (even more so) the United States, the enjoyment and discussion of motion pictures not primarily in the English language remains, sadly, a fringe activity, with one or two breakthrough productions in every decade gaining as much widespread recognition from the public as the most ordinary of Hollywood product.

My third decision is to devote time only to movies where the 'gangster' is the major character, the hero or antihero of the piece. There are, for want of a better term, many 'crime dramas' that touch on organised crime, but where the focus of the film is elsewhere. (To pick a particularly extreme example of such a movie, Tim Burton's *Batman* (1989) features several characters who are involved in organised crime, including a bravura Jack Palance, but the real focus of the movie is Michael Keaton as the lunatic orphaned guy in the cape and cowl.)

The 1930s is generally recognised as a 'Golden Age' for gangster pictures, titles such as *Little Caesar* (Mervyn Le Roy, 1931) *Scarface* (Howard Hawks, 1932) and *Angels With Dirty Faces* (Michael Curtiz, 1938) resonating with the general moviegoing public seven decades later. The reasons for the proliferation and popularity of gangster movies in America in that decade are complex, and have been much discussed. Essentially, though, they can be boiled down to a combination of a few needs on the part of the audience of cinemagoers. Depression-era poverty and deprivation meant audiences badly needed a vehicle for cinematic escape. This combined with a need for on-screen glamour and a desire to hit back at a society that many felt was failing them. An additional factor is the fudged moral landscape created by the further inequalities caused by the hypocrisy of the unenforceable 18th Amendment (Prohibition) and the criminal consequences of that. They're part wish-fulfilment fantasy, part hymn of outrage, part social melodrama, part aspirational tract, part horror movie and part Robin Hood-style search for a foundation myth for the United States' twentieth century. This combination of circumstances is what produced so many mini-classics in such a short time, although other contributions can be factored in, too. For one, the fact that Warner Bros gangster movies of the time were generally put together in a pacier way than other films of the period certainly helped. In addition, the streamlined, *über*-efficient methods of the Studio System – then in full swing and reliant, as it was, on long-term contracts – were certainly responsible for the sheer wealth of relevant product (how else would the same studio get *Little Caesar* and *The Public Enemy* out in the same quarter, after all?).

The thirties gangster movie is, therefore, where all the fascinations of what we'd consider to be a 'gangster film' come together, but, as I said, the genre does have a prehistory too. More than one academic study has cited *Little Caesar* as the 'first' gangster film, but contemporary reviews of the film see it as part of a trend already firmly in place. It's perhaps more accurate to say that it's the beginning of a cycle, or series, of such pictures across the 1930s, and that it contains – for perhaps the first time – enough of the themes, elements and iconography of what most people would recognise as a 'gangster film' to be fairly labelled one in the sense that we now understand it. It is, in a way, our own 'Year One'.

There had been films that featured gangsters before, of course, but none of them could be said to be overtly part of the same genre as, say, *The Godfather* is. They fit more in the 'connected' category I put Burton's *Batman* into above, in that they feature gangsters but are not portrayals of them. Examples of movies that contain gangsters, or portrayals of gang members and organised crime, would be pictures such as the silent Buster Keaton comedy *The High Sign* (Edward F Cline/Buster Keaton, 1921), which features the hapless hero working in a carnival controlled by the mob.

Perhaps the earliest extant American film to portray organised gang violence was made by D W Griffith, legendary director of *The Birth of a Nation* (1915) and the first technical genius of American film. His one-reeler, *The Musketeers of Pig Alley*, made as long ago as 1913 told the simple story of a New Yorker who is robbed while carrying the money he has gained by selling his beloved violin in order to feed his wife and ailing grandmother. Climaxing with a shootout between the two rival gangs, Griffith's film is technically superb but is clearly of only limited interest in relation to our topic. Its hero is the robbed, not the robber; the innocent man, not the criminal. Griffith's gangsters are also defiantly unromanticised and not at all glamorous, and there are no attempts to delve into who they are, or why they have done what they have done, and an absolute refusal to contemplate them as anything other than the enemy of society. The movie's real concerns are, in all honesty, elsewhere entirely.

A far more appropriate example can be found in *Underworld*. Josef Von Sternberg, the Austrian auteur behind *The Blue Angel* and others, made *Underworld* in 1927. With a screenplay by Ben Hecht (who had written the play on which *The Front Page* (Lewis Milestone, 1931) was based, and who was then currently developing one of the most successful careers in Hollywood) that won an Oscar at the very first Academy Awards, the movie remains an absolute classic of its kind. It concerns a love triangle among a gangster, his right-hand man and his 'moll'. An obvious inspiration for *Miller's Crossing* (Joel Coen, 1990), it has an obsession with its criminal figures' code of honour that marks it out as a prototype of the kind of film we instinctively reach for when discussing gangland thrillers, but it arguably remains more about the triangular romance, and the strains it places on a friendship, than what it is these people do to make money.

Another good example is *Doorway To Hell* (William Wellman, 1930), which, if not the actual precursor to *Little Caesar* and similar, pointed the way. Certainly it anticipates many of the concerns of the thirties Warners Bros gangster movies and is, indeed, directed by the man behind the camera on *The Public Enemy*. Crime is shown as a tragic outgrowth of contemporary social problems when the lead hood, Louie Ricarno, visits his childhood home and discusses how his brother died of typhoid in a street that is little more than a shanty town. The picture even anticipates *Caesar* and its protagonist directly, Ricarno being a small figure with a Napoleon complex who takes solace in dying in a haze of bullets rather than being captured. It also contains a version of the following decade's attitude that money is a cure-all. 'Money can buy anything,' says Ricarno at one point. *Doorway To Hell* ends, as *Little Caesar* begins, with a 'socially responsible' notice – in this case one that is impossible to read without hearing the voice of the *Twilight Zone* creator/presenter Rod Serling intoning it. Or maybe that's just me. These disclaimers would become a regular part of early-thirties gangster films largely, although not exclusively, those from Warner Bros.

For the most part, throughout the 1920s, crime thrillers dealt with the law enforcers and the victims of crime rather than the perpetrators (see **The Racket**, included here, as an example, for some interesting facts it throws up, and because it's typical). There was a subgenre of 'prison dramas', but even these were often redemption tales, or dealt with men wrongly imprisoned. It was genuinely *Little Caesar* that initiated, or at least popularised, the shift.

The gangster as a Robin Hood figure is a powerful notion. The idea that the gangster was romantically appealing to a country with a 30 per cent unemployment rate (officially, that is: history would show it to have been much higher) – because the character was that of a man who refused to play by society's rules and confronted 'the establishment' – has some credence.

The habit that the leads in gangster pictures have of disposing of their ineffectual leaders and taking control can be seen as a fantasy that an audience is willing to buy into in an era of apathy, defeat, disorientation and insecurity. Against this backdrop characters that were traditionally villains became heroes, perhaps because the institutions that America had long regarded as heroic no longer entertained the trust of the masses. The July 1931 issue of *Motion Picture Magazine* said, 'You can't tell the hero from the heavy . . . they get riddled with machine gun bullets or hanged or electrocuted . . . Our old heroes have grown sadly shop-worn and we haven't, as yet, any very satisfactory substitutes.'

In the figure of the gangster, audiences saw a man who was able to do what they could only dream about: make it to the gilded paradise using only his wits, although conventional morality demanded that he be ultimately punished for his actions, his success being material and thus transitory. It can almost be said that the gangster genre, involving as it does the purchase of earthly pleasure at the price of spiritual and moral damnation, can be seen as a kind of social pornography, at least in the sense that it's an outlet for urges that an audience possesses, but would condemn in others; an onanistic process ending in a hypocritical combination of almost physical catharsis and moral disgust.

This provides us with one of the chief interests, and also chief problems, of the genre. In order to present a story of organised crime in a sufficiently involving way the characters must, almost certainly, be human and sympathetic enough for the audience to be engaged by them, to want to follow their lives in order to see what happens to them. Yet these are inevitably going to be people who commit crimes, perhaps appallingly violent crimes, and there is a moral issue there. There's also the related, but distinct, issue of how to portray the glamorous lifestyle associated with ill-gotten gains (the wages of sin, you might call them) without making crime seem like a good idea to the audience. Additionally there's the more complex question of how to portray the process whereby someone embarks on a life of crime. Some pictures, such as *Little Caesar*, *Gangster No. 1* and *GoodFellas*, seem to choose to portray the gangster as an exceptional individual, one drawn to criminality by something within himself – these people are, deliberately and otherwise (see **GoodFellas**), portrayed as openly sociopathic, even depraved. Other films, such as *The Public Enemy*, take the almost diametrically opposite tactic, and portray people pushed into organised crime by social problems and the impossibility of surviving otherwise. The first of these options is more morally comforting, the second more socially aware. The first is more openly condemning; the second seems to say, 'There but for fortune go I' (see **Angels With Dirty Faces**). They are almost certainly equally dishonest, inadequate and inaccurate. The nature–nurture divide is a critical cliché of little value, and the more sophisticated gangster picture chooses to combine the two, acknowledging, crucially, that *means* are themselves corrupting whatever the intended *ends* may be. It also acknowledges that few would choose a life of danger, of almost endless confrontation (despite the financial rewards), if there were another way. Successful in simultaneously acknowledging the allure of an easy path to the highlife, *The Godfather* takes this to its ultimate conclusion and creates a dynastic tragedy from this raw material.

Among all this talk of the appeal of gangster films, however, something that should also never be forgotten is the market-led nature of Hollywood trends. *Little Caesar* is an exceptional motion picture, utterly compelling nearly three-quarters of a century after it was made, and its enormous success is ultimately more down to its quality than anything else. It's down to its evocative visuals, terrific pace and that magnificent central turn from Edward G Robinson. Like many other exceptional motion pictures that seemingly arrived out of the blue (*Star Wars* (George Lucas, 1977), *Moulin Rouge!* (Baz Luhrmann, 2001), *Psycho* (Alfred Hitchcock, 1960) and indeed many unexceptional motion pictures that simply made vast amounts of cash), it inspired a slew of imitations, created by an industry motivated, above all else, by *profit*. Whether any of these four movies fulfilled a psychological need that had been neglected, or created a niche for itself and products like it through its sheer quality, is a chicken-and-egg argument that could be dragged out until the end of time.

Commercialism is, of course, no disgrace. Film remains an innately commercial, crowd-pleasing medium, a populist art form, and only the painfully naïve or chronically un-self-aware could ever seriously suggest otherwise.

How to use this Book

As is traditional for the Virgin Films series, each motion picture given its own chapter within these pages has been divided up into a number of subcategories. In this case they begin with the title of the film and some principal production credits (usually in the form and order in which they come at the very beginning of the movie in question), followed by some or all of:

SUMMARY: A (usually brief) précis of what happens in the movie. The actual length will depend on all sorts of factors relevant to the film under discussion, including how well known the plot is, how complex a story the picture has and how important the details of the plot and plotting are to the way the movie unfolds.

THE PLAYERS: Potted career and life histories of the major actors in the picture, partially to ground the film in the context of the career of its major stars, but also as an illustration of the movie history we're moving through. People who appear in more than one film in this book will occasionally have their entry split across the several films in which they appear.

THE DIRECTOR: Some notes on the career of the director.

VISUAL INTEREST: Film is primarily a visual medium, so this is the catch-all category for everything from innovative cross-fades to cunning use of symbols. The place for discussion of a movie's visual elements.

QUOTES: Some choice snippets of dialogue, always a good way of getting one into the mood of the film under consideration. Who doesn't get an almost Proustian rush of 'Godfather'-ness when they read the words, 'Instead, you come into my house on the day my daughter is to be married, and you ask me to do murder. For money.' Exactly.

SOURCES TO SCREEN: The writing of the screenplay, obvious literary and filmic influences, anterior references, things like that.

CONTEMPORARY REACTION: How the film was received at the time of its release, incorporating reviews, public reaction, awards and even social repercussions. In terms of reviews I'll generally include (when possible and/or desirable) commentaries on the reviews from *Variety* and the *New York Times*, two of the longest-running continuous streams of movie reviews in America. Between them they provide a good indication of mainstream American opinion. I'll often supplement these two with other sources: often it'll be Roger Ebert of the *Chicago Sun-Times* (because, though he and I rarely agree, he always seems so genuine in his opinions – something often untrue of film critics) or whoever is currently reviewing pictures for *Rolling Stone* or British broadsheet newspapers (British tabloid film journalism is, trust me, not worth the effort).

TRIVIA: All the things you didn't know you didn't know.

SEX/MONEY/DEATH: The big catch-all: a discussion of the movie in terms of issues and ideas. It's what it's all about, after all.

THE VERDICT: In a genre largely concerned with crime and punishment, it might be remiss of me not to offer judgement. I'll be ever so quick, I promise.

The Racket (1927)

(Black and white, silent – 60 minutes)

Howard Hughes presents
Title cards written by Eddie Adams, Del Andrews,
Harry Behn
Adapted by Bartlett Cormack from his own play
Director of Photography: Tony Gaudio
Editor: Tom Miranda
Directed by Lewis Milestone

PRINCIPAL CAST: Thomas Meighan (Captain McQuigg), Marie Prevost (Helen Hayes), Louis Wolheim (Nick Scarsi), George E Stone (Joe Scarsi), John Darrow (Ames), 'Skeets' Gallagher (Miller), Lee Moran (Pratt), Lucien Prival (Chick), Tony Marlo (Chick's Chauffeur), Sam De Grasse (District Attorney), Burr McIntosh (Old Man), G Pat Collins (Johnson), Jim Farley, Henry Sedley (not known)

SUMMARY: A prohibition syndicate tries to elect a corrupt mayor who will do its bidding, while fending off McQuigg, the only uncorrupted police officer on the force, who is determined to bring them down.

THE DIRECTOR: Russian-born Lewis Milestone began his film directorial career shooting instructional shorts for the US army towards the end of World War One (titles include *The Toothbrush* and *Posture*, about how to brush one's teeth and stand correctly respectively). He spent the early 1920s shooting comedy shorts (such as *The Caveman* (1925) about a $100 bill cut in half and thrown out of a window) before graduating to more substantial material, including *The Garden of Eden* (1928), a visually sumptuous adaptation of the wisely comic stage play by Rudolf Bernauer and Rudolph Osterreicher. In the thirties he was responsible for *All Quiet on the Western Front* (1930) and *The Front Page* (1931), two of the best-remembered films of the era, and had an uncredited hand in *Scarface* (1932) – another. He worked into his sixties, his last two pictures being the original *Ocean's Eleven* (1960) and the Trevor Howard/Marlon Brando *Mutiny on the Bounty*.

SOURCES TO SCREEN: Newspaperman turned playwright Bartlett Cormack created scandal when, in 1927, he produced his Broadway play *The Racket*, starring Edward G Robinson. A savage attack on prohibition and the corruption resulting from it, it suggested that many police officers and other law-enforcement officials were turning a blind eye to crimes against the Prohibition-enforcing Volstead Act in return for cash favours. Notorious enough to be banned in Chicago, the play was turned into a film, thanks to the patronage of Howard Hughes. By all accounts a close adaptation of the play (within the constraints that all the dialogue of a very speech-heavy script had to be disposed of), the film was no less controversial. The film was remade in 1951.

TRIVIA: Nominated for Best Picture at the very first Academy Awards, *The Racket* remains one of only two films nominated for Best Picture unavailable to the general viewer. No copy of *The Patriot* (Ernst Lubitsch, 1929) is known to exist, despite extensive searching, and, while *The Racket* is thought to be held at UCLA, the copy is apparently unviewable.

Alibi (Roland West, 1929)

Another 'proto' gangster film of interest is Roland West's *Alibi* based on Elaine S Carrington and JC Nugent's play *Nightstick*. In *Alibi* the gangster figure, Chick Williams (played by Chester Morris), is the hero of the piece in the sense that he's the protagonist, but he is neither sympathetic in the manner that Cagney's gangsters would become (*The Public Enemy* et al.) nor compelling due to his monstrosity, like the anti heroes of *Scarface* or *Little Caesar*, he's simply a thug whose downfall is both a given and a cause for celebration. Chick Williams is a prohibition bootlegger who is released on parole. Returning to his life of crime, he plans the perfect alibi for a heist he is going to pull (hence the title). He takes a policeman's daughter Joan (Eleanore Griffith) to the theatre and then pops out of the performance to commit the robbery hoping that her evidence that she was with him all night will be considered watertight by law-enforcement officials. Unfortunately another policeman is killed during the robbery and because of both his reputation and his suspiciously good alibi, Williams is the prime suspect. An informer is sent to infiltrate his gang and he is caught. Faced with the prospect of death he cowers, no longer a tough guy, a broken, snivelling wretch.

Interesting in that it is a film that was prepared in two versions – one with sound, one without, for release simultaneously – *Alibi* was nominated for Best Picture at the 1930 Academy Awards. Morris was nominated for his performance and the art director William Cameron Menzies was also nominated, presumably for his realisation of a rooftop chase (which is not unimpressive now) and his occasionally delirious art deco set decoration, especially in the opening nightclub scene.

Some of the key aspects of this film, and the play on which it's based, would become staples of the genre. The anti-hero who turns coward (which, a decade later is already being subverted in *Angels With Dirty Faces*) and the attempt to create a compelling alibi through the use/abuse of an impressionable young girl (Brighton Rock, The Blue Lamp) are the two most notable examples of this.

Little Caesar (1931)

(Black and white – 79 minutes)

First National Pictures Present
Little Caesar
Novel by W R Burnett
Directed by Mervyn Le Roy
A First National Vitaphone Talking Picture
Continuity by Robert N Less
Screen Version and Dialogue by Francis Edward Faragon
Photography by Tany Gaudio
Edited by Ray Curtiss
Art Director: Anton Grot
General Musical Director: Erno Rapee

PRINCIPAL CAST: Edward G Robinson (Little Caesar, alias 'Rico'), Douglas Fairbanks Jr (Joe Massara), Glenda Farrell (Olga Strassoff), William Collier Jr (Tony Passa), Sidney Blackmer ('Big Boy'), Ralph Ince (Pete Montana), Thomas E Jackson (Sergeant Flaherty), Stanley Fields (Sam Vettori), Maurice Black (Little Arnie Lorch), George E Stone (Otero), Armand Kaliz (DeVoss), Nick Bela (Ritz Colonna)

SUMMARY: Minor hoodlums Joe Massara and his friend 'Rico' see a story in a newspaper about a local mob boss, 'Diamond' Pete Montana, who is being fêted by his contemporaries, and resolve to head to 'the city' to expand their lives of crime, because the unnamed conurbation is 'where things break big'. They join the mob run by Sam Vettori, and, while Rico rises through the ranks with astonishing rapidity, developing a reputation for brutality in the process, Joe returns to his true passion, dancing, and develops a relationship with his dancing partner, Olga.

Rico kills his driver, Tony, who has, in Rico's term, 'gone yellow'. Rico is granted the object of his grand ambition, the celebratory dinner, and he takes childlike delight in this. The publicity causes rival gang leader Arnie Lorch to set up an attempted assassination, which Rico survives.

Rico's revenge is swift and terrible: Arnie is forced out of the city and Rico takes his business. Rico is now only second to 'the Big Boy', who, it seems, controls the city from a legitimate vantage point as well as being in charge of organised crime (see **SOURCES TO SCREEN**). 'Big Boy' invites Rico to his mansion and offers him Pete Montana's territory. The next time the audience sees Rico he is living in luxury and is trying to persuade Joe to return to organised crime, saying that he needs a loyal lieutenant. Joe refuses, and Rico makes threats against Olga, who he says is responsible for Joe's 'going soft'. Later, Rico follows Joe to Olga's apartment, and she summons the authorities. Rico is unable to bring himself to kill Joe. Fleeing from the authorities, Rico is scammed out of $9,850 by an old woman, and is reduced to living in a fifteen-cents-a-night home for derelicts.

Enraged by a newspaper report that insults him and says he is finished, Rico calls the police station to boast; they trace the call and send men to apprehend or kill him. Rico dies beneath a hoarding advertising Joe and Olga's latest dance success.

THE PLAYERS: Born Emanuel Goldenberg, Edward G Robinson emigrated to America with his parents at the age of ten. Initially interested in becoming a rabbi, he developed an obsession with performing (he later asserted that he would act for free if necessary, such was his need to) at college and began acting professionally in 1913. Gaining Broadway exposure in two years, he would work in the theatre for another fifteen, as both actor and writer, before the movies beckoned.

His debut was a small part in *The Bright Shawl* (John S Robertson, 1923) a silent comedy, but it was as sound began to take hold that Robinson's expressive voice and almost palpable physical dynamism enabled him to establish himself in the medium. Although hardly five foot five tall, and far from a matinée idol in looks, he established himself as a major star after signing up as a contract player at the Warner Bros studio. Although he is remembered principally for his immortalisation of Rico Bandello in this picture, and his roles in *Double Indemnity* (Billy Wilder, 1944) and *Key Largo* (John Huston, 1948), his career was diverse and full, embracing such varied pictures as 1931's *Five Star Final* (which saw him reunite with *Little Caesar*'s director Mervyn Le Roy to play a tabloid newspaper editor afflicted with a conscience) and the alarmist SF classic *Soylent Green* (Richard Fleischer, 1973). He was exceptional in Arthur Miller's *All My Sons* (Irving Reis, 1948), *Kid Galahad* (Michael Curtiz, 1937), *The Sea Wolf* (Curtiz again, 1941) and *Dr Ehrlich's Magic Bullet* (William Dieterle, 1940), which was about the physician who cured syphilis. A noted art collector and remarked-upon philanthropist, he survived blacklisting during the McCarthyite communist witch hunts of the 1950s, and the long-term psychological problems of his eldest son, only to succumb to cancer in 1973. His autobiography, *All My Yesterdays*, was published posthumously, and the Academy of Motion Pictures Arts and Sciences chose to present his widow with a lifetime achievement Oscar for her late husband's career that same year. They had voted to present the actor with the award shortly before his death, but he had died before the actual ceremony could be held.

Douglas Fairbanks Jr never achieved the same level of movie-star status as the father he barely knew, but his long career is distinguished by the occasional outstanding performance, and it's quite clear that it was the roles he was given, rather than his own abilities, that inhibited him. Equally, his long semiretirement, performing, on average, little more than once a decade for the last forty years of his life, meant that the world rarely got to see what he could really do when given the opportunity. He was, however, one of Hollywood's most celebrated military heroes: his naval service in World War Two saw him awarded both the Silver Star and the Legion of Merit with V for Valor in Combat. He was a friend to presidents and monarchs: Franklin Delano Roosevelt made him a special envoy in 1941, and when he died Buckingham Palace expressed the Queen's personal sympathies. His best performances arguably came in *The Dawn Patrol* (Howard Hawks, 1930) the 1937 John Cromwell version of *The Prisoner of Zenda* (where he wickedly parodied his father), *Gunga Din* (George Stevens, 1939) and *Sinbad the Sailor* (Richard Wallace, 1947), in which he gave a far more giving and affectionate pastiche of the kind of performance that (by then the late) Fairbanks Sr had given in his own heyday. Two other pictures of his are particularly worthy of note: Ben Hecht's blacker-than-black comedy, *Angels Over Broadway* (1940), which Fairbanks also produced, and *Ghost Story* (John Irvin, 1981), his final big-screen appearance. In this he teamed up with three other 'living legends' in Fred Astaire, Melvyn Douglas and the producer/actor John Houseman. His long retirement saw him busy himself with social engagements and the composing of the two volumes of his autobiography, *The Salad Days* (1988) and *A Hell of a War* (1992). He died in New York in 2000. A decade before, he had, when interviewed, expressed his belief that few people realised he was still alive.

Theatre-trained Glenda Farrell was brassy, sexy and best known for her long-running role in the Torchey Blaine series of films, in which she played a wisecracking reporter. Although the character was not created for her, the gender was changed so that she could take the part ('she' had been a 'he' in Frederick Nebel's stories) and the character as she played it was obviously derived from her turn in the seriously neglected, disturbing, two-tone Technicolor masterpiece, *The Mystery of the Wax Museum* (Michael Curtiz, 1936).

Farrell's movie career waned at the start of the 1940s. This was a shame, given that her appearance, style of acting and essential persona seem far more modern than those of many of her far more successful contemporaries. She returned to the stage, although later screen roles of note include her Emmy-winning turn on television in *A Cardinal Act of Mercy* (1962) and an appearance as Elvis's mother in *Kissin' Cousins* (Gene Nelson, 1964). She died of lung cancer in 1969. She may not be the most famous of leading ladies of her period of film, but she helped define a certain kind of female lead that has not merely survived to the present, but prospered in the years between her films and now.

THE DIRECTOR: Born in 1900, San Franciscan Mervyn Le Roy was one of the many children rendered practically destitute by the great California earthquake of 1906. His first job was a paperboy, but the emerging film industry was always his goal. Initially a costumier, he worked his way up through the industry in order to become a director, serving as a lab technician and later as a camera assistant, with parallel stints as a gag writer and bit-part performer for good measure. Industry contacts (his cousin Jesse Lasky was a producer) had got him into the industry in the first place, and perhaps had a role in his gaining his first directorial feature, *No Place to Go*, which he shot in 1927, making him one of the youngest first-time Hollywood directors in history.

Known as the 'boy wonder' at the Warner Brothers studio, he was widely held to be a profitable populist capable of taking hold of any genre, but who lacked a distinctive cinematic style of his own. This is an unfair assessment of a versatile, and occasionally inspired, director whose reputation seems, bizarrely, to have been adversely rather than positively affected by the many different kinds of film of which he made a success.

He was credited as a great discoverer of talent, his movie star finds including Loretta Young, Clark Gable, Robert Mitchum and Lana Turner, and his movies-as-director including *Broad Minded, Five Star Final* (both 1931), *I Am a Fugitive From a Chain Gang!* (1932), *The World Changes, Gold Diggers of 1933* (both 1933), *Oil for the Lamps of China* (1935), *Anthony Adverse* (1936) and *They Won't Forget* (1937).

Made head of production at MGM in 1938, he returned to directing after the (now difficult to believe, but very real) initially disastrous box office of *The Wizard of Oz* (Victor Fleming, 1939), a project he'd enthusiastically backed. After taking over the epic *Quo Vadis?* (1951) from John Huston who'd left the project, Le Roy shifted his attention to musicals, including *Rose Marie* (1954). He then returned to Warner Bros, directing *The Bad Seed* (1956), *Gypsy* (1962) and *The FBI Story* (1959) among others. His final film, *Moment to Moment*, was made for Universal in 1966. Le Roy retired (save for giving John Wayne some uncredited help on 1968's appalling *The Green Berets*) and wrote his autobiography. He died from Alzheimer's disease in 1974.

VISUAL INTEREST: The picture opens with a shot of a book, a deliberate appropriation of the furniture of a more respected documentary and narrative medium. This conceit is just one of the things that make *Little Caesar* feel like that contradiction in terms, 'a silent film with sound'. It is very much one of those talkies that moves and looks like a silent movie. It even has more than one title card, as if the director were unsure that an audience would be capable of following a plot expressed through a film grammar that doesn't use them; and important thematic, plot and character information – such as 'Rico continued to take care of himself, his hair and his gun – with excellent results' – is conveyed through them regularly.

The entirely unrealistic lighting of the backlot streets (which has to be a conscious decision, compared with *The Public Enemy*, which was shot virtually simultaneously with almost identical equipment) has been commented on before; less remarked upon is the way the lights flashing behind

Vettori in the first scene cast an almost impressionistic pall across the room or how fundamentally unreal many of the interiors look (notice the jagged angular wall that appears to be going nowhere in Anthony's apartment).

The shot of Rico studying himself in the mirror at almost exactly his career's halfway point must be intended as a visual indication of the coming reversal in his fortunes, just as the earlier swift, steady moving away, upwards and outwards, from a spinning roulette wheel clearly symbolises the transitory nature of fame, and the spinning wheel of fate. Just as what goes up comes down (or 'Months passed – Rico's career had been like a skyrocket – starting from the gutter and returning there', as another caption card puts it), what goes around comes around, as the cliché goes.

Le Roy and the editor, Ray Curtiss, also use a large number of cross-fades in the piece, despite their being expensive, complex and time-consuming. This, combined with Le Roy's use of a far more 'roving' camera style than is typical of early talkies, and in addition to the elements mentioned above, creates a strange interiorised visual universe for the film to operate in. It's not quite as if the audience were inside Rico's head, but there's a sense in which this small man and his small world seem appropriate in this grimly claustrophobic setting. The audience certainly never sees the sky or anything approaching a product of the natural world.

It's well known that Robinson (a gentle artistic soul by all accounts) so intensely disliked firing guns that he visibly flinched every time he had to fire one. The solution Le Roy hit upon was to use make-up tape to fix Robinson's eyes open for certain scenes. The effect is to give Rico a certain wide-eyed, frenzied look in some sequences, one that is entirely to the film's benefit.

Robinson's performance is worth mentioning as a 'visual interest' in its own right, given that it keeps surprising audiences after seventy years of being pastiched and appropriated. With its deliberately contained physicality, hands-on-hips acting, swagger and sudden violence, it's an effective appropriation of much of the physical grammar of a child, placed in the service of a portrayal of unthinking evil and is a perfect complement to Le Roy's murky, purgatorial 'city'.

QUOTES:
Rico: 'I don't want no dancin' I figure on making other people dance.'

And, inevitably:

Rico: 'Mother of mercy, is this the end of Rico?'

SOURCES TO SCREEN: *Little Caesar* was one of the earliest talkies to present gangsters outside the confines – relatively comforting for audiences – of state penitentiaries (examples of such tales of incarceration include *The Last Mile* (Samuel Bischoff, 1932) and *The Big House* (George W Hill, 1932). According to contemporary press material, W R Burnett wrote his novel, upon which the film is based, in the aftermath of personal tragedy: a friend was shot and killed by gangbangers who were indiscriminately gunning down the audience at a Chicago club while trying to find and kill members of a rival gang.

Little Caesar is essentially a visceral, condemnatory portrait of Al Capone, who (as Rico does in both novel and screenplay) began as a mob bodyguard and rose through the ranks to become a crime lord second to none. Several incidents in the plot of both are supposedly taken from Capone's life: the character of Pete Montana is presumably derived from 'Big Jim' Colisimo, whom Capone had murdered during his own rise to prominence, whereas 'Big Boy' is clearly based upon the legendarily nest-feathering, bribe-taking 'Big Bill' Thompson, mayor of Chicago during much of Capone's reign, who was universally acknowledged to be in Capone's pay.

Of course, while Capone remains the archetypal gangster for many, there are aspects of Rico's story that are drawn from others sources: the dinner given in Rico's honour, for instance, is analogous to that held to celebrate the 'achievements' of Samuel J 'Nails' Morton and Dion O Bannion. Asked by Wallis to write the film script, Burnett declined; Robert Lord did a rough draft, but Wallis, finding it too sophisticated, assigned the experimental playwright Francis Edward Faragon to tone it down with some gangster lingo. Darryl Zanuck also had a hand in giving the story the right tone.

CONTEMPORARY REACTION: The January 1931 issue of the *New Yorker* devoted a great deal of space to *Little Caesar*, calling it an 'insight into the criminal mind', albeit one that was not 'so intensively nor thoroughly worked out . . . to be the final word on this absorbing topic'. This might count as the film-reviewing understatement of the decade. The reviewer approved of Robinson's performance, citing how the actor avoided fetishising the gangster milieu with a portrayal that takes pains to 'make the gunman certainly no hero' despite his operating 'in a world of appealing glamor'; 'very probably his analysis is accurate', the piece goes on to say, concluding that it is wise and appropriate to portray gangsters as unpleasant in order to avoid allowing audiences to become seduced by the riches that they acquire through their lives of crime. This is, of course, related to the central dichotomy of portraying a life of crime in a sufficiently entertaining way, and with characters understandable and human enough to maintain audience interest, without glorifying what they do.

The *New Yorker*'s fellow charter of East Coast life, the *New York Times*, reviewed the film on 8 January 1931, and noted the larger-than-usual crowds that accompanied the picture's opening at the Strand Cinema in the city. Of special note, felt the paper, was the 'wonderfully effective' performance given by Robinson, who managed to turn Rico into 'a figure out of Greek tragedy', taking a 'cold, ignorant, merciless killer' from the page and making him 'the plaything of a force greater than himself'. Douglas Fairbanks Jr, however, was judged to be less convincing, too 'nice' to play the cheap Italian thug he is supposed to be according to the plot.

Around a week later (14 January 1931 edition), *Variety* also reviewed the film, calling it 'gripping and interesting' comparing it favourably with the more 'romantic' *Doorway to Hell* (see **Introduction**) but declaring the characters to be 'stock' with the exception of Rico, although the script was praised for making him 'tough from the start' and not attempting to portray society as being to blame for his sociopathic nature, or to trace the path whereby he became a criminal and a killer. On the whole it was an 'astute handling' of the issues, but a film with 'no new twists' to complement its 'pace'.

TRIVIA: Despite its fine technical qualities, vast box-office takings and Robinson's bravura performance, *Little Caesar* was up for only one Academy Award: Best Writing, Adaptation, Francis Edward Faragon and Robert N Lee nominated. It failed to pick up the statuette.

The whole movie was produced for $700,000, a not inconsiderable sum for something that was far from a prestigious production for the studio at the time.

The movie was shot, finished and ready in 1930, but released in early 1931 in most states. There is little consistency between libraries and resources over which year *Little Caesar* should be considered to have been 'made'. This book chooses 1931.

SEX/MONEY/DEATH: It is perhaps because of the writer W R Burnett's personal experiences (see above) that the screenplay avoids overglamorising its protagonists and purchases our sympathy for the characters without making them humane, or even particularly human.

Robinson's Rico is not, like Capone, a sophisticated tactician and complex administrator. Rico revels in power for its own sake rather than as a means to an end, and he has no long-term goals of any kind. He has no agenda other than to be in charge, no creed other than 'have your own way or nothing', as he himself describes it, and he becomes hugely excited by the idea of getting people to 'do whatever you tell 'em' in his very first scene in the film.

Rico Bandello is a vicious, debauched toddler, with his pudgy fingers and squinting eyes and casual, needless violence. It is this immaturity of thought and sociopathic lack of understanding of the consequences of action that truly mark out the character of Rico and give him his power. Like a child, he seems somehow to fail to grasp the consequence of action. Everything that happens to him in the plot trammels out as a direct result of his initial decision to go to the city, 'where things break big'.

His delight in colour and splendour and his simple enjoyment of the moment are the more positive, endearing aspects of this childishness (watch Robinson, rarely ever better, in the scene where he admires the menu at the dinner given in his honour) but the negative connotations are far more prevalent.

When, after his fall from power, he hides in the home of an old hag, who seems in appearance and demeanour to have come straight out of 'Hansel and Gretel', he has somehow, from the very first second he appears with her, ceded all his authority and power to her. She is, as has often been commented upon, a sort of mother from hell, and when, having hidden it from him, she offers him a minute share of his own money if he's 'a good boy', the scene looks and feels like a portrayal of some small child being offered his allowance in return for mowing the lawn. It's emasculating, and something entirely in keeping with the general presentation of the character.

Rico's relationship with women is interesting inasmuch as he simply doesn't have one. His open disgust at women, and at any notion of femininity, is also distinctly pre-teen (emphatically not, as has been suggested, implicitly homosexual).

Farrell's Olga is beautiful and spirited enough that Joe's sudden collapse into passionate love for her (it takes him less than a minute of on-screen time to fall wholeheartedly for her charms) seems strangely plausible; but Rico is visibly and audibly revolted by her, both when they're on screen together and when he has to talk about her elsewhere. 'Love! Soft stuff!' he mutters more than once, and he uses the word 'molls' with a sneer and a touch of ironic contempt. Again, the association is playground, with Rico as the schoolboy appalled by 'nasty girls'.

This of course impacts on Rico's relationship with Joe. To call this 'homoerotic' would be, as noted above, spectacularly misplaced. Rico is asexual, a protohuman, beyond and beneath the concerns and emotions of the normal human world.

It is odd that, adhering to traditional notions of tragic heroism (that heroes and anti-heroes are destroyed by a single, epic personality flaw), has led seventy-plus years of film criticism to hold that it is Rico's compassion for Joey that is his undoing. It is the 'done thing' with regard to this film to argue that, by not killing Joey when he first attempts to leave the gang (something he would have done with any other gang member) Rico sows the seeds of his own destruction. His refusal to kill Joey creates the later situation where Joey betrays his old friend and this then naturally leaves Rico with no choice but to kill him because, by this point, not killing Joey would result, as it does, in Rico's fall. But much of the logic of this reading comes from Rico's own feeble justification for his fall: 'This is what I get for liking a guy too much,' he mutters to explain how he has come to a bad end. But how can it be that compassion is a bad thing? Clearly if human feeling comes into conflict with your lifestyle it's your lifestyle that's at fault, not your desire not to commit a murder. Like a retired politician or an exiled leader, Rico is incapable of seeing that it was what he did that was wrong. It's not a single mistake, or even a pattern of mistakes: it's the way he chose to live his life.

It's also inarguable that Rico's loyalty, his supposed saving grace, is a childish, immature thing: 'You're my pal . . . I need you. Nobody ever quit me. You're still in my gang . . .' he whines at Joey, sounding more like one of the Li'l Rascals than Al Capone.

'You're gonna be in on this and you'll like it!' he barks at Tony earlier, again with the thoughtless aggression of a petulant child, and his death, pleading for his mother beneath a hoarding celebrating the adult, fulfilling union of Joe and Olga, is really all the conclusion you need. The fact that their dance is called 'Tipsy Topsy Turvy', implicitly suggesting that this is also true of Rico's view on life, is just an extra cleverness, and Rico's odd pride in his own death, in squalor in the gutter – which he allows himself because he's fulfilled his own prophecy that the police would 'never put any cuffs' on him – is further indication of the picture's choice to present Rico's psychology as aberrant, as tipsy, topsy, turvy.

Yet, the iconic, memorable nature of that death is an inevitable consequence of the film's decision to present Rico as a remarkable individual – that's his ambition, of course, 'To be somebody!' as he says in his first scene.

The comparisons to Napoleon and Caesar that are made seem to set Rico apart from the normal mass of humanity, and there's little suggestion that Rico has turned to crime because of social problems – something that will become a recurring instance with the more Everyman characters who populate other thirties gangster movies. While the refusal to give some characters names ('the Big Boy') and the constant referral to the setting as the (generic) 'city' might seem to suggest an Everyman quality to Caesar Enrico Bandello, when combined with the above they more seem to elevate him to the level of iconic, grotesque, dangerous buffoon, if not quite an American Hitler, then an American Mussolini – and Il Duce, of course, always saw his role as akin to that of Caesar.

Warner Bros' more socially conscious conceptual follow-up, *The Public Enemy*, was already in advanced production, and would be out inside three months. 'Mother of mercy, is this the end of Rico?' Robinson legendarily asks. What no one seems to have ever pointed out is that in every sense that matters, the answer to that question is a very firm 'no'.

THE VERDICT: Warner Bros would make many gangster films throughout the 1930s, but this, arguably the first, remains just as arguably the best. Robinson's performance is a real powerhouse demonstration of his unique talents and the atmosphere of the picture remains unique. A bona fide classic movie.

The Public Enemy (1931)

(Black and white – 80 minutes)

Warner Bros Pictures, Inc.
& The Vitaphone Corp. Present
The Public Enemy
by Kubec Glasmon and John Bright
Directed by William A Wellman
Screen Adaptation by Harvey Thew
Photography by Dev Jennings
Art Director: Max Parker
Edited by EDW M McDermott
Wardrobe by Earl Luick
Vitaphone Orchestra conducted by David Mendoza

PRINCIPAL CAST: James Cagney (Tom Powers), Edward Woods (Matt Doyle), Jean Harlow (Gwen Allen), Joan Blondell (Mamie), Beryl Mercer (Ma Powers), Donald Cook (Mike Powers), Mae Clarke (Kitty), Mia Marvin (Jane), Leslie Fenton (Samuel 'Nails' Nathan), Robert Emmett O'Connor (Patrick J 'Paddy' Ryan), Murray Kinnell (Putty Nose), Snitz Edwards (Miller), Rita Flynn (Molly Doyle), Frank Coghlan Jr (Tom as a boy), Frankie Darro (Matt as a boy), Sam McDaniel (Headwaiter), Helen Parrish (Little Girl), Purnell Pratt (Officer Powers)

SUMMARY: The lives of Tom Powers and his friend Matt from childhood high jinks in 1909 through petty crime to murder and drink running during prohibition. Tom romances the blonde bombshell Gwen, whom he picks up in the street, and is slowly estranged from his family, including his more straight-laced brother Mike.

As rivalries between local gangs escalate Matt is killed, and Tom attacks Matt's killers, avenging his friend's death. Savagely injured in the gun battle, Tom is taken to hospital, from where he is kidnapped by his enemies and murdered. His mutilated body is sent to his home, where his mother is still excitedly awaiting his return.

THE PLAYERS: Born into poverty in Yonkers, New York, in 1899, James Cagney (inevitably referred to colloquially as Jimmy) began his showbiz career as a dancer, impersonating a woman in a chorus line. He was married once, in 1922, to Frances Vernon, at whose side he would remain until his death more than sixty years later. The 1920s saw Cagney move into more appropriate theatre roles, and it was a turn in the play *Sinner's Holiday* that impressed John G Adolfi enough for him to be offered the chance to recreate the part in his film version (1930). That led to his being offered a studio contract at Warner Bros, where minor roles in *Doorway to Hell* (Archie Mayo, 1930) and *Other Men's Women* (William Wellman, 1930) beckoned. Wellman subsequently cast him in *The Public Enemy* (see **TRIVIA**). The success of *The Public Enemy* saw Cagney's career in sudden ascendance, and – while he was ever disdainful of the term – he became effectively the first American superstar of the sound era (see, for instance, **Angels With Dirty Faces**).

Jean Harlow (just twenty when she made this film) had played bit parts for a few years (including opposite Laurel and Hardy in *Double Whoopee* (Hal Roach, 1928)) and had been the leading lady in the bootlegging melodrama *The Secret Six* (George W Hill, 1930) before landing the part of Gwen. A small but memorable, hugely sultry role, hers remains one of the movie's enduring images. *Platinum Blonde* (Frank Capra, 1931) cemented her as a sex symbol in the minds of the American public, and a flood of roles, many opposite Clark Gable, followed.

Perhaps the clearest indication of her meteoric rise to colossal fame can be found in the fact that a mere photograph of her, representing Oliver Hardy's girlfriend in the terrific *Beau Chumps* (James R Horne, 1931), aroused audience interest. Her face was well known enough to be the visual punchline of a joke in a film she had nothing to do with. She was so famous that everyone in every cinema was expected to know her instantly. Harlow (real name Harlean Carpentier) led a controversial life, eloping with and marrying an older man at sixteen, and then divorcing him two years later.

Her second husband, the German-born screenwriter/ director Paul Bern, was twice her age and committed suicide after 64 days of marriage. There was speculation that he was actually murdered, and Harlow has been attached to more than one conspiracy theory – all unproven. She married again in 1933, but was divorced eight months later. She died on 7 June 1937, having been hospitalised with ureic poisoning during the shooting of *Saratoga* (Jack Conway, 1937), which was finished using a double in long shots. She was 26.

THE DIRECTOR: William Wellman, three times Oscar-nominated as a director and winner of the Screenplay Oscar for *A Star is Born* (1937), was a descendant of Francis Lewis, a signatory of the Declaration of American Independence and hero of the Revolutionary War. Wellman too had fought, joining the French Foreign Legion before the US entry into World War One. His earliest movie work was as a bit-part actor, but he soon became a prop man and later a director.

Wings, his 1927 portrayal of wartime aviation, won the first ever Best Picture Academy Award, and was heavily

influenced by his own experiences as a flyer for Lafayette
Escadrille during the conflict. A friend of Douglas Fairbanks
Sr, who traded blows with his actors and once had a
stand-up fight with Spencer Tracy, Wellman was known as
'Wild Bill'. His films include the stirring *Beau Geste* (1939),
the comedy *Nothing Sacred* (1937) and the disturbing
lynching drama *The Ox-Bow Incident* (1943), as well as the
smash hit *The High and the Mighty* (1954).

VISUAL INTEREST: Less obviously indebted to the silent
era than *Little Caesar* in terms of technique (captions are
used only for dates, not for narrative clarity, for example),
Wellman uses lighting that is more suggestive of some kind
of objective reality than Le Roy's impressionistic smears.
The result (when combined with his use of exterior/stock
footage) is a film that has a visual style that is far closer to
what a general audience would now call 'realism' than that
of its near contemporary. (*The Public Enemy* does, however,
boast action sequences that are extraordinary in their pace
and structure, and beautifully, fiercely edited. Seventy years
after they were shot they retain the power to increase the
pulse rate of a viewer, which is no small achievement.)
The completed picture is, despite the fact that Wellman's
reputation is far greater than Le Roy's these days, a far less
visually arresting film than *Little Caesar* with considerably
less individual style; it appears, as a consequence, far more
dated than the more studio-bound picture.
Whereas *Little Caesar* is dark, and closeted, with never a
glimpse of natural light, much of *The Public Enemy* takes
place in reasonably bright light, recognisably the real
outdoors (and, unlike the case with *Little Caesar*, at least
some of the picture takes place in daylight). Wellman
perhaps sacrificed the absolute control afforded by sweaty
interiors for the verisimilitude offered by a mix of interiors
and exteriors. If so, he bought short-term success at the price
of the film's long-term worth. Visually, *The Public Enemy*
stands no comparison with *Little Caesar*, with only Cagney's

rain-soaked collapse, and the grim final frames truly lingering in the memory.

That said, the film's deliberate grappling with the moral and personal impact of crime, and its refusal to make its lead a mere grotesque, mark it out as groundbreaking, and there remains far more to enjoy in the picture for the more patient general viewer than in the majority of films of its era.

CONTEMPORARY REACTION: For something now held up as a classic of its kind, initial reaction to *The Public Enemy* was mixed with regard to almost every aspect of the production. On 21 April 1931 the *New York Times* reviewed the movie: 'weaker than most in its story, stronger than most in its acting' was the verdict, with Cagney and Woods adjudged 'remarkably lifelike' in their presentation of 'young hoodlums', although the reviewer was utterly unimpressed with Jean Harlow's 'essaying a turn as a gangster's mistress'. The most interesting aspect of the review is that it draws the reader's attention to the vast disparity between the way Warner Bros said that the film should be viewed (i.e. as a cautionary fable) and the way the audience reviewer Mordaunt Hall saw the film: they 'laughed frequently and with gusto' – amused, but appalled by Cagney and Woods for 'slugging disloyal bartenders, shooting down rival beermen, slapping their women crudely across the face'. This is in some contrast to the review in the May 1931 issue of *Reel Journal*, which was confident that the picture was 'absolutely serious from start to finish and was meant to be taken seriously by the audience'. *Reel* felt it to be 'a good moral picture', one 'not for children', but only because 'they will not understand it'. The magazine was particularly impressed that Cagney's and Woods's characters were neither portrayed as 'fantastic figures' nor obviously based on any real individual, instead being believable Everymen in 'conditions as they actually exist today' in an on-screen representation of the real 'life of crime which the gangsters lead'.

The picture on the whole was clearly 'meant to awaken honest citizens to the gangster tyranny prevalent in large cities today'. *Variety* (29 April), with rather less gravity, declared enthusiastically, that *The Public Enemy* was the 'roughest, toughest and best' gangster film the reviewer had seen. He felt that this would either enhance or seriously damage the box office, depending on how the public reacted, morally speaking. *Variety* noted with some glee that the climax was 'a shudder' and spent much less of its word count on the moral implications of what was on screen. Another point of disagreement between *Variety* and the *New York Times* came when the paper went on to praise the picture for having 'comedy as well as rough stuff' and declared Beryl Mercer's Ma Powers 'too mincing' (the *New York Times* had picked her performance out as a highlight).

TRIVIA: Edward Woods and James Cagney swapped roles during rehearsals: Wellman was convinced that Cagney was better for the bigger part and the more obvious natural star. It has been said that the difference between the two men's subsequent careers (Cagney is an icon; Woods petered before the 1930s had drawn to a close) proves the wisdom of Wellman's decision, and there is obvious truth in this orthodoxy, but Woods is excellent in support, and it would have been interesting to see what he might have made of the role. This is an interesting version of the movie's own argument, of course. Did the man make the part or the part make the man?

Like *Little Caesar*, *The Public Enemy* was nominated for the Screenwriting Oscar for its year. John Bright and Kubec Glasmon were named. Bright, incidentally, went on to write for the Basil Rathbone *Sherlock Holmes* series.

SEX/MONEY/DEATH: Comparisons between *The Public Enemy* and *Little Caesar* are frequent and inevitable. The same studio produced them, and their active production virtually overlapped. Darryl Zanuck ran production of *The*

Public Enemy at Warner Bros' Sunset studio, while Hal Wallis was in charge of *Little Caesar*, made at Warners' suburban Hollywood facility in Burbank. One followed hard upon the other at the box office, and essentially, between them, birthed Warner Bros a decade of gangster pictures.

Each also created a great movie star. Equally, they share similar fascinations and iconography, and are – even if only at face value – 'about' the same thing: the rise and fall of a gangster who dies as a result of his affection for a fellow hoodlum whom he has known since before he turned to crime.

However, this consensus is misleading, as technically, morally and philosophically they are very different films (see also **VISUAL INTEREST**). The most important difference between the narrative approach of *Little Caesar* and that of *The Public Enemy* is that Wellman's film seems to be genuinely attempting to examine the process whereby people are led into a life of crime. Rico in *Little Caesar* is a sort of carnival grotesque, a monster with only a tangential relationship with psychological reality. He has no family, only one friend to speak of and is already a murderer by the time the audience first encounter him. Tom in *The Public Enemy*, on the other hand, is introduced while a child, and has a large and extended family, all of whom the audience get to know to a lesser or greater extent. (It has been suggested that making Tom an Irishman in an era when organised crime sat almost entirely in the hands of Sicilians is born of a conscious desire to invoke the clichés of warm Irish family atmosphere when the plot requires it.)

The audience see the formative experiences of Tom's childhood, from joking horseplay with his siblings and neighbourhood girls to his being savagely beaten by his policeman father for his first foray into petty crime. (Indeed this is a thematically useful, almost symbolic, representation of the younger generation of the early twentieth century being battered by the forces of conformity.)

Tom's character is, for most of the picture, essentially defined by, and through, his relationship with his brother, whose own life acts as a dramatic counterweight to Tom's story. A little older than Tom (and perhaps, then, a product of slightly better times?), Mike is nearly as much a conformist as Tom is a rule breaker. Straighter even as a child (he chides Tom for a comic incident with roller-skates, for example), he's later described by his younger brother as 'too busy going to school', where he is 'learning how to be poor'. Tom plays society's game by its own rules, working hard, going to college and even enlisting when World War One rolls around.

Matt's reward for this conformity is not to fly as high as Tom, but then he doesn't end up being delivered, bloodied and bullet-ridden, to their mother at the film's ending. If grinding poverty and the avoidance of an early death are the only rewards for doing the right thing, then there is assuredly something wrong with society – and it's by subtly pushing this angle that *The Public Enemy* achieves its own kind of moral equivalence.

One of the most famous exchanges in the picture comes when Matt says to Putty Nose, 'If it hadn't been for you we might have been on the level.' Tom says, 'Sure, we might have been ding-dings on a streetcar.'

What this seems to be saying is that, while Tom has a personable culpability for his life of criminal endeavour (he is, after all, cynical about the idea that he could ever have avoided it, whereas Matt is wistful at the notion), a society in which the poor cannot imagine any worthwhile fate for themselves that can be achieved honestly must bear much of the responsibility also. For an individual to be responsible to his society, society must be responsible to the individual. This sophistication, perhaps now passed into cliché, is what sits at the heart of the best of the Warner Bros gangster movies, and makes it possible to sympathise with characters like Tom to a far greater extent than it is possible to root for Rico in *Little Caesar*, who remains, essentially, engaging only on a purely visceral, emphatically not humanitarian level.

The exchange is about, and the remark addressed to, Putty Nose, the oddly affectionate petty fence to whom Tom and his buddy Matt sell stolen goods as children. Putty clearly acts as a father figure, an alternative to the stentorian presence of his biological father. Although the character is clearly written as far more sinister, Murray Kinnell plays him with a chuckling playfulness that, while perhaps dishonest – for this is a man who is using children to assist his criminal endeavours, and isn't even recompensing them appropriately – adds to our understanding of Tom's descent.

There surely isn't, as some commentators seem to think, a contradiction between the individualistic nature of Tom's personality and crimes and the film's hastily written disclaimer's twice-asserted belief that *The Public Enemy* of the title is a social problem. Clearly Tom is an Everyman, and as the audience observe his journey they see all that contributes to the destination he ultimately reaches. The point is not so much that anyone could be Tom: it's that anyone could find themselves walking their own individual path to a similarly sordid and hollow fate. In the context, the title seems more complex, and a kind of pun: the Enemy is the Public and the Public is the Enemy – not two sides of the same coin, but one society embroiled in a divisive confrontation with itself. In this light the quotation from the Bible that begins *Little Caesar* ('For all they that take the sword shall perish with the sword' – Matthew 26: 52) seems infinitely more appropriate when applied to this picture.

THE VERDICT: A handsome, well-acted, well-intentioned picture that is now obviously a product of its time, *The Public Enemy* doesn't transcend its more dated aspects in the way that *Little Caesar* does. When compared to later Cagney pictures like *Angels With Dirty Faces* it is much harder to imagine a mainstream, early 21st century audience enjoying *The Public Enemy* without 'making allowances' for it. It is rather shapelessly structured and, the ending aside, contains nothing that could be considered shocking, or even mildly disturbing, for a modern audience. Cagney's performance is, despite make-up that seems effete to modern sensibilities, absolutely outstanding and it's very easy to understand how this picture made him a massive star.

Disclaimer

Later release prints of *Little Caesar* and *The Public Enemy* begin with a rolling caption card that mentions how both films had 'a great effect on public opinion' due to the way they 'brought home violently the evils associated with prohibition' and 'suggested the necessity of a nation wide house cleaning'. It went on to say that the two leads were 'not two men, nor are they, merely characters, they are a problem that sooner or later we, the public, must solve'. It's an indication of how keen Vitaphone were to make clear that they did not see their crime films as irresponsible, or the criminals presented within as aspirational – even though there's clearly an element of that to them. The open denunciation of prohibition, and the labelling of it as a mistake by government is merely another example of the studio attempting to appear responsible. *The Public Enemy* goes further than *Little Caesar*, with another caption (labelled 'Foreword') following on from the opening credits. This states, at some length, that the film's ambition is to 'honestly depict an environment that exists today in a certain strata of American life' (rather than to glorify the criminal, one assumes). It goes on to say that the story of Tom Powers is 'essentially a true story', deliberately placing the character in the milieu of the Everyman. This is especially ironic, given that, while the entirely believable life of Tom Powers is made up, the extraordinary career of Rico Bandello is largely based on real events.

Behind Bars

Another sub genre, one popular early in the twentieth century, is the 'criminals behind bars' movie. While to a modern filmgoer the above phrase is more likely to conjure up the unfortunate mental image of cheap, cable television-produced, soft-core pornography, the prison movie was once an area where compelling, aberrant characters could be presented in a manner that was 'safe'. Audiences were assured by the simple fact that these characters were in a penitentiary yet simultaneously, hypocritically, thrilled by their exploits in trying to escape, to either be reunited with a loved one or gain some kind of revenge. This is a formulaic genre, with few films that really stand up today, but a good example of this kind of movie is *20,000 Years In Sing Sing* (Michael Curtiz, 1932). Running at only 78 minutes this quickie is not Curtiz's best film (or even his best film of the year!) but it's notable in that it features, for the only time, the romantic pairing of Bette Davis and Spencer Tracy. Tracy's character Tom Connors is sentenced to prison for various mob-related crimes, but is convinced that his highly paid legal team – and corrupt city contacts – will get him free on parole soon enough. Unable to stop being a 'big shot' even in prison, he runs into trouble with the (admittedly Draconian) regime inside and is confined to solitary where he is further mistreated. Eventually even the possibility of parole is removed; he will have to serve out every day of his sentence. After his girlfriend Fay (Davis) is injured in further mob-related activity, Connors is given compassionate leave to visit her under the 'Honour System': he must meet an appointment with prison authorities to be taken into custody again, or become a wanted fugitive. While out, Connors encounters rival gangster Joe Finn, they fight, and Fay shoots Finn. Connors is blamed by the authorities for the death, and is executed in the electric chair.

A rattling melodrama, *20,000 Years In Sing Sing* allows audiences to feel for its protagonist by showing him battling against a system that is just as corrupt as he is, but also substantially larger and more powerful; this is the classic pattern for 'underdog' gangster films. By showing him as defeated by his love for Fay, and being executed for a crime he did not commit, the movie becomes as morally ambiguous as it can while adhering to a moral code that insists that criminals cannot be sympathetic and must be punished.

Scarface – The Shame of the Nation (1932)

(Black and white – 90 minutes)

Howard Hughes Presents
Scarface
From the Book by Armitage Trail
Screen Story by Ben Hecht
Continuity and Dialogue by Seton I Miller, John Lee Mahin, W R Burnett

United Artists Picture
Co-Director: Richard Rosson
Editorial Adviser: Douglas Biggs
Photography: Lee Garmes and L W O'Connell
Settings: Harry Oliver
Film Editor: Edward Curtiss
Sound Engineer: William Snyder
Musical Directors: Adolph Tandler and Gus Arnheim
Production Manager: Charles Stallings
Directed by Howard Hawks

PRINCIPAL CAST: Paul Muni (Tony), Ann Dvorak (Cesca), Karen Morley (Poppy), Osgood Perkins (Lovo), C Henry Gordon (Guarino), George Raft (Rinaldo), Vince Barnett (Angelo), Boris Karloff (Gaffney), Purnell Pratt (Publisher), Tully Marshall (Managing Editor), Inez Palange (Tony's Mother), Edwin Maxwell (Detective Chief)

SUMMARY: Bodyguard Tony 'Scarface' Camonte murders kingpin crime boss Big Louie Costillo. Johnny Lovo, the new big shot, appoints Tony to be his first lieutenant in recognition of this service. Tony, who has a creepy, obsessive (and perhaps inappropriately intentioned) relationship with his younger sister, Cesca, also has designs on Lovo's moll, Poppy.

Tony starts a gang war with the Irish mob of a neighbouring district and develops an equally unnatural love of the machine gun. Soon even Lovo fears him. When Lovo begins to suspect Tony's designs on Poppy, he plots to dispose of his dangerous lieutenant. Tony's pal Guarino kills Lovo. Now Tony is in charge. Tony takes a vacation, but on his return he discovers Cesca has left her mother's house. She's moved in with Guarino. Twisted up with jealousy, Tony kills Guarino. Cesca tells him that they married while he was away. She calls him a butcher. Tony runs away. Cesca follows him and threatens him with a gun. Then the police arrive. Instead of shooting Tony, Cesca embraces him. She's proud to die by his side. She is then killed in an exchange of gunfire.

A gas attack by police forces Tony towards them; the police disarm him and he begs not to be killed. As they try to arrest him, he flees, and is cut down by gunfire.

THE PLAYERS: Born Meshilem Meier Weisenfreund in Austria in 1897, Paul Muni emigrated to America as a child and worked much on the stage (particularly in Yiddish theatre) before his Oscar nomination for his very first screen role as a man on death row in *The Valiant* (William K Howard, 1929). *I Am a Fugitive From a Chain Gang!* (Mervyn Le Roy, 1932) gained him a second Oscar nomination, and the title role in *The Story of Louis Pasteur* (William Dieterle, 1935) finally gained him the award. (He would be nominated again for *The Life of Emile Zola* (Dieterle again, 1937) and for *The Last Angry Man* (Daniel Mann, 1959), his last movie and a part specially written for him.) An extraordinary actor who made fewer movies than many of his contemporaries, he eschewed stardom and concentrated on performing (though he was often dismissive of what 'acting' was). Muni may be unique in that his major place in Hollywood history was gained solely through committed performances in prestigious pictures. He studiously avoided pot-boilers and populist entertainment. He disliked making movies and was as often on the stage at the height of his powers as he was in front of a camera. He semiretired in 1953 and quit for ever after *The Last Angry Man*, feeling that his health and perhaps his talent were failing him. He died in 1967 from a heart problem that had plagued him all his life.

One of the great 'nearly men' of Hollywood history, George Raft nevertheless performed his coin-flipping trick in pictures as diverse as this one, *Some Like It Hot* (Billy Wilder, 1959) and *Casino Royale* (1967: *Royale* had many directors; Raft worked with Val Guest). He was born in Hell's Kitchen (Now Clinton), New York, in 1895 and as a young man was a regular hoofer at the El Fay nightclub while it was run by Texas Guinan (see **The Roaring**

Twenties). He often played hoods, and his associations with the likes of Guinan and real-life gangsters such as Bugsy Siegel were latterly an impediment to his career. He turned down the roles assumed by Humphrey Bogart in both *High Sierra* (Raoul Walsh, 1941) and *The Maltese Falcon* (John Huston, 1941), as well as parts in *Casablanca* (Michael Curtiz, 1942) and *Double Indemnity* (Billy Wilder, 1944).

Wide-eyed, beautiful and a clearly very capable actress (as well as a professional dance instructor) Ann Dvorak was the daughter of the silent-movie star Ann Lehr. She fought with studio bosses over roles and money and, despite the patronage of Howard Hawks, this remains essentially her only major screen role (although *G Men* (William Keighley, 1935) with James Cagney arguably comes close). She was neither the first nor the last talented young woman to have a career crushed beneath the mechanical wheels of Old Hollywood (see **The Roaring Twenties** for a particularly dispiriting example). She married an Englishman and came with him back to Europe. She was a volunteer ambulance driver throughout World War Two and died in 1979.

THE DIRECTOR: Howard Hawks was a director with a clean and uncluttered visuals style, and a persuasive way with actors. He is constantly cited as a pivotal influence by filmmakers who have followed him. He made three films with Cary Grant that dwell for ever in the collective unconsciousness of moviegoers (*Bringing Up Baby* (1938), *Only Angels Have Wings* (1939), and *His Girl Friday* (1940)) and two with Humphrey Bogart (*To Have and Have Not* (1944) and *The Big Sleep* (1946)) that will do likewise. Stars whose screen immortality he shaped include Lauren Bacall and Marilyn Monroe (he directed *Gentlemen Prefer Blondes* (1933) featuring 'Diamonds Are a Girl's Best Friend') and he directed the magnificent western *Rio Bravo* (1959), starring a rarely better John Wayne and a never-better Dean Martin. He was an outrageous storyteller (some might say outright liar), and his mythmaking skills were apparent off screen as well as on. His anecdotes and sound bites provide a collage of half-truths and 'spin' for anyone attempting to work their way with any objectivity through Golden Age Hollywood.

VISUAL INTEREST: The opening shot is a slow pulling down and away from a lamppost as its light goes out and is hugely impressive. Later in that scene Tony appears for the first time, in shadow, deep in the right-hand corner of the picture. His entrance is barely noticeable. The sweeping, arcing camera then moves to allow Tony to continue to move entirely in silhouette as he moves to murder Costello.

There's a fabulous 'luxury shot' of a machine gun firing savagely as the pages of a calendar splatter away and out of the frame.

Colossal attention is paid to lighting throughout: note the Venetian-blind effect across the walls when Tony is quizzed by the police, or the smears against the wall when Cesca rails at Tony for killing her husband. Even the dark band across the close-up of the tickertape reporting the warrant for Tony's arrest makes the screen suddenly more three-dimensional than those in almost any other film of the era. Cesca's approach towards Tony, gun in hand, tears staining her face, is still remarkably beautifully lit even today.

The X-shaped scar on the title character's face (which also appears under the credits at the beginning of the film) is used as a physical indicator/presager of on-screen murder in a way that borders on magic realism. Gaffney is killed at the bowling alley and his death occurs just after he has rolled a strike (marked on the score sheet with an X, of course). Cesca wears a dress with crossed straps. When Tony kills the seven leading hoods, the camera drifts up to show what is either an industrial beam or a bridge, formed by seven metal crosses interlinking with one another. When the corpse is thrown from the taxi to announce the beginning of a gang war, the body lands upon an X-shaped shadow.

QUOTES:

Tony: 'In this business there's only one law you gotta follow to keep out of trouble. Do it first, do it yourself and keep on doing it.'

Tony: 'There's business just waiting for some guy to come and run it right. And I got ideas.'

Guarino: 'We're workin' for Lovo, ain't we?'
Tony: 'Lovo? Who's Lovo?'

Tony (To Cesca): 'Listen, I don't want anybody kissin' my sister, do you understand? . . . I don't want anybody puttin' their hands on you.'

Tony (looking at the sign that says 'The World Is Yours'): 'Someday, I'll look at that sign and I'll say, "OK, she's mine." '

SOURCES TO SCREEN: The playwright Ben Hecht wrote his screenplay in eleven days, drawing on his own experiences as a newspaperman during Prohibition. He worked from the 1930 novel *Scarface* (by Maurice Coons, writing under the nom-de-plume of Armitage Trail), although in truth there is little resemblance between that book and Hecht's final script, despite their both being based on the life of Al Capone. (Tony Camonte is a Capone analogue; Johnny Lovo is the notorious Johnny Torrio; and Costillo is a stand-in Big Jim Colosimo.) The St Valentine's Day massacre is recreated faithfully when Camonte kills seven leading gangsters; there's a murder in a hospital (where Capone had the incapacitated Legs Diamond killed); and the 1920 killing of Deanie O'Bannion in a florist's is represented also.

Of course, Capone was already in jail by the time the film came out, doing eleven years for tax evasion, the only crime they could pin on him. He was let out on parole in 1939 and died of syphilis in 1947 – a fate no less sordid, though considerably less iconic, than Tony Camonte's end.

CONTEMPORARY REACTION: *Variety* (24 May 1932) found *Scarface* 'powerful and gripping'. In a review that assumes that *Scarface* will probably be the last gangster film for some considerable time, the paper saw the picture as 'strong for adults' and emphatically 'not for children', mixing 'more blood with rum' than all previous bootlegging dramas combined. It found the picture to be 'moral', though with no 'blaming of the environment' for gangsters' antisocial behaviour (such 'blaming' is automatically assumed to be a bad thing by the piece) and an emphatic closing condemnation of gangster rule ('And what are you going to do about it?' as the disclaimer goes).

Of course *Scarface* was far from the last gangster picture, but if all had gone to plan it could have been the first, or the first talkie at least. It was finished and ready for release in late 1930, which would have seen it steal a march on *Little Caesar* by a month or so, but Hawks and Hughes got into fights with various organisations promoting 'decency' and were accused of 'glorifying' gangsterism.

Many changes were demanded, and made, before the film was allowed to be released. The process dragged on for over a year. The subtitle was added (an earlier suggestion had been to call the film *The Menace*) and the long, apologetic disclaimer was added to the beginning. A few extra scenes were shot. One showed Tony Camonte's mother disapproving of her son's actions while talking to her daughter. This occurs as Mother takes Cesca upstairs, after Tony has screamed at her for demonstrating sexuality. Although largely in the style of the rest of the film, the camera angle on the set changes for no reason, and suddenly, and there are subtle differences in the set, hair and make-up. The lighting and the 'look' of the film grain also shift slightly.

Other additional scenes, all three featuring denunciatory speeches, were added along the film's length. The first features a chief of police and the second and third a newspaper editor. Hawks refused to have any involvement in this shooting and the scenes were directed by Richard

Rossen, who gained the vainglorious 'co-director' credit for his uninspired and shoddy censorship-inspired hackwork.

To a modern sensibility, these scenes are far more noxious than anything in the movie itself. The first apologises for the precepts of the Hays Code (then being written – see box below) and the others go on to blame the public for gangsterism, refusing to let any blame fall on the corrupt police force: 'Don't blame the police. They can't stop machine guns from being run back and forth across the state lines!' And they even verbally assault moviegoers who are enjoying the picture the scenes have been shoe-horned into.

As well as additions, there were also some subtractions, one of the most obvious being the removal of Cesca's line, 'You're me and I'm you – it's always been that way', from moments before her death. This doesn't simply make her a less active accomplice, but it also removes her final acknowledgement of the sheer impropriety of her brother's feelings towards her – a thread that has subtly snaked its way throughout the film. The most serious changes were made to the ending, which was completely reshot without Hawks or Muni's consent or involvement.

In this Tony is tried and sentenced by a criminal court, having been captured but not killed in the final shootout. The judge reads out a long condemnation of Tony's character and calls him more guilty than 'any criminal who has come before me for sentence'. He is sentenced to death for being 'ruthless, immoral, and vicious'. 'There is no place in this country for your type.' Tony, seen only in close-ups of his feet, or in long-shot, is then graphically hanged.

What these additional scenes actually do, rather than ameliorate the violent content of the film, or make Tony less 'heroic' (something he isn't in the first place), is excuse the authorities for any responsibility for a society in which such things can happen. The censorship is about self-defence, not about the protection of audiences.

The film ultimately did poorly at the box office (it was banned in several states, and showings were delayed over a

year in Chicago) and was withdrawn from circulation by
Howard Hughes. It wasn't rereleased until 1979. No print of
the unmutilated version is known to exist. The version
available on video and syndicated to television keeps
Hawks's ending, but retains the other alterations.

SEX/MONEY/DEATH: Like Rico of *Little Caesar* Tony is
a monster from the moment he's first seen. Smug, calm,
calculating and cold, he is, again like Rico, more a force of
nature than a recognisable human being. Mocking and
sneering his way through killing after killing and seemingly
incapable of human feeling, he also has only a tangential
relationship with human reality.

It is difficult to see how anyone, in any audience, could
identify with or wish to be like Tony Camonte. His life of
crime doesn't visibly bring him financial rewards or material
possessions (he gets a new dressing gown – but so what? –
and he seems to live with his mother throughout). His
attractiveness to women doesn't seem to increase as a result
of his gangster status and Poppy – whom he pursues – is
clearly portrayed as herself psychologically aberrant for
being (if Karen Morley's performance is anything to go by)
aroused by his violence and sociopathy. To put it bluntly,
who would want to be the object of the affections of a
madwoman?

Maybe it's Tony's contempt and sarcasm that made
censors feel that he would be perceived as a hero, but he's a
stupid person, mocked as often as he's mocking, who
doesn't understand what the word 'effeminate' means and
who takes 'tacky' to be a compliment.

Another aspect of the film that adds to Tony's vileness is
the inappropriateness of his relationship with his sister,
whom he initially seems merely overprotective of.
Eventually, even their mother acknowledges that his
obsession has drifted beyond the fraternal. ('Sister! Ha! To
him you're just another girl!' she says.) The scene, for
example, where he tears her dress to reveal her underwear

while screaming at her would be overtly sexualised and violent in a film of the period even without the implicitly incestuous content. Her decision to help him escape and to go down fighting with him, and indeed this whole thread, seems to have largely escaped the censors' attentions. Presumably, they didn't notice it, felt it was sufficiently flagged as 'bad' or (more alarmingly) didn't see it as particularly wrong.

THE VERDICT: Although the finished product was a mutilated masterpiece (the additional sequences uniformly dreadful), Hawks's original cut of *Scarface* was not the endorsement of the gangster lifestyle or the call to immorality that the Christian right complained of at the time. It was a compulsive portrayal of an aberrant figure who suffers the ultimate punishment for his transgressions. The extant film is often sadly unsubtle, smug and reactionary, thanks to the censorship interference, but the beauty of Hawks's compositions and Muni's performance shine through regardless.

Scarface (1983)

Remade by Brian De Palma, from a screenplay by Oliver Stone, the 1983 *Scarface* stakes a claim for its own place in the history of the genre by casting Michael Corleone himself (Al Pacino) in the lead and upping the ante in terms of violence. Pacino is excellent, although it is an early example of the 'overblown' performances that would dominate his later career. De Palma wisely largely avoids his frequent Hitchcock pastiche in favour of a murkier visual style. The major difference between the two in storytelling terms is that Stone's screenplay makes Tony Camonte 'Tony Montana', a Cuban refugee, fleeing Castro's regime, who earnestly attempts to make an honest living in America before turning to drug dealing and crime. Despite the best efforts of all concerned, it stands no comparison with even the censored version of Hawks's film.

The Hays Code

Because it is such a complex subject, any discussion of what has become popularly known as 'the Hays Code' (or often just 'the Code') that runs for fewer than several tens of thousands of words is inevitably going to be perfunctory and shallow. The following is offered merely as a rough guide to the basic concept for those unaware of the Code and its long-lived and, frankly, derogatory influence on American film.

Initially American films were unregulated, and there were no controls on content and/or what was represented on screen. In 1922, after a series of Hollywood scandals (involving more than one suspicious death, and the first firm emergence into the public consciousness of the idea that those in the film industry may be leading a hedonistic lifestyle), the film industry decided to begin to regulate its own product. This self-censorship was partially motivated by fear of the very real emergent possibility that the government might itself choose to regulate the industry through legislation. Some Catholic groups had begun to call for all Catholics to boycott the entire medium of film because of its moral turpitude. Compared with this sort of organised pressure, the notion of self-regulation was almost appealing.

Will Hays, a former US postmaster general with strong government credentials (he was a one-time chairman of the Republican Party, then in the middle of an uninterrupted fourteen years in office, with three separate successive elected presidents in Harding, Coolidge and Hoover), was installed as the chief executive and figurehead of the newly created MPPDA (Motion Picture Producers and Distributors of America Inc.). Hays's government contacts and unimpeachably conservative views, rather than any specialised knowledge of film, were the chief reasons for his selection.

Hays wrote the first MPPDA Code, with which he soon became synonymous. Issued in 1930, it contained a vast number of instructions and guidelines to which any film had to stick in order to gain a PCA (Production Code Administration) seal of approval. Without any such seal, a film couldn't be distributed to cinemas.

The Code, which is freely available online in a number of versions (it was revised several times during its lifetime), is, to twenty-first-century eyes, an astonishingly severe, aggressively religiously motivated and, at times, outright racist document. What the Code terms 'sex between the races' – i.e. virtually any physical contact between men and women of different skin tones – is identified as a sexual perversion as gross as paedophilia and as serious a breach of Code etiquette as 'showing the genitals of children', for example. Inconsistently applied, and subject to constant revisions, the Code remained in force until the mid-1960s.

> The main impact on the gangster picture of the Hays Code was very simple. After 1934, all criminals shown in motion pictures had to be either portrayed as seeing the error of their ways and redeemed or justly punished by the law. Preferably both.

Afraid to Talk (Edward L Cahn, 1932)

Afraid To Talk is the kind of film that the Hays Code (see The Hays Code **box**) was arguably *really* trying to dispose of. While not horribly violent or overtly sexy according to the manners of the time, it is a searing attack on the corruption of the period, and it pulls no punches at all in illustrating how the law enforcement, and City Governance, organisations of the day were as effectively criminal as the more easily recognisable 'gangster' archetype. In it, an innocent bellboy at a hotel (Eric Linden) is destroyed by the massed forces of City Hall and local gangsters because he happens to witness a pay off being made; simultaneously a corrupt District Attorney (an elected state-employed prosecuting council) conspires with corrupt policemen to ensure that the mobsters who are bribing them don't get busted.

Afraid To Talk is not about an individual man of action or a portrayal of an aberrant psychology, like *Little Caesar* et al., and it does not ask the audience to sympathise, even slightly, with its mobster characters. It is, however, a far more direct attack on the establishment of the period that was responsible for creating, and perpetuating, many of the problems ordinary citizens faced on a day-to-day basis. It's the kind of picture that it was far more difficult to provide alternative versions of after the Hays Code really began to bite. The more action/character-orientated gangster thriller proved easily transferable into other, subtly different, milieu with much of the violence retained; strangely once the violence was meted out by government employees in pictures, it became less disapproved of by the censors. The dramatic 'furniture' of the gangster film, such as violence and revenge, became more acceptable once the underlying logic, rebellion against authority, had disappeared – even though it was the furniture that was officially objected to most. *Afraid To Talk* is a rare example of a film where the underlying logic is more important than the mere furniture and the desire to entertain.

G-Men (William Keighley, 1935)

G-Men is a fine example of the kind of films Hollywood studios were prompted to make following the introduction, and subsequent tightening up, of the Hays Code. It is a vehicle for Jimmy Cagney's pugnacious tough guy persona, as developed in *The Public Enemy* et al., but it sees Cagney working for the Establishment, not against it. The movie's tagline 'Hollywood's Most Famous Bad Man Joins the "G-MEN" and Halts the March of Crime!' gives an indication of how this picture was sold. There are all the thrills one expected from Cagney, but they are presented in a more 'socially responsible' (arguably actually merely 'establishment flattering') manner. Cagney plays 'Brick' Davis, a young law school graduate whose way through college is paid for by a Mob Boss. Encouraged to go into public service by his college roommate Eddie Buchanan, 'Brick' demures. However, when Eddie joins the FBI, he is killed by criminals. Brick, having found a leaflet lying in the gutter that suggests honest citizens should apply to join the bureau, enrols to avenge him.

Many of the fascinations of the gangster picture are featured in *G-Men* (Cagney himself, a 'loner' hero in moral torment, a climactic gunfight, a revenge plot) with, as noted, the significant difference that the movie's hero operates on the opposite side of the law. Although entertaining, and packed with action typical of the period, *G-Men* is arguably inhibited by the unmistakable whiff of propaganda that surrounds it. Production was approved of, and supervised, by FBI head J Edgar Hoover, who assigned FBI agents to the film to make sure that the film represented the agency in the manner in which he wanted it represented. The film also marks a sea change in the bureau's procedural behaviour and relationship with the public: during the course of the picture FBI agents are armed for the first time (something happening contemporaneously in reality) and they are, again for the first time, given the power to arrest suspects without getting the permission of local enforcement authorities.

The picture made over $1 million at the box office and was rated a success by both Hoover and audiences. It was hugely influential in its own way – it is the first time a major star played an FBI agent as a heroic lead – and the establishment of this archetype led, indirectly, to its subversion in television series such at *The X-Files* (1993–2002). *G-Men*'s 'authorised' nature, however, can best be illustrated by the simple fact that it was re-released in 1949 to celebrate the FBI's 25th anniversary.

Angels With Dirty Faces (1938)

(Black and white – 97 minutes)

Warner Bros Inc Pictures Presents
A First National Picture
Directed by Michael Curtiz
Screen Play by John Wexley and Warren Duff
From a Story By Rowland Brown
Music by Max Steiner
Dialogue Director: Jo Graham
Photography by Sol Polito, ASC
Film Editor: Owen Marks
Art Director: Robert Haas
Gowns by Orry-Kelly
Sound by E A Brown
Musical Director: Leo F Forbstein
Orchestral Arrangements: Hugo Friedhofer

PRINCIPAL CAST: James Cagney (Rocky Sullivan), Pat O'Brien (Jerry Connolly), Humphrey Bogart (James Frazier), Ann Sheridan (Laury Ferguson), George Bancroft (Mac Keefer), Billy Halop (Soapy), Bobby Jordan (Swing), Leo Gorcey (Bim), Gabriel Dell (Pasty), Huntz Hall (Crab), Bernard Punsly (Hunky), Joe Downing (Steve), Edward Pawley (Edwards), Adrian Morris (Blackie), Frankie Burke (Rocky as a boy), William Tracey (Jerry as a boy) Marilyn Knowlden (Laury as a child)

SUMMARY: Ghetto children 'Rocky' Sullivan and Jerry Connolly break into a rail freight car. Happened upon by security, they flee. Jerry jumps a fence, but Rocky is caught. Rocky goes to a juvenile detention centre, and when he emerges embarks on a life of crime – from bootlegging to murder, if we are to believe the headlines that are shown. More than a decade passes. Rocky goes to jail for three years after being convicted of a heist, but is assured by his lawyer, Frazier, that his share of $100,000 will be waiting for him when he gets out.

After his release Rocky returns to the area where he lived as a child and is reunited with Jerry – now a priest – and Laury, a girl whom he once teased. He also goes to see Frazier, who is now working for a man called Keefer, another big-time hood. Rocky asks for a job, but Frazier is secretly planning to have him killed.

Rocky falls in with a group of kids and they come to idolise the glamorous gangster, who feeds them treats and plays basketball with them. After a failed hit, Rocky confronts Frazier – stealing money and papers related to his illegal business dealings and court cases – and manages to secure for himself a position in Keefer's organisation, thanks to trickery and a faked kidnap. He gives the kids money for running items for him and donates money to Father Jerry, so that the priest can build a recreation centre. Jerry refuses the money and begins a public campaign against all mobsters, including his old friend, because he's frightened of the influence they have on children.

Because of this, Frazier and Keefer want Jerry killed, but Rocky won't countenance it. Rocky kills Frazier and Keefer to protect Jerry, and then goes on the run. Captured and tried, he is to be executed for murder. On death row Jerry visits Rocky and asks a favour: he wants him to die a coward, so that the kids in the old tenements will no longer revere him, and look for better role models. Rocky refuses: pride is all he had. Yet, later, when confronted with the chair, Rocky breaks and dies begging for his life, screaming and pleading for mercy he knows can never come. The kids gather over the paper, reading about Rocky's fear. Jerry comes to see them, and they ask him if Rocky really died screaming. He tells them he did.

THE PLAYERS: Since becoming a star, James Cagney had kept busy, with Warner Bros ordering him into star vehicles (mostly crime pictures). These included *Taxi!* (Roy Del Ruth, 1932), in which he showed off his perhaps surprising ability to speak Yiddish, *The Crowd Roars* (Howard

Hawks, 1932) and the wonderfully entitled *The Mayor of Hell* (Archie Mayo, Michael Curtiz, 1933).

Despite his talent, the studio's lack of imagination had taken hold of his career and he'd quickly found himself repeating the same character over and again in formula pictures; an exception is his stellar turn as a dancing producer/performer in the musical *Footlight Parade* (Lloyd Bacon, 1933). Cagney began pushing the studio, demanding more challenging, more interesting roles and – crucially – more money than that to which he was contractually entitled. By 1935 he had also incurred the wrath of the Warner Bros head, Jack L Warner, by becoming involved in the creation of an actors' rights group, later to become the Screen Actors Guild. Warner Bros appears to have given in to at least some of his demands. So, while his determined and incorruptible FBI agent in *G-Men* (William Keighley, 1935 – see previous box) was little distinguishable from his gangster roles (save that he was now on the right side of the law), he also got to play pilots in *Ceiling Zero* (Howard Hawks, 1936) and *Devil Dogs of the Air* (Lloyd Bacon, 1935) and was cast, perhaps surprisingly – but in this critic's opinion most effectively – as Bottom in Warner Bros all-star version of Shakespeare's *A Midsummer Night's Dream* (William Dieterle, Max Reinhardt, 1935). Clearly these newly granted opportunities weren't enough, as shortly afterwards he cut out on Warner Bros before his contract had ended (an action that was the height of vulgarity in Hollywood's eyes).

Along with his brother William (a sometime actor himself), Cagney set up his own production company within the independent distributing company Grand National Pictures. The aim was personally to develop and produce the kinds of picture that Warner Bros had never let him make. Perhaps as importantly, he'd also own a portion of the profits of any film he made, rather than working for a salary.

His first Grand National picture, *Great Guy* (John G Blystone, 1936), was blandly cut from the same cloth as the

Warner Bros vehicles he'd been trying to escape, and perhaps suggested that he was really more interested in the profit-share aspect of his new venture than the actor's-craft part. His next project, though, a musical, *Something to Sing About* (Victor Shertzinger, 1937), was something that Warner Bros would almost certainly never have let him anywhere near (it's a very different film from *The Footlight Parade*, despite their both being musicals) but it was overly expensive and only a modest hit, failing to go into profit.

Perhaps sensing defeat, Cagney took his next project, this picture, back to Warner Bros, where it was given a lavish production by a studio that was keen to have its once most bankable star back on its lot. *Angels* was a smash hit, and earned Cagney an Oscar nomination.

Pat O'Brien, thought of as Old Hollywood's finest 'professional Irishman', was actually born in the Midwest (although of Irish stock) and genuinely considered the priesthood as a vocation before embarking on an acting career that would see him constantly 'frocked up' as one man of God or another. Unlike his pal Cagney (they were close off screen as well making nine movies together), O'Brien was a political conservative who openly, loudly and publicly supported General Franco during the Spanish Civil War. Equally unlike Cagney, he was a studio employee who accepted rote assignments, standard wage packets and roles tailored to his screen image uncomplainingly.

He'd come from the stage too. He'd been playing Walter Burns in Ben Hecht's *The Front Page* on the New York stage, and was asked to reprise his role in the 1931 Lewis Milestone movie adaptation. However, somewhere along the line the studio made a mistake, and he was offered the other lead, Hildy Johnson, instead. Presumably fancying the chance to play the other guy's role or, characteristically, not wanting to upset the apple cart, he accepted the part anyway.

Aside from *The Front Page* and *Angels*, O'Brien is best known for his role as the fast-talking (though most of his characters were fast-talking) eponymous football coach in *Knute Rockne, All American* (Lloyd Bacon, 1940), delivering the famous speech where he demands that his demoralised players win a big game for 'the Gipper' (future president Ronald Reagan). (Your author, though, is hugely fond of his turn in the Deanna Durbin vehicle *His Butler's Sister* (Frank Borzage, 1943).)

It's another measure of his conformist nature that, whereas most actors would balk at being so closely identified with one role, O'Brien cheerfully spent his retirement repeating, word for word, gesture for gesture, that speech at after-dinner engagements. His last film was also Cagney's (big-screen) swan song, *Ragtime* (Milos Forman, 1981) an adaptation of E L Doctorow's novel of sexual jealousy and murder in pre-World War One America.

Humphrey Bogart is an icon – even more than Cagney – a movie star whose image, face, voice and persona resonate. The simple fact that there are half a dozen stories that claim to be the 'true' version of how he suffered the partial facial paralysis that caused his trademark half-sneer and lisp is all the proof you need of his near-mythic status.

Born 25 December 1899 into a wealthy Manhattan family, he was expelled as a teenager from Philips Academy School, where he'd been doing premed, and went on to serve in the US Navy through World War One. After the war he became a stage manager and bit-part player in theatre, graduating to full-time acting by the early twenties. Minor film roles followed, including a stint at Fox, where he made shorts. He was released before his contract came to an end.

In 1936 the screen adaptation of the Broadway hit *The Petrified Forest* proved his way into the movie big time when its star, Leslie Howard, demanded that Bogart be hired to reprise his stage role in Archie Mayo's film. Bogart was impressive in the picture, and gained a contract at Warner Bros on the back of it. His signature performances in *The Maltese Falcon* (John Huston, 1941) and *Casablanca* (Michael Curtiz, 1942) followed hard upon his fruitful collaborations with James Cagney here and in *The Roaring Twenties* (1938) and *Bullets or Ballots* (William Keighley, 1935). *To Have and Have Not* (Howard Hawks, 1944) paired him with Lauren Bacall for the first time. They would marry, have children and dabble in politics together for more than a decade before his untimely death from cancer. Together they led protests against the House Un-American Activities Committee (he famously commenting that McCarthy would try anyone who'd ever scratched themselves during the national anthem) as well as appearing in *The Big Sleep* (Howard Hawks, 1946) and the magnificent, yet underrated, *Dark Passage* (Delmer Daves, 1947), defining a new kind of on-screen partnership in the process. Other Bogie (and it is 'Bogie', not 'Bogey', as anyone who has seen his autograph can attest) films that dwell in the collective unconsciousness of moviegoers include *Key Largo* (John Huston, 1948), *The Treasure of the Sierra Madre* (John Huston, 1948) and his Oscar-winning performance in *The African Queen* (John Huston, 1951). He was buried in California, and his coffin contains a gold whistle placed there by Bacall.

THE DIRECTOR: Born in Budapest in 1886, Michael Curtiz had been an actor and successful director of silents in Northern and Eastern Europe before and after World War One – such as *Atlantis* (1913) – before going to America. Influenced by German expressionists and with an on-set authoritarian style modelled on the likes of Von Sternberg, he was nonetheless an uncomplaining Warner Bros contract director who accepted whatever script, in whatever genre, he was given. This led both to his being sneered at by those who feel a great director should demonstrate a consistent worldview and, more fortunately, to his becoming one of the primary shapers of America's celluloid dreams.

His pictures included horrors such as *The Mystery of the Wax Museum* (1933, one of the most underrated films of the 1930s); swashbucklers such as *Captain Blood* (1935), *The*

Adventures of Robin Hood (1938) and *The Sea Hawk* (1940, arguably *the* three seminal influences on the modern action movie); the legendary musical *White Christmas* (1954); and the Joan Crawford melodrama *Mildred Pierce* (1946), among many others. He garnered Academy Award nominations for *Four Daughters* (1938) and *Yankee Doodle Dandy* (1942), as well as for this picture, and won an Oscar for directing *Casablanca* (1942), a troubled production that nevertheless remains rightly held up as one of the best films ever made in America. He died in 1962.

VISUAL INTEREST: 'Skilful' rather than 'showy' is probably the best description of Curtiz's direction here. The montage that establishes Rocky's life of crime after he comes out of the juvenile detention centre is effective, but less eye-boggling and nowhere near as conceptually complex as the ones in, say, *The Roaring Twenties*. There's a casual realism to much of the film's outdoor (backlot) scenes, a faintly contrived normality that seems to be an offshoot of production-line filmmaking. A nice luxury-shot feature, though, is the more or less direct duplication of the early crane shot (which leads the audience to Rocky and Jerry for the first time) utilised when the Dead End Kids are first introduced. It's a neatly done visual signifier that these boys are now at the same point in their lives as the leads were in the introductory sequences, and that they will have to make similar choices, in perhaps harder times.

The ending, although morally soporific, seems, to modern eyes, to be a strong indictment against America's continued enthusiasm for the legislated murder that is the death penalty. Huge, almost pseudo-Langian, shadows thrown against the wall, tears from O'Brien and screams from Cagney raise the hackles on the back of the neck and chill the blood even after fifty-odd years. It's predictable, but appropriate also, that in the final shot Father Jerry leads the boys both physically and morally upwards, and indeed towards a shining light.

QUOTES:
Rocky: 'What we don't take we ain't got.'

Rocky: 'Say your prayers, mugs . . .'

Father Jerry: 'Say a prayer for a boy who couldn't run as fast as I could.'

SOURCES TO SCREEN: There are points of comparison between *Angels* and other Warner Bros gangster films – and not just those starring Cagney. The central relationship between two men echoes *Little Caesar* and Rocky's death seems to be a deliberate reaction against that ethos. Another obvious source is *Dead End* itself (see box on page 60) and it is the combination of two eminently bankable Warner Bros properties (Cagney and the Kids) that provides the least satisfying elements of the film to a modern audience. The teen actors are – at best – passable, and much of their comic play is risible. Only when Cagney joins them do these scenes come alive, and when he's absent they genuinely drag. Despite the Oscar nomination, the script is a little underdeveloped with regard to the character of Laury, who is frustratingly simplistic, despite a strong performance from Ann Sheridan, and doesn't really have a function within either the narrative or iconography of the piece.

CONTEMPORARY REACTION: *Variety* (26 October 1938) didn't think much of a film that would become regarded as a classic piece, and it was the juvenile leads, rather than Cagney (a fading star, then) and Bogart (not yet a star) that they saw as being at the centre of the picture and its failure. 'A typical Dead End Kids picture' said the paper describing it as 'no bonfire'. The ending came in for particular scorn with Cagney's simulated cowardice 'completely implausible' and his redemption 'hokey'. The *New York Times* was more positive. On 28 November the paper's regular critic Frank S Nugent approved of the 'human story' at the heart of the 'savage melodrama' and maintained, in opposition to *Variety*, that the picture had a 'realistic point of view' on organised crime and made up for the 'familiarity of the ground' it was treading with 'surprising twists of plot and character'. The film as a whole was 'picturesque and dramatic' and featured a performance from Cagney that could be labeled 'his best'. A month or so later, when summing up the whole of 1938, Nugent and his fellow New York Critics left the picture out of the list of the year's ten best, but it made the runners up list of five. Cagney won the New York Film Critics Award for the Best Performance by a Male Actor, although this decision was apparently only reached after a record nine ballots of those entitled to vote. Strong box office, and positive word-of-mouth made sure opinion of the feature held closer to the *Times* than *Variety* and, by March the following year, it had been nominated for three Academy Awards, the aforementioned one for Cagney, one for director Curtiz and one for the screenplay – although none of those translated into actual awards at the ceremony.

SEX/MONEY/DEATH: The fact that Jerry chooses to become a priest and Rocky chooses to become a gangster has been used to argue that this picture moves away from blaming societal problems for the rise of the gangster. Of course, nothing could be further from the truth: 'There but for the grace of God goes I,' says O'Brien's priest at one point, the implication being that not merely his faith but his decision to become a churchman is all that saved him from a life of crime.

Indeed, the montage that establishes his career's progress leads directly on from the 'foolish' (rather than evil) petty criminal high jinks that Rocky and Jerry commit together. Is the more likely implication that had Jerry rather than Rocky been caught, then their roles in life would have been reversed? Rocky's decision to not die 'heroically' (or at least in a manner that the children would regard as 'heroic') at the end of the film, it has been argued, affirms his free will. But that is the free will of an adult, not a child trapped in a ghetto, and the choice he makes – die screaming or die quietly – isn't really much of a choice at all. Should the analogy, then, be that, just as Rocky had no choice but to die and could choose only the manner of his dying, he had no choice but to be born poor, but it was only the decision to be *bad* that was his? This doesn't make it impossible that he felt *forced* into being a career criminal, though, and the fact that, a decade and a half later, children are in the same position suggests that there really is – and was – no hope in crime alley.

Not everyone can become a priest, after all, and Jerry's decision to become one comes after Rocky's initial incarceration; until that moment they are much the same kind of boy. Jerry's comment that Rocky is a 'boy who couldn't run as fast as I could' makes it clear the priest himself sees the two of them as indistinguishable up to that point.

But no, even this seems wrong, feels wrong, when one watches the picture. Rocky's decision to die in a manner that will turn children away from his path may not affirm that he had free will all along: it may actually be the only choice he has ever been able to make for himself, the only moment when he had any choice at all. If these children are presented with an alternative, they will grow up to be better people than he was. Rocky knows that he had no good examples when he was growing up, and that this contributed to his near inevitable fall. By refusing to provide the children with a role model – albeit negative – and instead implicitly telling them to follow the less exciting, more low-key but ultimately better path offered by Father Jerry, he is not merely dying for his sins, but dying to prevent theirs. He gives up his reputation and the kind of immortality that the leads of *Little Caesar* and *Scarface* were desperate to embrace in order to do some good. It's not quite a self-sacrifice, but it's an entirely selfless, redemptive act, which sits comfortably among the constant religious iconography of the piece.

Rocky isn't a particularly bad man by the standards of on-screen gangsters (even on-screen gangsters played by

Cagney). His crimes largely consist of racketeering and profiteering, providing things society wants but denies itself the chance to acquire legally. It's hard to see that owning a nightclub is an innately criminal activity anyway, and Rocky is dragged back into crime during the course of the film only because he has no opportunities to make money legally.

Although Rocky does corrupt the neighbourhood boys' perceptions of who they want to be, he does so unknowingly, believing that being like him is the only way they can survive. There's a sense in which he's always doing what he believes to be the right thing for them. This is why his final decision to destroy his own memory – to die saving the boys from having him as a hero, pretending to be 'yellow' and squealing in the chair – is entirely in character. It is not, as some contemporary critics felt, an unconvincing final reversal of character, but the entirely appropriate end to a story that Cagney himself had developed, perhaps as a conscious – and *socially* conscious – reaction to his own previous screen image.

THE VERDICT: A slightly muddled film with some redundant characters and grating 'children' indulging in poor comedy of the 'gee, shucks' variety, this is granted immortality by another tremendous Cagney performance, terrific support from Bogart and (especially) O'Brien and a final half-hour that builds to an execution scene of astonishing horror.

The Dead End Kids

In 1937 the successful stage production *Dead End* (concerning children in a ghetto environment who hero-worshipped a character played by Humphrey Bogart) was adapted into a motion picture. Samuel Goldwyn of Metro Goldwyn Mayer signed the six principal 'child' actors (they were all actually well into their teens) on two-year contracts. They were Bill Halop, Bobby Jordan, Leo Gorcey, Gabriell Dell, Huntz Hall and Bernard Punsly.

Soon, though, Goldwyn sold their contracts on to Warner Bros, thanks to a combination of an inability to find an appropriate second vehicle and the off-screen misbehaviour of some of the 'Kids' (such as Gorcey's persistent traffic violations). Warner Bros made *Crime School* (Lewis Seiler, 1938) with the group and then, presumably due to the same problem of developing the right vehicle that Goldwyn had found, lent Hall, Dell, Punsly and Halop to the rival studio Universal to make *Little Tough Guy* (Harold Young, 1938), which, though cheap and uninspired, was a substantial financial success.

Warner Bros recalled the four from Universal and – reuniting them with Gorcey – put them into the Cagney project *Angels With Dirty Faces*. The group then made *Hell's Kitchen* (Lewis Seiler, Ewald Andre Dupont), *They Made Me a Criminal* (Busby Berkeley) and *Angels Wash Their Faces* (Ray Enright, all 1939) but none was a great success. *Angels Wash Their Faces* is a particular oddity. Conceptually and thematically something of a sequel to *Angels With Dirty Faces*, the movie even features Ann Sheridan from the former movie in a role in which, while she has a different name, is essentially the same character. Shortly afterwards, the Kids' contracts were quietly dropped by the studio. There were various other iterations of the 'Dead End Kids' notion from other studios in the immediately following years, usually involving much of the core group from *Dead End* (billed as, for example, 'The Bowery Boys') indulging in adolescent man-child high jinks. One version of the group also featured Leo Gorcey's younger brother David.

The Amazing Dr Clitterhouse (Anatole Litvak, 1938)

As with *G-Men* and *Bullets or Ballots* this is another example of a studio, in this case Warner Bros, trying to find a way to make a gangster movie without making a gangster movie. A successful play by Barré Lyndon was adapted into a movie script by (later) noted director John Huston and John Wexley. The play, which had starred Cedric Hardwicke, was a tale of a high society doctor who wants to develop a cure for crime, which he believes to be a treatable behavioural illness. In order to gather data on how criminals act and behave he begins committing crimes himself (he measures his heart rate, respiration, etc., during heists) and, while robbing a safe at a party, comes across a gang who are trying the same thing. He joins the gang in order to study its members but comes into conflict with the group's erstwhile leader, Rocks.

The film version sees Edward G Robinson replace Hardwicke and Humphrey Bogart take on the role of Rocks. While it has been suggested that Robinson does not approximate Hardwicke's laconic style sufficiently to make the film version a success, he is very funny in the film, albeit in a deadpan manner. The additional textual frisson caused by the doctor plotting to end all crime, while slowly being seduced by the lifestyle, must surely though be of interest to many viewers. Clitterhouse's noble motives, the picture's comic nature and the confirmed 'badness' of Bogart's portrayal of Rocks make *The Amazing Dr Clitterhouse* a strong, but utterly peculiar, example of the length Warner Bros were prepared to go to make films that would appeal to their core audience without violating the Hays Code.

The Roaring Twenties (1939)

(Black and white – 100 minutes)

Warner Bros Presents
Jack L Warner in Charge of Production
A Warner Bros Picture
Executive Producer: Hal B Wallis
Associate Producer: Samuel Bischoff
Screen Play by Jerry Wald, Richard Macaulay and
Robert Rossen
From an Original Story by Mark Hellinger
Dialogue Director: Hugh Cummings
Director of Photography: Ernie Haller, ASC
Film Editor: Jack Killifer
Sound by E A Brown
Art Director: Max Parker
Wardrobe by Milo Anderson
Make-Up Artist: Perc Westmore
Special Effects: Byron Haskin ASC, Edwin DuPar, ASC
Orchestral Arrangements: Ray Heindorf
Musical Director: Leo Forbstein
Directed by Raoul Walsh

PRINCIPAL CAST: James Cagney (Eddie Bartlett), Priscilla Lane (Jean Sherman), Humphrey Bogart (George Hally), Gladys George (Panama Smith), Jeffrey Lynn (Lloyd Hart),

Frank McHugh (Danny Green), Paul Kelly (Nick Brown), Elizabeth Risdon (Mrs Sherman), Ed Keane (Henderson), Joe Sawyer (The Sergeant), Joseph Crehan (Michaels), George Meeker (Masters), John Hamilton (Judge), Robert Elliott (First Detective), Eddie Chandler (Second Detective), Abner Biberman (Lefty), Vera Lewis (Mrs Gray), Narration by John Deering

SUMMARY: Eddie Bartlett returns from World War One to find depression, Prohibition and personal unemployment. Accidentally drawn into liquor running, he soon begins to brew his own rotgut, making more and more money and becoming a bigger and bigger fish. He romances Jean Sherman, not knowing that she is more interested in his lawyer and wartime friend, Lloyd, and ignores the advances of his business associate, the sassy Panama Smith.

Jean and Lloyd go on to be married, and Eddie's fortune collapses, owing to a combination of the Wall Street crash and the end of Prohibition. The remains of his criminal empire are taken over by his former lieutenant (and another army pal), George Hally. Eddie goes back to driving a taxi, but slides into alcoholism and depression. He kills George in revenge but is in turn killed by George's men.

THE PLAYERS: Beautiful and capable of attracting an audience's empathy with the slightest movement of her face, Priscilla Lane was a Warner Bros contract player in, for the period, 'racy' dramas such as *Yes, My Darling Daughter* (William Keighley, 1939), which was about an unmarried couple's weekend away together. Lane made an average of four films a year between 1938 and 1943. She was always the highest-billed woman in the cast, and appears to have been groomed by the studio for great things.

She worked with Alfred Hitchcock (on *Saboteur*, 1942), Michael Curtiz (*Four Wives*, 1939) and Frank Capra (she was Cary Grant's love interest in the rightly much-loved *Arsenic and Old Lace* (1944)). In *Brother Rat* (Keighley

again, 1938) she played against the future US president
Ronald Reagan. She was equally adept at comedy and
drama and gives strong performances in all her movies. She
is exceptional in *The Roaring Twenties* and the
above-mentioned Hitchcock and Capra films. Tragically, she
made an enemy of Warner Bros' studio head, Jack Warner,
by demanding a rise and better treatment from the studio,
and her career was over by 1948. She died in 1995 aged
eighty, having never returned to screen acting.

THE DIRECTOR: 'Uncle' Raoul Walsh was a student of
D W Griffith and worked for his mentor as both actor and
assistant director (he played John Wilkes Booth, Abraham
Lincoln's assassin, in *The Birth of a Nation*, 1915, and the
title role in 1914's *The Life of General Villa*). His own early
films from this period include *Regeneration* (1915) a grim
depiction of tenement life clearly indebted to his master (that
said, which film director isn't?), which is also the only early
Walsh to remain extant. *The Thief of Baghdad* (1924),
starring Douglas Fairbanks Sr, was a spectacular success and
made Walsh a major force in American film. He wrote,
directed and starred in *Sadie Thompson* (1928), acting
opposite Gloria Swanson, and was due to write, direct and
star in *In Old Arizona* (1929), the first outdoor talkie, but he
lost an eye in an accident during filming and was replaced by
Warner Baxter, who, to add insult to injury, won an Oscar
for his performance. The thirties saw Walsh direct westerns
such as *The Big Trail* (1930) and begin to specialise in
portraying the bygone world of the previous century in films
such as *The Bowery* (1933) and *Klondike Annie* (1936).

VISUAL INTEREST: After beginning with a shot of the
globe, the picture feels compelled to demonstrate that it is
set in what was then already history, and the audience are
invited to slide back in time, leaving a present represented by
pictures of Franklin Delano Roosevelt and Hitler, travelling
through a recent past represented by President Hoover and

depictions of the Depression, to a hugely impressive and handsomely mounted World War One trench-warfare sequence, where Cagney, Bogart and Jeffrey Lynn swap one-liners and make each other's acquaintance while trapped in a shell hole.

While *Variety* commented on its release that the film was 'dated', they surely must have been talking about the subject matter rather than the technique on display. The montages are superb, mixing stock footage, an excitable voiceover that prefigures television announcers and specially recorded footage in a number of lightning-fast, edited sequences (less than a minute each) that convey huge amounts of information both visually and through sound (the spinning camera that circles around the Tommy gun, demonstrating the power of this weapon while sound track rat-tat-clack-clacks with the noise of bullets being spent, for example). The portrayal of the Wall Street crash of 1929 is particularly spectacular: semiexposed pictures compete with each other for space, demanding the audience's attention, and creating an atmosphere of confusion. A giant tickertape machine then takes up most of the screen. It looms towards the audience against a photographic background of New York, and then begins bearing down on an exaggerated foreground area of stairs not unlike those of a church, on which crowds dozens of people wait to be crushed.

The immediately following shots of paper falling down towards the panicking populace deliberately echo the tickertape parade the audience see near the beginning of the picture, as animated dollar signs spiral downwards in an obvious metaphor. Finally, a pyramid of what looks like sand collapses, a metaphorical symbol of the collapse of prosperity, before the New York stock exchange slides into the floor with a drunken shudder that, viewed now, seems impossibly reminiscent of the fall of the World Trade Center. It's breathtaking.

Walsh's action sequences are really pulse-raising, too, better even than those in *The Public Enemy*, with the large budgets running to no fewer than three trucks for the heist sequence, and plenty of cars and guns available to the production. There's a real scale to the movie, as befits its epic ambition to portray a decade.

At the other end of the scale, the cloistered, claustrophobic gunfight in the Spaghetti Restaurant is terrific, climaxing in Eddie's shooting a man through a closing door. Eddie's own final flight from George's men, ending in his pitiful staggered run and fall up and down the steps of a church, is even more powerful, and Walsh's camera is ever steady.

Also worthy of mention is the utterly chilling moment when George kills his former army sergeant, whom he has come across during a heist. Bogart – cackling with sudden cruelty, 'Well, if it ain't my old sergeant!' with one half of his physicality subsumed by an utterly black shadow – provides a truly striking, arresting image that suddenly reminds you of George's dark side in the perfect combination of performance and camera technique.

QUOTES:
George: 'There's one thing to pass a law, and another thing to enforce it. There'll always be fellows wanting a drink.'

Jean: 'Aren't you going to tell me about the war, and how you suffered?'
Eddie: 'You'll never know how we suffered.'

George guns down a German soldier Lloyd has estimated to be around fifteen years old, moments before the armistice comes into effect, with a sinister witticism: 'He won't be sixteen.'

Eddie: 'I don't go into speakeasies.'
Texas: 'Well, some people like spinach.'

Texas: 'I'm sick of watching you try to put out that torch you carry for her with a load of cheap hooch.'

Jean: 'He used to be a big shot.'

SOURCES TO SCREEN: Mark Hellinger's 'screen story' for the picture was originally entitled *The World Moves On* and drew directly on his personal experiences – he had been a newshound in New York during Prohibition and had known the people on whom his thinly fictionalised characters are based, and frequented speakeasies all over the city.

Panama Smith was openly based on the actress and nightclub hostess Texas Guinan, and there is some physical resemblance between Gladys George in character and the star of such silent westerns as *The White Squaw* (1920) and *The Girl of the Ranch* (1919). Guinan died of complications from an operation in 1933.

Eddie Bartlett is largely based on Larry Fay, the twenties bootlegger who strenuously objected to being labelled as such. Operating out of plush offices in New York, he made and lost a fortune during Prohibition and was arrested and charged 41 times across the decade. Although Eddie Bartlett's story is closely modelled on Fay's, the differences between fiction and fact are worth noting here. Fay wasn't a war hero, and, while he got into booze running, and later bootlegging, by chance, and as a result of cabbing, he got out quickly, within two years, and turned his talents to the even less savoury pursuit of robbing drunken taxi passengers.

Like Eddie, Fay also moved into club ownership, running the El Fey Club, which opened in 1924 and was on West 47th. In 1929, Fay became involved in the New York Milk Chain Association. In the late 1920s, two dairy giants handled nearly all of the bottled milk in the city. Fighting for the scraps were 300 small independents, of which Fay helped organise 94 into a competitive group. Fay was making $900 a day by mid-1930, until a criminal investigation resulted in his indictment. Despite being acquitted he left the milk business.

During the Depression Fay, like many, lost his fortune, and less than a year after his milk-related operation closed he was reduced to working as a manager in someone else's club (Casa Blanca on West 56th Street). There he was murdered by a drunk and disgruntled employee on New Year's Eve 1931. He had three dimes in cash on him.

As well as these factual cues *The Roaring Twenties* seems to go out of its way to refer to previous Warner Bros gangster pictures. Eddie's reference to himself as a 'Big Boy' recalls the nameless generalissimo of *Little Caesar*, while the refrain from the song 'I'm Forever Blowing Bubbles', which drifts across the 1919 sequences, is obviously designed to evoke *The Public Enemy*, for which it was the theme tune. Equally, George's comment, 'You must have been reading about Napoleon', seems designed to remind viewers with long memories of both *Little Caesar* and even *Doorway To Hell*.

CONTEMPORARY REACTION: *Variety* didn't think much of *The Roaring Twenties* upon its initial release; it conceded, though, that Cagney's performance was 'dynamite' if a little too reminiscent of that he gave in *The Public Enemy* (which was then, eight years before, more than a quarter of the whole history of popular cinema). Although the picture contained 'plenty of shooting and killing' and was noticeably expensive, it was also 'overlong'. And so it is for a film in 1939, but it's packed with incident, never once sags in terms of pace, and has an enormous amount of ground, both in terms of social change and character development, to cover. The *New York Times* of 11 November 1939 was equally underwhelmed by the picture, calling it 'egregiously sentimental', full of 'annoying pretentiousness' and 'false dignity'. The reviewer felt that there had been too many gangster movies for anyone to seriously attempt an 'epic handling' of the issues involved as Walsh had here tried to do; he was also aggrieved that the twenties, 'already the most thoroughly cinematised (sic) decade', had provided the setting for a film made in the advanced, modern days of 1939. *The Roaring Twenties* was not nominated for any major awards.

SEX/MONEY/DEATH: Eddie Bartlett is pushed into a life of crime by an accident (he's given some gin to run in his cab, and takes the parcel as a fare without knowing what it is), through disenfranchisement (his imprisonment for his unknowing crime embitters him), and because he has no other choice. The movie goes out of its way to show Eddie seeking honest work upon his return from the war, and to portray his becoming corrupted by the way he makes his money. With some subtlety, however, the picture is capable of portraying him as aggressive, clipped and stentorian with his employees while still being charming, sweet and old-fashioned when romancing the innocent and unknowing Jean.

The narrator is quite keen to portray the criminality of the decade of the title as being directly linked to Prohibition ('an unpopular law' foisted on 'an unwilling public') and to claim that the public of the Prohibition era looked on 'the bootlegger as an adventurous hero'. Accordingly, initially at least, crime in this picture is largely victimless, people who want alcohol being sold alcohol by people who have it. The only sufferers are the federal government (represented by a corrupt, easily bribed and alcohol-consuming policeman), who have banned something innocent for needless reasons. The screenplay even decides to have its cake and eat it, declaring excessive drinking a result of Prohibition, with college students and even schoolchildren who would otherwise 'never have drunk' being turned on to alcohol by its newly illicit nature.

Yet, as the world of the picture darkens and 'corruption, violence and murder' become commonplace, Eddie's character becomes darker, too, and the audience see him involved in some quite shocking (for the period) acts of violence – although he never quite descends to George's level of lip-smacking glee. Even when he discovers that Lloyd and Jean are having an affair he is incapable of hurting either of them. Instead, a sudden burst of dramatic, yet half-hearted, violence is followed by a grim facial expression, and acceptance of this new fact.

Eddie is probably the most complex and compelling central protagonist of any of Warner Bros thirties gangster pictures. He doesn't choose the bootlegging life, and, even as he becomes good at it, successful from it and accustomed to it, Cagney always manages to suggest that he's ill suited to it. 'You can get to like anything,' Eddie says with a shrug at one point, while reflecting on his new lifestyle, but he doesn't sound terribly convinced as he does so. Cagney is brilliant throughout the picture, subtly shading from a decent young man who has seen much that is distressing through a period of real darkness to a renewed humanity, followed by absolute disintegration.

It's also worth noting the one-way sexual tension between Eddie and Panama: she openly says that she's drawn to him because he reminds her of a man she loved who went to war in France and never came back, but he never seems to notice the implication. During their later conversations, as she advises him on his behaviour towards Jean, there's an unspoken subtext that arises out of her obvious interest in him (watch her reaction to his totally noneroticised response when she snugly, sensually grasps his hand).

Another interesting aspect of the picture is its unflinching depiction of the production of illicit alcohol. Eddie makes a crack about a bathtub, and minutes later the audience actually see it being made. The list of ingredients is grim to hear. On another occasion illicit hooch is referred to by the distinctly unpleasant term 'tiger sweat'.

It could be said that *The Roaring Twenties* is needlessly elegiac in its evocation of a period that was, at the time of its production, a mere twenty years gone. However, there's an equally strong argument that it successfully takes a long view of the period for the first time in a major motion picture, with subtle characterisation that avoids making the hoods simple monsters but doesn't absolve them from blame for their lives of crime.

THE VERDICT: Grievously underrated, beautifully made and beautifully performed, *The Roaring Twenties* sees the Warner Bros gangster series leave the 1930s on a real high with, ironically, a powerfully downbeat conclusion.

The disclaimer

'It may come to pass that, at some distant date, we will be confronted with another period similar to the one depicted in this photoplay. If that happens, I pray that the events, as dramatised here, will be remembered. In the film, the characters are composites of people I knew, and the situations are those that actually occurred. Bitter or sweet, most memories become precious as the years move on. This film is a memory – and I am grateful for it.'

There's an ambiguity in the final sentence of that: it is unclear to the audience whether Hellinger is grateful to be free of these times, grateful that they are just memories, or whether he is grateful for the memories, because it means that he lived through the era and got to experience its good aspects.

Brighton Rock (1947)

(Black and white – 89 minutes)

Associated British Picture Corporation Presents
The Boulting Brothers Production of
Brighton Rock
From the Novel by Graham Greene
Made at Welwyn Studios, Great Britain
Screenplay by Graham Green and Terence Rattigan
Associate Producer: Peter De Sarigny
Director of Photography: Harry Waxman
Art Director: John Howell
Production Manager: Gerard Bryant
Camera Operator: Gilbert Taylor
Assistant Director: Gerald Mitchell
Editor: Peter Graham Scott
Sound Recordist: Frank McNally
Costumes: Honora Plesch
Make-Up: Bob Clarke

Sound Editor: Audrey Bennett
Music Composed and Conducted by Hans May
Produced by Roy Boulting
Directed by John Boulting

PRINCIPAL CAST: Richard Attenborough (Pinkie Brown), Hermione Baddeley (Ida Arnold), William Hartnell (Dallow), Harcourt Williams (Prewitt), Wylie Watson (Spicer), Nigel Stock (Cubitt), Virginia Winter (Judy), Reginald Purdell (Frank), George Carney (Phil Corkery), Charles Goldner (Colleoni), Alan Wheatley (Fred Hale), Carol Marsh (Rose), Lina Barrie (Molly), Joan Sterndale-Bennett (Delia), Harry Ross (Brewer), Campbell Copelin (Police Inspector), Mary Stone (Waitress), Norman Watson (Racecourse Evangelist)

SUMMARY: A gang killing in interwar Brighton leads to a revenge murder organised by 'Pinkie' Brown's gang, but it goes wrong. As Pinkie sinks into a paranoid despond, and begins murdering potential witnesses and those of his own gang who disagree with his plans, local busybody Ida Arnold begins investigating what she sees as inconsistencies in the 'official version' of that day's events that the gang have sworn to the enquiry.

Pinkie seduces, and later illegally marries (they are too young to marry without parental consent), Rose Brown, an innocent waitress who is aware, though she doesn't know it, of some aspects of his cover-up. He knows that if he can get her to feel he loves her, and that she is beholden to him, she'll never tell on him even if she does work out the truth. Eventually, he decides to kill her, convincing her that a joint suicide is their only way out of the difficulties they face as a couple.

Pinkie's last remaining henchmen, Dallow, is appalled by this potential action against an innocent, and summons the police, who rescue her. Pinkie leaps off the pier into the water and to his death rather than be taken alive by the police.

THE PLAYERS: It isn't hyperbolic to claim Richard (later Sir, now Lord) Attenborough as one of the most significant figures in the history of British film (and one of the most significant Britons to work in American film). His career as an actor and latterly director in film spans well over half a century. He made his on-screen debut in Noël Coward's *In Which We Serve* (1942), a stirring example of wartime propaganda distinguished by many fine performances. He went on to further small roles in *A Matter of Life and Death* (Michael Powell, Emeric Pressburger, 1946). His first headlining role was in the Boulting brothers' *Journey Together* (1946) and next as Ted Peters in *Dancing With Crime* (John Paddy Carstairs, 1947), a less sophisticated 'spiv' crime picture, which can be seen in some ways as a dry run for this film.

Attenborough continued to work as an actor in many films both good and bad, but never turned in an inappropriate performance, before turning to directing in 1969 with *Oh! What A Lovely War!*, a savage indictment of the way World War One was fought. It swept the board at the BAFTAs and won Attenborough a Golden Globe. Further films followed, minor successes such as *Young Winston* (1972, with Simon Ward as the politician as a young solider, journalist and MP) and the (frankly, rubbish) psychological horror film *Magic* (1979), before winning a Best Director Oscar for *Ghandi* (1981), depicting the life of the murdered Indian politician, activist and man of peace.

Later films as director include *Cry Freedom* (1987 – a life of the anti-apartheid activist Steve Biko), *Chaplin* (1992) with Robert Downey Jr, and *Shadowlands* (1993) with Anthony Hopkins as C S Lewis, all of which demonstrated his preference for subjects founded in recent historical events, and his mythmaking skills. At the time of writing, he is chairman of RADA and president of BAFTA but may be most recognisable to some audiences as John Hammond, the man who brought the dinosaurs back to life in *Jurassic Park*

(Steven Spielberg, 1993) and *The Lost World: Jurassic Park* (Steven Spielberg, 1997).

William Hartnell was a major star of British film either side of the World War Two. Starting in 'quota quickie' comedies, he was versatile enough to play the 'wronged man' (*Murder in Reverse* (Montgomery Tully, 1945)) and the romantic lead (*Strawberry Roan* (Maurice Elvey, 1944)) as well as the tough guys and sergeants he became typecast as in films such as *Carry On Sergeant* (Gerald Thomas, 1958) and TV series such as *The Army Game* (1957–8, 1960–1). His best on-screen performances came in *The Yangste Incident* (Michael Anderson, 1957), *Hell Drivers* (Cy Endfield, 1957) and *This Sporting Life* (Lindsay Anderson, 1963). The last of these led to his being offered the title role in a new BBC children's SF series. *Doctor Who*. He played the part of the Doctor over three years, appearing in 130 episodes, before retiring, owing to a combination of ill health and a series of clashes with the series' new producer, with whom he did not see eye to eye. He returned to the series over Christmas/New Year 1972–3 to film four brief cameos to celebrate the programme's tenth birthday. He died in 1976 after a series of strokes brought on by arteriosclerosis from which he had suffered for many years. His life is commemorated by a 'blue plaque' at BBC Television Centre and a mounted wall bust at BAFTA in London.

THE DIRECTOR: John Boulting, with his producing partner/often co-director/twin brother Roy, is most associated with the satirical, socially conscious light comedies they made, such as *I'm All Right Jack* (1959) and *Heavens Above*! (1960). The brothers divided their time equally between comic and more serious pictures, shooting wartime stories such as *Journey Together* (1946) – the story of the invention of radar – and the bomb thriller *Seven Days To Noon* (1950). As a producer John was latterly responsible for Roy's *The Family Way* (1966), the famed

kitchen-sink drama starring Hayley Mills, her father John
and Hywel Bennett.

VISUAL INTEREST: A visually odd, but entirely
stimulating, combination of dark, shadowy, impressionistic
smears for the night scenes and crisply shot daytime
sequences, *Brighton Rock* benefits greatly from the vast
amount of location filming undertaken for the production.
There are frequent visual unorthodoxies (such as the sudden
fast-swinging pan from Dallow and co. by the bar to the
police by the door near the film's end) and some moments of
genuine inspiration: the reflection of the corpse of Spicer in
the glass of the skylight above Pinkie's head (Pinkie has just
pushed him to his death) must have taken forever to set up
and execute with 1940s techniques, but it's worth it for the
image of Spicer lurking, dead, behind Pinkie's shoulder. This
is just one of the many moments of technical ingenuity that
are used to help create visual supporting evidence for
Prewitt's drunken assertion that they are actually in hell. The
dreamy, hallucinatory atmosphere of the long-lensed
deep-focus scenes where Pinkie is told that Spicer (whom he
is certain is dead) is actually alive and in the next room is
another.

The most showy of these is the ninety-second
tour-de-force journey through the appropriately entitled
'Dante's Inferno' ghost-train ride, where Pinkie murders
Fred. The promoter calls it '90 seconds of pure terror' and in
the cinema, with the sound cranked up, that's not an
inaccurate description – it's certainly deeply disturbing as
the water charges towards the viewer, accompanied by
horrific, cacophonous laughter. Another vital difference
between the day and night sequences in *Brighton Rock*
comes in the vast difference in focus. The daytime scenes are
(usually) wide-angled, filled with bustling people and
movement, the light is flat and open and there's a feeling
that, despite the vileness the audience are witnessing in
close-up, there is something good left in this place. At night,

with the camera usually pushed in near to the action, with snarling close-ups in constant usage, and grim industrial-looking metal shoved into every possible frame, it's a very different story. Even the public areas, such as the bar Dallow frequents, seem crowded, heated, oppressive and inhumane – and it always seems to be raining.

A notable luxury shot, which adds enormously to the picture's atmosphere, is the train seen ploughing along the bridge in silhouette as Pinkie and Dallow visit Brewer's house at night. Clearly contrived (presumably with models), it nevertheless looks marvellous.

QUOTES:

Ida: 'He hadn't any folks to make a fuss, only a second cousin in Middlesbrough. And he was in Middlesbrough!'

Pinkie: 'These atheists don't know nothing. Of course there's a hell, flames, damnation torments . . .'
Rose: 'And heaven too?'
Pinkie: 'Perhaps . . .'

Pinkie: 'It wouldn't be a proper marriage – not like when the priest says it.'

Ida: 'I've got to save that girl.'
Corkery: 'She doesn't want to be saved.'
Ida: 'What does that matter?'

Prewitt: 'A hag with a passion for tinned salmon. Can you imagine that, madam? Tinned salmon!'

Pinkie: 'When I was a kid, I swore I'd be a priest.'

Rose: 'I wouldn't want to be saved, if he was lost.'

SOURCES TO SCREEN: Before looking at the book on which the film is based, it's also worthwhile considering *Brighton Rock* in the context of the American gangster films on which it so clearly relies for further cultural context. The movie was known in America on release as *Young Scarface* and, while there are similarities to **Scarface**, it also has much in common with **The Public Enemy** and **Little Caesar**, the touchstones of gangster cinema of nearly two decades before. Like Rico, Pinkie seems asexual, uninterested in any of the spoils of crime except for the power that a criminal existence enables him to wield. Also like Rico, he sees a Pyrrhic victory in dying rather than being taken alive by the law.

Like all the above pictures, *Brighton Rock* opens with a lengthy caption that seeks to find a social context for its drama. It's odd that *Brighton Rock*'s caption insists that the story takes place between World Wars One and Two (the period when the novel was written), since there's nothing in the story to mean that it *must* take place before World War Two. Indeed, if set at the time of the film's production, the story fits more neatly into the era of the 'spiv' and British movies about criminals benefiting from the postwar retention of rationing in the same way as American gangsters had previously benefited from Prohibition. Pinkie's death cry of 'Mother' naturally seems to echo Rico's.

Graham Greene's co-written screenplay is an adaptation of his own 1938 novella (which he himself dismissed as 'an entertainment'). As one might expect of a self-adaptation, there's a dignity and respect in it that ensures that the essence of the story's themes remains intact, along with the transplanted plotline. Those who suggest that *Brighton Rock* lacks the religious subtext associated with the prose version have obviously never paid attention to the picture's dialogue or the visual iconography the Boultings invoke constantly (see **VISUAL INTEREST**). Barely a scene manages to go by without someone invoking heaven, hell, redemption or damnation (see **QUOTES**). Prewitt is frequently found quoting from *Macbeth* or *King Lear*, and even at one point invokes the ending of Christopher Marlowe's *Dr Faustus* ('Why, this is hell, nor am I out of it'), implying strongly that the dark and rain-lashed streets of this coastal town, awash with violence and fear as much as water, are as much a home of the damned as the eternal fires themselves. Greene's tortured Catholicism seeps from nearly every frame of this picture, which ends, after all, with a slow pan into a crucifix hanging on a wall.

Many have complained about the screenplay's alteration of the ending of the book. The novella ends with Rose about to listen to the record that Pinkie has made for her in the recording booth – but the book actually ends before the needle is placed on the vinyl. This suspended enigma – the audience knows what's coming but the character doesn't – is a deeply unpleasant, downbeat ending. Rose is unaware that the record, which she has never heard, is actually of Pinkie telling her he hates her, and that he despises her for her innocence and her protestations of love for him. In the film, the audience actually get to see her listen to the record, which, presumably, owing to Pinkie's attempts to destroy it earlier by bashing it against a table, sticks, and she believes that what he actually recorded was the words 'I love you' over and over again. Pilloried as a studio-inspired 'happy ending' this is, of course, not so much an alteration of the novella as simply the film continuing its narrative for longer than the book does.

What also needs to be pointed out is that the film's ending, although it seems happier, is actually far bleaker than the novella's. The final scene of the film sees Rose absolutely unrepentant for her sins, both carnal and emotional, with Pinkie entirely convinced that his love for her has made all of her life worthwhile. This isn't helped by the nun who is counselling her, who insists that 'any love' is of value. This, of course, combined with the distortion of Pinkie's last message means that Rose will go through her life believing that Pinkie loved her, that their life together, brief though it was, had some value. Her lack of repentance, even if contributed to by ignorance, arguably means that, in Greene's own philosophy, she's as damned – damned despite her kindness and innocence, damned by the actions of others, more or less. Greene's moral universe was a cruel one, though it revolted him often. The addition to the ending of *Brighton Rock* is a superb example of it and is, frankly, entirely to the benefit of the picture's complexity.

THE VERDICT: A visually disturbing, entirely British absorption of the iconography of the 1930s gangster movie, shot through with a blacker-than-black worldview and a tortured, terrified religiosity. One of the half-dozen best British films ever made.

White Heat (1949)

(Black and white – 114 minutes)

Warner Bros Pictures Present
A Warner Bros First National Picture
Screen Play by Ivan Goff and Ben Roberts
Suggested by a Story by Virginia Kellogg
Director of Photography: Edward Carrere
Film Editor: Owen Marks
Sound by Leslie G Hewitt
Set Decorator: Fred M MacLean
Wardrobe by Leah Rhodes
Special Effects by Roy Davidson (Director), H F Koenekamp,
ASC
Orchestrations: Murray Cutter
Make-Up Artist: Perc Westmore
Music by Max Steiner
Produced by Louis F Edelman
Directed by Raoul Walsh

PRINCIPAL CAST: James Cagney (Arthur 'Cody' Jarrett), Virginia Mayo (Verna Jarrett), Edmond O'Brien ('Vic Pardo' (Hank Fallon)), Margaret Wycherly (Ma Jarrett), Steve Cochran ('Big' Ed Somers), John Archer (Philip Evans), Wally Cassell (Giovanni 'Cotton' Valletti), Fred Clark ('The Trader' (Daniel Winston))

SUMMARY: Escaping after a daring train heist – in which one of the gang is hideously burned – Cody Jarrett and his gang (which includes his wife and his mother) hide out in an old house before heading out under the cover of a storm. Cody is devoted to his mother, who continually tells him that he'll one day be at 'the top o' the world'. Cody turns himself in for another crime (one he did not commit) in order to have an alibi for the robbery he did.

In prison he is given a cellmate who calls himself Vic Pardo, but he's actually Hank Fallon, a federal agent who specialises in infiltrating prisons and making his way into the confidence of crooks. While in prison, Cody, who suffers seizures and fits when distressed, discovers that his beloved mother has died and that his wife has left him for his former henchman, 'Big Ed'. Together 'Vic' and Cody escape prison and, after Cody has murdered Ed and 'won' back his wife, 'Vic' and Cody plan a heist based around a 'Trojan Horse' trick involving an empty fuel tanker. 'Vic' rigs up a device so that his colleagues can track him, and the authorities arrive during the robbery, just after another criminal acquaintance of Cody's has unexpectedly recognised 'Vic' as Hank. The gang are killed in a shootout and a visibly deranged Cody hides atop a huge tank containing flammable substances. Thanks to the firefight, it explodes and Cody burns up, screaming to his absent mother about reaching 'the top o' the world!' at last.

THE PLAYERS: Since *The Roaring Twenties*, Cagney had continued his career at Warner Bros, making his first ever western in *The Oklahoma Kid* (Lloyd Bacon, 1939) and trying his hand at comedy with *The Strawberry Blonde* (Raoul Walsh, 1941) with Olivia de Havilland and Rita Hayworth (it's a film in which Cagney gives a tremendous performance). The last film of this, his second stint at the studio, was *Yankee Doodle Dandy* (Michael Curtiz, 1942), a glorious, roaring biopic of the musical impresario George M Cohen. Although long for the time, it made a fortune and won Best Picture at the Academy Awards. As he sang, danced, joked and emoted his way through the piece, Cagney's less obvious talents suddenly reached the widest possible audience. He took home a thoroughly well-deserved Oscar for the film.

After leaving Warner Bros, Cagney worked as an actor-for-hire for a few years. Again trying to introduce more variety into his career, he picked his parts carefully and made few films. He starred in *Johnny Come Lately* (William K Howard, 1943) as a wandering drifter who saves aged Vinnie McLoud's newspaper from collapse; *Blood on the Sun* (Frank Lloyd, 1945) as an American editor in 1930s Japan, uncovering Imperial Japanese militarism; *13 Rue Madeleine* (1946), in which he was a secret service instructor with a double agent in his class who then pursues his rogue pupil into occupied France; and *The Time of Your Life* (H C Potter, 1948) a screen version of William Saroyan's play about bored men trapped in the town of their birth. It was unloved at the time, but its atmosphere of *ennui* was later a declared influence on both Fellini and George Lucas. Following *White Heat*, Cagney picked up his productivity. In 1955 alone he gained another Oscar nomination, this time for playing Doris Day's husband in *Love Me or Leave Me* (Charles Vidor, 1955); he impressed as the comically vile captain in *Mister Roberts* (John Ford, Mervyn Le Roy, 1955); and, for an encore, he reprised his Oscar-wining role of George M Cohan for a cameo in *The Seven Little Foys* (Melville Shavelson, 1955), another Broadway biopic.

He also showed real talent for directing, making *Short Cut to Hell* (1956), an adaptation of Graham Greene's *A Gun For Sale* (his only film behind the camera), and played an entirely different kind of movie legend in *Man of a Thousand Faces* (Joseph Pevney, 1957), in which he memorably portrayed Lon Chaney in a film that could never be called an accurate portrayal of the late silent star's life.

His self-stated 'retirement' film was *One Two Three* (Billy Wilder, 1961), a farce in which he played, with astonishing energy, a man trying to reconcile the demands of his job (marketing Coca-Cola in West Berlin) with chaperoning his boss's daughter through her romance with a communist. Thirteen years later he was awarded a Lifetime Award by the American Film Institute and the ceremony was shown on television. Still full of energy and life (he was 76), he danced across the room to accept his award.

Five years later, after he'd apparently been ordered by his doctor to become more active (he'd done little since completing his autobiography, published in 1975, except paint and entertain at home), Cagney came out of his twenty-year retirement to appear in Milos Forman's *Ragtime* (1981), giving a marvellous performance as a police commissioner, Rheinlander Waldo. Its release meant he'd headlined films across six decades. It seemed destined to be his swan song but in 1984 he made a final screen bow in the sentimental TV movie *Terrible Joe Moran*. Between agreeing to do the part and shooting it, he suffered a stroke and, while he recovered quickly enough to play the role, his voice was weak and much of his dialogue was redubbed later. Nevertheless, it's an avuncular performance of warmth and dignity, which, if not a fitting final role for such a pre-eminent star, shows he was always willing to try to add a few new strings to his bow. He died in 1986.

Versatile and appreciated professionally for it, though he was not immediately recognisable to the public, Edmond O'Brien was the creepy pressman in *The Barefoot Contessa* (Joseph L Mankiewicz, 1954 – starring Humphrey Bogart), for which he won an Oscar. Other memorable roles include that of the poisoned hero of *DOA* (Rudolph Mate, 1950) and that of John Frankenheimer's right-wing nuclear-paranoia/political conspiracy thriller *Seven Days in May* (1964), for which he was Oscar-nominated. He died, from Alzheimer's disease, in 1986.

THE DIRECTOR: Since the last time he and Cagney had teamed up to portray organised crime, Raoul Walsh had directed the visually impressive (if historically inept) war film *Objective Burma!* (1945) with Errol Flynn (the picture, which shows American troops reconquering Burma, caused a mini-riot when insensitively screened to the British Indian servicemen who'd actually done the fighting). He'd also shot the episodic, characterful western, *Cheyenne* (1947), and the utterly bizarre, flashback-heavy and genre-assaulting *Pursued* that year. Although he continued to work until the 1960s (he retired in 1964 at the age of 68), *White Heat* is his last film of real note. He died in 1980 at the age of 93, having been instrumental in the popularisation of the filmic medium and been one of the founders of the Academy of Motion Picture Arts and Sciences. (For earlier career details, see **The Roaring Twenties**.)

VISUAL INTEREST: As much an immediately identifiable product of the late forties/early fifties as *The Public Enemy* is of the opening years of 'talkies', *White Heat* is blessed with bags of location filming, with valleys and train sidings shot from a medium height, and far from close up, making everywhere Cody goes lush and windswept. Unlike his work on the artificial yet lavish **The Roaring Twenties**, Walsh seems determined to spend as much time as possible in the wild outdoors – a reflection, perhaps, of Cody's inner turmoil and an appropriation of the literary device of pathetic fallacy, whereby the outside world reflects the emotional state of characters within the drama.

Once Cody is in prison, Walsh makes the inside of the penitentiary a space that reflects the inside of Cody's mind in a different way: jagged ceilings and looming shadows that bear down on the viewer and actors, and bars and bands that throw long dark shadows. Cagney's collapse in the prison factory is a tour de force of loud noises, abstract footage of machinery and blurring lights.

There's an unusual pace to the film: outside prison the scene and camera setup changes are surprisingly rapid; inside, a slower, more fixed-camera approach is preferred and cuts are slower. Also, as Cody's mood darkens, so does the lighting of the film, with the picture increasingly murky, purgatorial and night-set after Ma's death with striking contrasts between artificial light and very real darkness dominating all the interiors (the scene where Cody kills is beautifully dripping with menace).

The close-ups on the revolving 'tracker' discs on the top of the government agents' cars are peculiarly precise, and the whole 'tracking' sequence is a marvel of cross-fades, short scenes with no dialogue and high, wide, establishing tracking shots. The finale is, naturally, spectacular with Cagney rolling around trapped in his own delusions atop a huge metal globe. On a less favourable note, the sets for the inside of the train in the early scenes are simply rubbish.

QUOTES:

Cody: 'If I turned my back long enough for Ed to put a hole in it, there'd be a hole in it.'

Cody: 'I don't know ya, and what I don't know I don't trust.'

Cody: 'I want something to eat!'
Doctor: 'You've sent away two meals already.'
Cody: 'That's why I'm hungry now!'

Cody's breakdown begins in earnest: 'A copper? A copper! How do you like that, boys? A copper. And we fell for it. *I* fell for it!'

And, inevitably, Cody: 'Made it, Ma, top o' the world!'

SOURCES TO SCREEN: As with many crime films of the period, the central figures are very loosely based on real people. In this case Cody is based on Arthur 'Doc' Barker, who also involved his mother in the criminal gang that he ran with his brother Fred and their mutual friend (they'd met in prison) Alvin Karpis. Fred Barker died resisting arrest on 15 January 1935, his mother alongside him, both gunned

down by FBI agents led by the then assistant director, E J
Connelley. 'Doc' had been arrested a week before, having
been uncharacteristically caught outside without a gun. He
was sentenced to life imprisonment on a sample charge of
his involvement in a criminal kidnapping/extortion. In 1939
he attempted to escape from Alcatraz, where he was being
held, and was shot dead by prison guards. They recorded his
last words as, 'I'm all shot to hell.'

Cagney himself reportedly suggested a plot outline
roughly based on the combined lives of these two men when
he intimated to Warner Bros that he was amenable to
returning to the studio for what has been called his 'Indian
summer' gangster film. The studio's choice of Walsh as
director seems to have also been influenced by a desire to
please their returning star – Walsh and Cagney had worked
together twice before and had an amicable creative
partnership. They would work together again subsequently.

CONTEMPORARY REACTION: *Variety* (31 August
1949) was in a nostalgic mood, feeling it had been 'too long
since James Cagney has spit a bellyful of lead' or 'laced a
guy's kisser'. Cagney's return to the gangster milieu was sure
to be 'red hot box office' but it didn't have anything more
interesting to say. The *New York Times*' critic Bosley
Crowther was also positive about the picture. Writing on 3
September 1949 he praised the appropriateness of the title,
which he saw as relating to the 'thermal intensity of this
film'. This was Cagney's finest performance, one of
'conviction, confidence, courage, power', and 'cruelly
vicious' to boot. The film was 'one of the most explosive . . .
ever played' and achieved 'technical perfection' with its
'crisp documentary style'. The only aspect of the production
he found unsatisfactory was the relationship of Cagney and
his 'Ma' (seen by many later viewers as the key to the
picture). This was 'not entirely convincing as truth' –
Crowther found it improbable that a man so dependent on
his mother could grow to be so cruel. The only major award

the picture was nominated for was an Oscar for Virginia Kellogg for her contribution to the screen story.

SEX/MONEY/DEATH: At its heart, and like *Scarface – The Shame of the Nation*, *White Heat* is a detailed study of an aberrant personality – in this case that of 'Cody' Jarrett, perhaps the all-time 'mummy's boy' with a overreliance on his mother that, while it doesn't seem to cross over into an *actual* Oedipus complex, is certainly unhealthily obsessive. 'Always lookin' out for your Cody, aren't you?' he asks her early on as she sits in his lap and she strokes his hair, soothing his troubled mood. A possible epileptic, Cody has fits when upset, but those who are profiling him for law-enforcement agencies insist at a number of points in the picture that these are psychosomatic.

His father died in a lunatic asylum, the audience are told, and as a child Cody faked 'attacks' to gain his mother's attention. His spectacular breakdown, a combination of weeping, thumb-sucking, rolling around on the floor and sudden violence when he hears of her death, is a splendid demonstration of the level of his derangement. The whole plot thread is a neat inversion of the clichés of crime ('his mother didn't love him'). Pudgy at fifty years of age, with his physically contained, hands-by-his-sides, infantile movements, Cagney resembles more Robinson's Rico Bandello (*Little Caesar*) than his own Eddie Bartlett (*The Roaring Twenties*). The fact that he dies screaming for his mother, and that Cagney had a hand in shaping the movie's overall theme, can only strengthen the idea that this is the actor having a crack at the 'other' gangster archetype.

While the mother-fixation is a real part of Cody's character, it shouldn't be considered its totality. Unlike Rico, Cody is at least capable of some adult feeling, at least to start with. Cody's relationship with his wife Verna is largely healthy and explicitly based on mutual sexual attraction (or as explicitly as it could be given filmic strictures of the time), and, while he is capable of both loyalty and disloyalty, neither is an obsession for him. Conversely, he's clearly dreadful with money: much is stolen through the course of the film, and more is discussed as having been stolen before, but neither he nor his family seems to have much in the way of real possessions.

This is also a man who is vigorous, a sensualist who enjoys good food and physical action (there's no reason for him to jump on a moving train at the opening: he knows it's slowing down) and nature (he picks and sniffs flowers). Though not well educated (he knows the story of the Trojan Horse, but only in abstract terms, like a folk memory), he's a fine strategist and his only real flaw as a tactician is that his ego won't let him see that anyone is smarter than he is (and 'Vic' *is* smarter than he is). In all fairness, for most of his life, no one has been smarter than him. He's also brutal, but fairly so (he never kills anyone without a reason, though his reasons – such as the engineer's having heard his name – are cruel).

Cagney gives a creepy performance, full of suppressed energy and sudden violence; he's also seedy, something he'd never really been before. Cody's discussion with 'Vic' about 'talking to Ma' (she's dead by this point and he's been wandering along through the dark) remains deeply disturbing viewing: a man slowly slipping into real dementia in sweaty close-up, harshly lit in the dark, with the personality-warping implications of Cody's obsession with his mother and his outright paranoia made clear by every twitched facial muscle on Cagney's unapologetically middle-aged face.

THE VERDICT: A cunning blend of pop-psychobabble, family drama and gangster clichés that has a riveting performance from Cagney at the centre, this is a minor masterpiece with a finale that is, both literally and figuratively, truly explosive.

The Blue Lamp (1950)

(Black and white – 84 minutes)

The J Arthur Rank Organisation Presents
An Ealing Studios Production
Released through General Film Distributors Ltd
Made at Ealing Studios, London, England
The Events and Characters portrayed in this film are
fictitious and any similarity to any incident, name or
individual is coincidental.
Screenplay by T E B Clarke
Original Treatment by Jan Read and Ted Willis
Additional Dialogue by Alexander MacKendrick
Associate Producer: Michael Relph
Production Supervisor: Hal Mason
Director of Photography: Gordon Dines, ARPS
Editor: Peter Tanner
Second Unit Photographed by Lionel Baines, FRPS
Unit Production Manager: L C Rudkin
Art Director: Jim Morahan
Music Director: Ernest Irving
Sound Supervisor: Stephen Dalby
Camera Operator: Chic Waterson
Assistant Director: Harry Kratz
Produced by Michael Balcon
Directed by Basil Dearden

PRINCIPAL CAST: Jack Warner (PC George Dixon),
Jimmy Hanley (PC Andy Mitchell), Dirk Bogarde (Tom
Riley), Robert Flemyng (Sgt Roberts), Bernard Lee (Insp.
Cherry), Peggy Evans (Diana Lewis), Patric Doonan (Spud),
Bruce Seton (PC Campbell), Meredith Edwards (PC
Hughes), Clive Morton (Sgt Brooks), Frederick Piper (Alf
Lewis), Dora Bryan (Maisie), Gladys Henson (Mrs Dixon),
Tessie O'Shea (Herself)

SUMMARY: Young gangster Tom Riley, one of a new
breed of ruthless and violently inclined career criminals,
murders PC George Dixon. Thanks to a sometimes strained

alliance between uniformed police, CID and regular criminals (who feel that Riley has 'gone too far' in killing a policeman) and the evidence of his girlfriend, Riley is captured.

THE PLAYERS: Jack Warner (born Horace Waters) had previously had a solid career in small-scale British cinema, and was popular as Joe Huggett in the series of comic films revolving around a holidaying family that began with *Holiday Camp* (Ken Annakin, 1948). He'd already made something of a career of playing policemen, having been one in *It Always Rains on a Sunday* (Robert Hamer, 1948) and *Dear Murderer* (Arthur Crabtree, 1947), among others. After *The Blue Lamp*, he'd play policemen again in *The Quatermass Experiment* (Val Guest, 1955) and *The Ladykillers* (Alexander MacKendrick, 1955), before taking the title role in the television series *Dixon of Dock Green* (1955–78, 430 episodes) which – despite Dixon's being killed during the course of *The Blue Lamp* – was a vehicle not just for Warner's policeman persona but actually for the character from the film. He died in 1981 at the age of 84. At his funeral real members of the Metropolitan Police Force he'd represented on screen for so long carried his coffin.

Dirk Bogarde (who became Sir Dirk Bogarde in 1992) had a career in film spanning seven decades, six as a star, and is best remembered by the British public as Simon Sparrow in the *Doctor* series of light comedies that began with *Doctor in the House* (Ralph Thomas, 1954). A subtle, versatile performer, he was always willing to take risks on screen, and looked for difficult and challenging roles his entire life.

Parts such as the gay barrister in *Victim* (Basil Dearden, 1961), the eponymous, monstrous lead in *The Servant* (Joseph Losey, 1963) and the former concentration camp guard involved in an obsessive, abusive, sadomasochistic sexual relationship with a camp survivor in *The Night Porter* (Lilian Cavani, 1974) demonstrate the extent to which he saw acting as a craft rather than a profession,

and how far he was willing to go to practise that craft.
Probably his finest performance was in *Death in Venice*
(Luchino Visconti, 1974), an almost wordless portrayal of
infatuation.

After completing *Despair* (Rainer Werner Fassbinder,
1979), Bogarde retired to France, where he wrote several
volumes of autobiography and well-received fiction. He
ventured out of retirement four times only, each time
tempted by that new, exciting, risky part.

Bernard Lee is instantly familiar to anyone who has ever
switched on the television during a British bank holiday.
He's James Bond's boss 'M' in every Bond film between *Dr.
No* (Terence Young, 1962) and *Moonraker* (Lewis Gilbert,
1979). He also notably appeared in the Orson
Welles/Graham Greene postwar thriller *The Third Man*
(Carol Reed, 1949).

THE DIRECTOR: Basil Dearden worked as a stage director
before getting into film as an assistant to director Basil
Dean. He worked as a writer (on films such as the
jewel-robbery thriller *This Man Is News* (David
MacDonald, 1938)) and second-unit director (on, for
example, *Penny Paradise* (Carol Reed, 1938)) before getting
the chance to helm films himself. Notable pictures include
the crime caper *The League of Gentlemen* (1959) and
Khartoum (1966) with Charlton Heston as General Gordon.
He also directed several episodes of the enjoyably ludicrous
Roger Moore/Tony Curtis vehicle *The Persuaders!* (1971).
He was one of many fine British film directors to work in
filmed serial television, due to the decline of the British film
industry (Roy Ward Baker and Charles Crichton are other
examples). He died in a car accident in 1971.

VISUAL INTEREST: The film begins with a close-up of the
eponymous lamp outside a police station and a pan down
into a dark street. Initially, Dearden's technique is
pseudo-documentary, using still photographs of newspaper

headlines (all fictional, incidentally), voiceovers and specifically demonstrative incidents (Dixon directs a man to Paddington Green Station; Jimmy is taken in by a small boy who just wants a free treat of a jam roll) to illustrate what life for these policemen is like. It's an approach that surely added verisimilitude to the picture at the time, although now it seems almost comically thorough.

Elsewhere, though, there's an obvious collision of a very Americanised technique and very English locations that is arresting for an audience. The initial car chase, backed by the ringing sound of a police car's bell, is terrific. Despite the mention of Ealing Studios in the credits, the vast majority of the film is clearly shot on location, with crisp daytime photography adding to the presentation of the story as being 'real'. There's a profound contrast between this and the murky darkness of the night streets down which these policemen tentatively walk. At night London becomes a different place in this picture: smoke fills the alleys, darkness creeps in around the few points of light. It's a visual invocation of the fact that the film seems to see civilisation as being under siege. The smoky rooms through which Riley passes when he is trying to set up crimes are a very British kind of dingy: cheap wallpaper and uninspiring food, games and people. Everything is, appropriately, very slightly shoddy. It's this world, seen here chronistically, that is evoked in films such as **Gangster No. 1**.

CONTEMPORARY REACTION: When the picture finally arrived in America (where it can't have been expected to do terribly well given that it's a such a squarely British take on an essentially very American genre), reviews were generally very good. *Variety* found this low-key British movie 'solid' rather than 'lavish' but 'well knit' all the same, with 'action, drama and suspense' and 'spectacular car chase' all put in the service of a serious portrayal of 'a new generation of thieves and murderers'. Dirk Bogarde was singled out for praise. The *New York Times* of 9 January 1951 saw Bosley

Crowther recognising the picture's nature as a 'warm, affectionate' tribute to the London policeman while praising the way it 'assumes the characteristics of a documentary' in order to tell its story. He was also impressed with the sharp volte-face that the film undergoes around the time Dixon is murdered, when the previously 'benign' picture, operating in a 'stunningly naturalistic style', begins 'racing pell-mell' to its conclusion, much to the shock of the 'bland observer' in the theatre. Again Dirk Bogarde was praised for his 'unhealthy and malevolent' performance. Crowther finished by bemoaning the film might be too essentially British to make as much of an impact in America as it should. The film won the British Academy Award for Best Picture and was nominated for the Golden Lion at the Venice Film Festival.

SEX/MONEY/DEATH: Screenwriter Clarke had himself served in the Metropolitan Police during World War Two, and he brought both an understanding of police terms and methods and – less ideally – a high-handed assumption of moral righteousness to his screenplay. The police force he writes of is entirely idealised. In fact, this is virtually a PR film with the message that the police are friendly, decent and honest, live in tidy, if humble, homes and exist entirely within ethical values. The criminals are scruffy, erratic, indulge in sex before marriage (Diana's appearance, drying her hair, standing in her underwear in front of two male friends is positively indecent by the standards of early-fifties British film) and live in dark squalor. It is, of course, as much a police-procedural drama as it is a gangster film; but it only really comes to life when Bogarde's insouciant, squinting thug comes on screen. It's also a portrayal of the new, postwar underworld that is clearly indebted to (and at points probably derived from) *Brighton Rock* (both film and novella), itself a series of improvisations around the tropes of the thirties Warner Bros films.

The twitchy relationship between the gangster killer and his hysterical girl links the two pictures, as does the condemning portrait of a morally bankrupt youth element unable to live up to the moral standards of the previous generation. The hunting down of Riley at the end is also obviously sourced in desperate chases that conclude so many earlier films.

The Blue Lamp lacks Brighton Rock's tortured religiosity but substitutes for this an attempt at verisimilitude. The film is trying to be both 'typical' (and Riley is a perverse anti-Everyman) and a portrayal of an aberrant human being. It's as resolutely unglamorous in its portrayal of crime as Brighton Rock is and is perhaps even more straightforwardly condemning. There is some recognition that social difficulties have caused the young to become criminals (and that rationing and austerity have, like Prohibition in America two decades before, created an atmosphere that allows criminality), but there's little discussion of it.

It's also oddly elegiac, deeply nostalgic for the prewar world of criminality. Thugs like the Bogarde character are specifically said to be dangerous because of their lack of discipline and their lack of understanding of what the code of civilised conduct for a 'criminal' is. The collaboration the other criminals give the police so that they can successfully capture Riley is, in retrospect, bizarre. There is also no criticism – implicit or explicit – in the film's characters' casual condoning of wife beating (something repeated in the Dixon of Dock Green TV series, incidentally) and the implicit racism and classism of the script. The poor are shown to be morally dubious for their lack of trust in the police, and children are seen to be inappropriately suspicious of authority; this is specifically said to be something that may cause problems in the future.

The Blue Lamp is a film that very strongly believes in a community and its values, and it believes that community and those values to be both eternal and temporarily under siege. As the American gangster film was experimenting with moments of near surrealism, and providing moments of outright psychodrama (**White Heat**), the British version is not so much looking backwards (although this is nowhere near as sophisticated a film as *Brighton Rock*) as demonstrating a refusal to contemplate the future to be very different at all, either socially or filmically, from the past.

THE VERDICT: Paternalistic, smug, old-fashioned, but visually striking, *The Blue Lamp* lacks wit or characterisation and is potentially hilarious if watched in the wrong frame of mind. It is also a tremendous example of British filmmaking and a uniquely British 'take' on the genre.

Robin and the 7 Hoods (1964)

(123 minutes)

Screenplay by David R Schwartz
Producer: William H Daniels
Associate Producer: Howard W Koch
Executive producer: Frank Sinatra
Director of Photography: William H Daniels
Songs by Jimmy Van Heusen and Sammy Cahn
Score by Nelson Riddle
Editor: Sam O'Steen
Production Designer: LeRoy Deane
Set Decoration by Raphael Bretton
Costume Design by Don Field
Directed by Gordon Douglas

PRINCIPAL CAST: Frank Sinatra (Robbo), Dean Martin (Little John), Sammy Davis Jr (Will), Bing Crosby (Allen A Dale), Peter Falk (Guy Gisborne), Barbara Rush (Marian Stevens), Victor Buono (Sheriff Alvin Potts), Hank Henry (Six Seconds), Robert Foulk (Sheriff Octavius Glick), Allen Jenkins (Vermin Whitouski), Jack La Rue (Tomatoes), Robert Carricart (Blue Jaw), Joseph Ruskin (Twitch), Phil Arnold (Hatrack), Harry Swoger (Soupmeat), Bernard Fein

(Charlie Bananas), Richard Bakalyan (Robbo's Hood), Sonny King (Robbo's Hood), Phillip Crosby (Robbo's Hood), Al Silvani (Robbo's Hood), Harry Wilson (Gisborne's Hood), Caryl Lee Hill (Cocktail Waitress), Mickey Finn (Bartender), Richard Simmons (Prosecutor), Edward G Robinson (Big Jim)

SUMMARY: While his loyal lieutenant 'Robbo' is out of town crime boss 'Big Jim' is murdered by another lieutenant, Guy Gisborne, who then takes over all the rackets himself; taking half of all bootlegging and gambling profits without consulting the other gang leaders. Robbo returns and with his friends, John, Will and Alan, works to bring down Guy, singing and dancing merrily as they do so. Robbo woos Big Jim's long-lost daughter, Marian, and devotes the profits of his crime empire to an orphanage in order to be less of a bad guy. Marian betrays Robbo and takes control. John, Robbo and Will become department store Santa Clauses.

THE PLAYERS: Born 12 December 1915 in New Jersey, Francis Albert Sinatra became one of the most celebrated entertainers of modern times. A singer-turned-actor, he was an instinctual rather than trained screen actor who was mostly content to play variations on his singing persona, but when he put the effort in, such as in *From Here to Eternity* (Fred Zinnemann, 1953), *The Man with the Golden Arm* (Otto Preminger, 1955) and *The Manchurian Candidate* (John Frankenheimer, 1962) he could produce outstanding screen performances.

The first of the above (a role written for Eli Wallach and for which Sinatra had to beg after a vocal-chord haemorrhage temporarily derailed his singing career) gained him a Best Supporting Actor Oscar. His unofficial, but real, leadership of the informal group known as the Rat Pack (himself, Sammy Davis Jnr, Dean Martin, Joey Bishop, Peter Lawford) brought him a social profile to match, and he had a string of high-profile marriages and love affairs. He died in 1998.

The thinking, drinking man's Rat Packer Dean Martin did everything Sinatra did, but he was funnier (he recorded country-and-western albums as Dean 'Tex' Martin despite openly never having even *been* to Texas). Born 7 June 1917 as Dino Paul Crocetti to an Italian American family in Ohio, he couldn't speak English until he was five years old. Initially known to the public as half of a partnership with the comedian Jerry Lewis (in movies such as *At War with the Army* (Hal Walker, 1950) and in the duo's popular radio series), he went solo after personal arguments split the partnership in 1957. He was confidently expected to sink into obscurity. Instead he became a top singing star, an icon of cool and a respectable actor (his performance as a drunken sheriff's deputy with everything to prove in *Rio Bravo* (Howard Hawks, 1959) arguably surpasses anything Sinatra ever put on film).

Other strong performances include those in *The Young Lions* (Edward Dmytryk, 1958) and *Sergeants 3* (John Sturges, 1963). Emotionally broken by the death of his son in an accident in 1987, he spent the last few years of his life in virtual seclusion. He died in 1995.

The magnificent Sammy Davis Jr was a performer since childhood. Born 8 December 1925 in New York City, he never attended school and was billed through much of his early career as a 'performing midget' to get around labour laws. He could sing, he could dance, he could even act (a bit) and his film appearances don't do his talents justice with the possible exception of his final movie *Tap* (Nick Castle, 1989), with Davis bringing dignity to the role of an over-the-hill song-and-dance man. It was in guest slots on television (such as on *Rowan & Martin's Laugh In*) and on stage in cabaret that Davis shone. He courted controversy all his life, refusing to play down the disadvantages America extended to a black, Puerto Rican, Jewish, one-eyed man (he lost his left eye in a car crash) and enraged some with his marriage to the white actress Mai Bitt. He remained a star until the day he died of throat cancer (he smoked up to a hundred cigarettes a day) in 1990.

Peter Falk is Columbo in the seemingly indefinitely running, rerunning and perpetually revived detective series of that name (the character has no confirmed first name), but there's more to him than that. A former merchant seaman, who lost an eye to cancer at the age of three, he was born in New York on 17 September 1927. Those who might like a chance to evaluate his versatility are pointed towards his performance as Reverend Theo in *The Lost World* (Stuart Orme, 2001) for BBC Television (with Bob Hoskins as Professor Challenger), his appearance in *The Princess Bride* (Rob Reiner, 1987) as the grandfatherly storyteller or his cameo as himself in Wim Wenders' *Wings of Desire* (1987).

THE DIRECTOR: Born in 1907, Gordon Douglas (a former child actor, and later joke writer) found early success as a film director with Laurel and Hardy mini-classic *Saps At Sea* (1940), in which the duo make a meal for an escaped convict out of odds and ends (including Stan's belt) after they become trapped on a boat with him. He also shot the utterly bizarre propaganda/slapstick burlesque *The Devil with Hitler* (1942) in which the board of directors of Hades threaten the Devil with being replaced by Adolf Hitler, whom he is now less evil than. The Devil then resolves to persuade the dictator to commit a good deed in order to save his own infernal seat. Featuring a lot of jokes about Hitler's skills as a housepainter, this is not the sort of film that turns up on Bank Holiday afternoons these days.

Douglas had experience of Robin Hood tales, having directed the acceptable *Rogues of Sherwood Forest* (1950) with John Derek in the lead. Before coming to *Robin*, he had been working with Bing Crosby's old partner Bob Hope on *Call Me Bwana* (1963), a film now better known for its ostentatious product placement in *From Russia with Love* (Terence Young, 1963 – the films shared the Harry Saltzman/Albert R 'Cubby' Broccoli production stable) than for anything Hope did on screen in it. He also directed

Them! (1954), a well-thought-of SF tale, and *I Was a Communist for the FBI!* (1951), clearly the film with the best title ever given to a motion picture. He died in 1993.

VISUAL INTEREST: Existing in a brightly coloured world of anachronistically cut suits and period-appropriate hats, *Robin and the 7 Hoods* displays a directorial style that is, at best, unobtrusive. It just hangs back and lets the actors do their stuff. Sammy Davis Jnr dancing on a bar, singing into camera while machine-gunning gambling chips has a certain visual fascination, but there's no real input from the director or editor in putting it there.

The title sequence, though, is a riot of boxes, severe black backgrounds and artwork presenting the principal players to the audience accompanied by parping, groovy music and the sound of gunshots. Objectively, it's easily the most worthwhile piece of the film. The speakeasy which 'transforms' into a mission hall is a peculiar, and impressive, bit of set decoration.

QUOTES:

Little John: 'When your opponent's sitting there holding all aces, there's only one thing left to do. Kick over the table!'

Guy: 'Here was a man with no enemies. Sure, he had a lot of friends that didn't like him, but you can't please everybody.'

Robbo: 'If you could shoot pool with that tongue of yours . . .'
Little John: 'I tried that. I don't like the taste of the chalk.'

Will: 'I like the fun of reaching for a gun . . . my kind of prank is walking in a bank and going "Bang! Bang!" '

Robbo: 'I'd rather keep you as an enemy: as long as I hate your guts I know I got good taste.'

Little John (rummaging through the rubble of a destroyed bar): 'A hundred thousand hangovers down the drain.'

SOURCES TO SCREEN: It's not so much a case of 'blink and you'll miss him' as 'stare in disbelief that he's doing this' when Edward G Robinson makes a lengthy cameo at the beginning of the film as 'Big Jim', the mob boss disposed of by Guy Gisborne, kicking off the plot in the process. The scene is partially a parody of the 'celebration dinner' scene in *Little Caesar* and Robinson cheerfully blends his familiar Rico mannerisms with a sort of avuncular Father Christmas-like air and some Michael Caine-style pointing to achieve an effect that is hallucinatory in its dizzying inappropriateness.

'Big Jim' is clearly named for 'Big Jim' Colisimo – the inspiration for many of the 1930s Warner Bros pictures; there's a mention of the St Valentine's Day Massacre of 1929, too. Otherwise reality is very far away in this film.

There is something ingenious about the way that Robin Hood and Little John's fight with quarterstaffs (as related in almost all iterations of the legend) is turned into a pool contest, but the way that the plot of the movie both refers to the Robin Hood story (John knows of the legend) while echoing aspects of it, and having characters named after figures from it, is either a mature deconstruction of the nature of fiction or an indication of the cheerfully random nature of the piece. Probably a bit of both.

CONTEMPORARY REACTION: Released on 26 June 1964 and later nominated for two music-related Oscars (Best Music, Song, Jimmy Van Heusen (music), Sammy Cahn (lyrics); for the song 'My Kind of Town' as performed by Sinatra and for Nelson Riddle's score), the picture picked up neither, losing out to *Mary Poppins* (Robert Stevenson, 1964) for the song gong and André Previn's work on *My Fair Lady* (George Cukor, 1964) for the score. Neither of these can, for a change, be argued with. Schwartz's screenplay was nominated for Best Written Musical by the WGA but didn't win. Initial reviews were mixed. *Variety,* on 6 August 1964, expected the film to make 'solid money' due to the way it 'stacked up nicely as mass entertainment', but felt that it was, on the whole, 'a let down without any particular merit'. Peter Falk was labelled a 'pure gem' for rising above the material, and the paper noted that Barbara Rush was 'beautiful to look at'. The *New York Times*' Bosley Crowther called the picture a 'minor musical whimsy' with a 'just too cunning title'. Overall it was 'an artless and obvious film' but 'mildly amusing' and at least the 'usual Sinatra arrogance' was absent from the lead's performance.

THE VERDICT: An entire movie predicated on a silly pun and the audience's presumed affection for the three Rat Packers here present, *Robin and the 7 Hoods* should work far less well than it does. It's almost irresponsibly lightweight and stupid, both thoroughly self-indulgent and half baked, and yet it somehow works. This is chiefly due to Sinatra's ability to wear a suit and the irrepressible, impossible cool of Dean Martin, who is, admittedly, assisted by a script that chooses to give him virtually all the good lines. An example of how far away from all sense and sanity a gangster picture can go, *Robin and the 7 Hoods* should be seen to be believed. Would you prefer it if I'd included *Bugsy Malone*?

The Italian Job (1969)

(99 minutes)

Paramount Pictures
An Oakhurst Production
Written by Troy Kennedy Martin
Director of Photography: Douglas Slocombe
Production Designer: Disley Jones
Associate Producer: Bob Porter
Music: Quincy Jones
Edited by John Trumper
Production Manager: Trevor Kavaanagh
Second Unity Director: Philip Westler

Directed by Peter Collinson

PRINCIPAL CAST: Michael Caine (Charlie Croker), Noël Coward (Mr Bridger), Benny Hill (Professor Peach), Raf Vallone (Altabani), Tony Beckley (Camp Freddie), Rossano Brazzi (Beckerman), Maggie Blye (Lorna), Irene Handl (Miss Peach), John Le Mesurier (Governor), Fred Emney (Birkinshaw), John Clive (Garage Manager), Graham Payn (Keats), Michael Standing (Arthur), Stanley Caine (Coco), Barry Cox (Chris), Harry Baird (Big William), George Innes (Bill Bailey), John Forgeham (Frank), Robert Powell (Yellow), Derek Ware (Rozzer), Frank Jarvis (Roger), David Salamone (Dominic), Richard Essome (Tony), Mario Valgoi (Manzo), Renato Romano (Cosca), Franco Novelli (Altabini's Driver), Robert Rietty (Police Chief), Timothy Bateson (Dentist), David Kelly (Vicar), Arnold Diamond (Senior Computer Room Officer), Simon Dee (Shirtmaker), Alistair Hunter (Warder), Lana Gatto (Mrs Cosca)

SUMMARY: Recently released from prison, career criminal Charlie Crocker plans and executes the audacious theft of $4 million worth of gold bullion from a bank in Turin during an international football match between England and Italy. Thanks to financial and logistical help from the contacts and resources of the imprisoned crime lord Mr Bridger, and despite the best efforts of the Mafia, Crocker's gang make their escape from Turin in a small fleet of minis, before moving on to a bus, where they pose as football supporters. However, poor driving leaves the gold-filled coach hanging off the edge of a cliff, leaving Crocker unable to retrieve his bounty without overbalancing the vehicle and killing himself and his team in the process. The credits roll with the gang's fate uncertain.

THE PLAYERS: Film legend, self-made man and knight of the realm, Sir Michael Caine has pursued a career that has embraced many projects of varying quality, but he remains one of cinema's true icons. Born Maurice Joseph Micklewhite in 1933 in south London, he worked in the theatre as a stage assistant and playing minor roles before doing his national service, during which he served in Korea. His major film debut was in *Zulu* (Cy Endfield, 1964) and he went to headlining status in *The Ipcress File* (Sydney J Furie, 1965) and *Alfie* (Lewis Gilbert, 1966). *Alfie* won him the first of six Oscar nominations. Often mocked, usually for reasons of class-related snobbery, Caine has made no secret of the fact that he has often taken film jobs purely on the basis of how much money they pay. He has famously commented that, while he has never seen the truly execrable *Jaws – The Revenge* (Joseph Sargent, 1967), he *has* seen the house the proceeds built for him. Despite this, he has arguably given more great performances in more quality films than any other working film actor of his generation, and that despite his 'enjoying' a fallow career period in middle age (something, to be fair, that is true of many actors, for example Sean Connery).

Exemplary Caine performances include, but are not limited to, those in **Get Carter** (Mike Hodges, 1971), *Sleuth* (Joseph L Mankiewicz, 1972), *The Man Who Would Be King* (John Huston, 1975), *Educating Rita* (Lewis Gilbert, 1983), *Quills* (Philip Kaufman, 2000), *Last Orders* (Fred Schepisi, 2001), *The Quiet American* (Philip Noyce, 2002), *Little Voice* (Mark Herman, 1998), *Hannah and Her Sisters* (Woody Allen, 1987) and *The Cider House Rules* (Lasse Hallström, 1999), the last two of which both won him Academy Awards.

Even more impressive is the career of Noël Coward, writer, director, actor, songwriter, singer and raconteur – all of these and more. Born in 1899, he was an actor by the age of six, a writer before he was out of his teens. His plays include *This Happy Breed*, *Relative Values*, *The Vortex*, *Private Lives* and *Bitter Sweet*. He was co-director (with David Lean) of the stirring wartime propaganda classic *In Which We Serve* and he gave the phrase 'poor little rich girl' (among many others) to the English language.

In 1930 he was the highest-earning living author in the world and his play *Hay Fever* was the first work by a living writer to be produced at the National Theatre. His greatest achievement remains, perhaps, the play *Blithe Spirit* (he certainly thought so). Coward is magnificent in *The Italian Job*, and his final scene, showing him being applauded for his many achievements by a vast audience, is a fitting capstone to his life in art.

Inexplicably popular, especially in the USA, Benny Hill is considered to be one of the first comedians to use the medium of television effectively, rather than simply recreate stage or radio routines on the small screen. His life was marked by vast commercial success and, less happily, much personal tragedy. *The Italian Job* remains his only significant big-screen work, indeed arguably his only significant work of any kind. His performance in this picture is, in all fairness, excellent.

THE DIRECTOR: Peter Collinson scripted and directed *The Penthouse* (1967), a languid adaptation of the Scott Forbes play, before turning in a far more impressive adaptation, the filmed version of Roger Smith's television play *Up the Junction* (1968). During the 1970s he directed a variety of small films, often with international casts. He died, at the age of 44, from cancer in 1980.

VISUAL INTEREST: The lush and long opening scene of the car traversing the Italian countryside is elegant and wonderfully scored. Moments later there's a marvellous visual joke as dozens of Mafia hoods remove their hats in tribute to the man they've just killed. Croker drives an Aston Martin DB5, the cool car of sixties Britain – as driven by James Bond in *Goldfinger* (Guy Hamilton, 1963), for example. Bridger's moving silently around the prison to the strains of 'The British Grenadiers' is a joy.

The frenetic pace of the chase sequences has been noted – and the small lapses in continuity are entirely forgivable in the context of seeing real vehicles performing real stunts in real environments and in real time. In this post-CGI age the primacy of *The Italian Job*'s chase scenes is almost shocking. The crisp clean lighting of the scene where Charlie travels past the South Bank on the back of a milk float – and in which the then newly constructed concrete buildings look glorious – can only be a vast surprise to those of us who've seen only the decaying filthy hulks they've become. The visual is also useful, of course, in establishing the difference between the world as it was when Charlie went into prison, and the world he's returned to.

QUOTES:

Mr Bridger: 'I hope he likes spaghetti. They serve it four times a day in the Italian prisons.'

Charlie: 'The car belongs to the Pakistani ambassador . . . Typical, isn't it? I've been out of jail five minutes and already I'm in a hot car.'

Charlie: 'You were only supposed to blow the bloody doors off.'

Salesman: 'You must have shot a lot of tigers.'
Charlie: 'Yes, I used a machine gun.'

Camp Freddie: 'If it's the Bank of England it's out – Mr Bridger is very worried about the state of the country's economy.'

Camp Freddie: 'Now, Butch Harry, tell us about Fulham.'
Butch Harry: 'Well, Fulham, a bit dodgy at the minute.'

Charlie: 'When I went in, that [suit] was all the go.'
Adrian: 'What did you do? Life?'

TRIVIA: Screenwriter Troy Kennedy Martin was the co-creator of, and one of the principal screenwriters for, the British police procedural TV series *Z Cars* (1962–5, 1967–78). He began his career in the 1950s with one-off TV plays, and later contributed to *The Sweeney* (the creation of his brother, Ian) and *Colditz*, before scripting the widely revered British television drama *Edge of Darkness*.

Michael Caine has asserted that the characters get out of their predicament at the end of the film by restarting the van's engine. The van's engine runs until the petrol is all exhausted and – because the petrol is at the back – this loss of weight is enough to even out distribution of mass across the coach, allowing the characters to clamber out of the doors to safety.

SEX/MONEY/DEATH: The script for *The Italian Job*, although witty and well paced, does not exactly demonstrate the interest in social justice and keen awareness of issues that one would normally associate with the writer Troy Kennedy Martin (see **TRIVIA**). It could be said, with some justice, that, despite the ambiguity of the deferred ending, the moral of the story is 'stealing is cool and clever, especially if one steals from foreigners'. Even more so than *Robin and The 7 Hoods*, *The Italian Job* is an unrepentant portrayal of organised crime. It's virtually impossible to recall, when thinking about the picture, that genteel Mr Bridger has people killed during the course of the plot or to square the relaxed, amusing image Caine projects with the kind of man Charlie Crocker must be. The answer is, of course, that *The Italian Job* is primarily a 'caper', a comedy, and a deliberately un-self-aware one at that (a glance at the screenwriter's CV indicates that any shallowness on display must be a deliberate choice).

While probably objectively morally reprehensible in its resolute refusal to engage with any of the issues surrounding its subject matter, *The Italian Job* remains one of the most simply enjoyable, pleasurable motion pictures ever (virtually every scene has at least one quotable line, as anyone who's been in an English pub in the years since the film's release can tell you). It's also so deliriously odd – and in an entirely unforced way. Examples of this include the funeral scene, the recurrent comical musical motifs, the constantly reused cliché iconography (the hoods in dark glasses, for example) and the strangeness of the table at which Camp Freddie always seems to sit surrounded by underlings.

Then there's the simple fact that there's a character called 'Camp Freddie' at all. In addition to that, the movie has the reel of film on which Roger's posthumous message to Charlie is relayed, Caine's constant lapsing into comic voices and impersonations, and many odd comic vignettes (the professor's sister, Charlie's tailor, Charlie fetching his car). It *is* a gangster movie also, something I've occasionally questioned while compiling lists for this book. Bridger is a godfather, Croker a career criminal, the heist is an organised crime put together by professional gangsters. They come up against the Mafia, of course, who refer to their rivals as 'the London Mob' throughout.

The Italian Job is important, even if it isn't particularly deep or clever, because of what its being made at all says about the filmic portrayal of organised crime (and never mind its elevation to 'national treasure' status). Its inclusion in this book is for the following reasons. First, it is, as noted above, the perfect unrepentant gangster movie, in which there are no consequences and everything is 'just a bit of fun'. However, unlike in the equally unrepentant *GoodFellas*, it never makes a claim to being set in the real world, but takes place in a sort of Wodehouse-inspired Avengersland, with criminals as heroes and a kind of warm, boisterous amorality. Second, it's the high water mark of English post-World Cup triumphalism, a 'criminals triumph' movie that grows not out of deprivation or social problems, but out of a period of affluence and self-confidence.

THE VERDICT: *The Italian Job*'s sharp suits and sharp wit, its self-consciously London-centred nature and its celebration of a certain idea of masculinity (the 'ordinary bloke') would be seminal influences on virtually every British film made about crime thereafter – including all the ones that follow it in this book. They may deconstruct it, reference it, revere it or refute it, but they all know it. *The Italian Job* is the party for which *Get Carter* is the inevitable hangover.

Get Carter (1971)

(112 minutes)

Metro Goldwyn Mayer Presents
A Michael Klinger Production
Michael Caine in
Get Carter
Screenplay by Mike Hodges
Based on the Novel *Jack's Return Home* **by Ted Lewis**
Music Composed and Played by Roy Budd
Lyrics by Jack Fishman
Director of Photography: Wolfgang Suschitzky
Production Designer: Assheton Gorton
Film Editor: John Trumper
Production Supervisor: Robert Sterne
Directed by Mike Hodges

PRINCIPAL CAST: Michael Caine (Jack Carter), Ian Hendry (Eric Paice), Britt Ekland (Anna Fletcher), John Osborne (Cyril Kinnear), Tony Beckley (Peter), George Sewell (Con McCarty), Geraldine Moffat (Glenda), Dorothy White (Margaret), Rosemarie Dunham (Edna), Petra Markham (Doreen), Alun Armstrong (Keith), Bryan Mosley (Cliff Brumby), Glynn Edwards (Albert Swift), Bernard Hepton (Thorpe), Terence Rigby (Gerald Fletcher), John Bindon (Sid Fletcher), Godfrey Quigley (Eddie), Kevin Brennan (Harry), Maxwell Dees (Vicar), Liz McKenzie (Mrs Brumby), John Hussey (Architect), Ben Aris (Architect), Kitty Atwood (Old Woman), Denea Wilde (Pub Singer), Geraldine Sherman (Girl in Café), Joy Merlin (Woman in Post Office), Yvonne Michaels (Woman in Post Office), Alan Hockey (Scrapyard Dealer), Carl Howard ('J')

SUMMARY: Jack Carter returns to his home town of Newcastle to attend his brother Frank's funeral. Convinced that his brother, who died while drunk in an accident in his car, was murdered, he begins working his way through the underworld of Newcastle, trying to find out who was responsible for his brother's death. He discovers that his brother was killed by Eric Paice, who was working on orders from local big time gangster Cyril Kinnear at the time.

Frank had himself discovered that his daughter Doreen had performed in a pornographic film made by and for Kinnear. He'd been told this by Cliff Brumby, another local gangster, who hoped that Frank would kill Kinnear in his rage (Kinnear had been threatening Brumby's business interests). Carter kills Brumby and then arranges for Kinnear to be arrested by the vice squad. He kills Paice himself, after first making him drink a bottle of whisky, which is what Paice did to his brother. Carter is then shot dead by an assassin hired by Kinnear. His body lies spread-eagled on the deserted shore, brown water lapping at it.

THE PLAYERS: Ian Hendry was the eponymous hero of *Police Surgeon* on ATV in 1960–1 and the original lead in *The Avengers* the following year. His film career, for which he left the popular series, never took off in the manner in which he expected it to, partially due to a self-confessed alcohol problem.

John Osborne is better known as the writer of *Look Back In Anger* the 1956 play that revolutionised British theatre. He had begun his career as an actor, however, and he and Caine had worked together before, when both were struggling to find stage work. Despite his success as a writer, Osborne always retained his love for acting and agreed to do this film on the strength of the script.

Bryan Mosley played Alf Roberts in British TV's *Coronation Street* for decades. Bernard Hepton had major roles in all the truly great British television series of the 1970s, including *The Six Wives of Henry VIII*, *Elizabeth R*,

I, Claudius, Secret Army and *Colditz*. Britt Ekland, a model, had formerly been married to Peter Sellers and would make an appearance in the James Bond film *The Man with the Golden Gun* (Guy Hamilton, 1974).

THE DIRECTOR: With this picture, Mike Hodges made his debut directing feature films, having previously worked in television. The entire production of this film, from the buying of the book rights to the release, lasted a mere 36 weeks. The shoot itself was only 40 days – a remarkable rate of work, even for the time. Since *Get Carter* Hodges' chequered career has taken in the screamingly camp, thoroughly enjoyable post-*Star Wars Flash Gordon* adaptation of 1980 and the light British comedy *Morons from Outer Space* (1985) as well as the tremendous Clive Owen starring *Croupier* (1998), which also featured *ER*'s Alex Kingston.

VISUAL INTEREST: Hodges's directorial style takes advantage of opportunities offered by shooting the film on location. The girls' marching band were simply spotted by Hodges in the street, and he immediately began shooting film of them. His (and the lighting cameraman Wolf Suschitzky's) use of light is sparing. It's often dark and what light there is often comes from naked, bright light bulbs that swing, glowing, in the background of shots. He also makes use of almost abstract close-ups, such as that on the screws going into Frank's coffin or on Caine's eyes.

There's an obvious attempt to evoke the silent saloon bars of classic westerns as Carter, a native but one who has become a stranger, goes into the bar and orders a pint of bitter in a thin (i.e. a straight) glass. It's worth noting that one of the extras in this scene has five fingers and a thumb on one of his hands (there's a whacking great close-up showing it). It certainly adds to the feeling of strangeness.

At Frank's funeral, the film deliberately hints at its predecessors in its genre by the ostentatious use of six, even then, antique cars in the funeral procession. This suggests the gangster pictures of the thirties in a subtle but deliberate way. The funeral itself is virtually empty, which doesn't actually make sense given the large number of cars. Both scenes work visually of course.

The film begins with a wide shot of a man standing in the centre of a wide window: Jack Carter stands alone. The unrestrained, tasteless opulence of the apartment is displeasingly bland and vulgar and that's before the audience realise that this small crowd of dapper, dour people are watching a series of pornographic slides. There's a close-up on the operating machinery of the slide projector, then another, and another, to suggest the mechanical nature of Jack's thought processes and that of the pornography. They're all laughing without humour at the show; no one even seems to be aroused. It's an effective beginning, which sets the style of the piece and the visual tone appropriately.

The train journey over which the opening credits are spelled out seems to take a whole day, beginning with the light of the late morning and ending with the smudging dark of early evening. This emphasises the distance between London and Newcastle (although it isn't really all that far) and highlights the efforts that Carter is going to. It's shot almost entirely handheld and was done on a single train journey as the cast and crew travelled north to get to their Newcastle locations.

Late in the film there's a spiralling car run, up and up the inside of a multistorey car park, which echoes the corkscrew plot structure, the sense the audience gets of going round in circles in this film, seeing only fragments of sense rather than the whole picture.

QUOTES:
Carter: 'You're a big man, but you're in bad shape. With me, it's a full-time job. Now behave yourself.'

Carter: 'Do you wanna be dead?'

Carter: 'Do you know a man called Albert Swift?'

Larry: 'Clever sod, aren't you?'
Carter: 'Only comparatively.'

Carter: 'How's school?'
Doreen: 'I left last year.'
Carter: 'What're you doing now?'
Doreen: 'Working in Woolworth's.'
Carter: 'That must be very interesting.'

CONTEMPORARY REACTION: *Variety* (20 January 1971) thought *Get Carter* an 'excellent drama of cinema vengeance' that, although violent and brutal, was 'genuinely artistic' in 'the way in which the gore was handled'. The 'excellent direction', 'spare score' and 'rare artistry' of the production helped it build to a 'logical, if ironic, climax' despite the 'generally negative characters'. The *New York Times* (4 March) saw Vincent Canby, one of the younger, hipper generation of film critics then emerging in parallel with the 'New Hollywood' movement, call the film 'persistently and consistently interesting'. He particularly liked the way it contrasted the myths surrounding gangsters and hitmen with 'the facts of the dismal life' of one man who is of those professions to provide an 'irony that is both entertaining and complex'. Canby picked up on Carter's reading of *Farewell, My Lovely* and noted how Carter presumably saw himself as a modern inheritor of Raymond Chandler's heroic characters when he was actually 'more like one of Chandler's crook characters'.

Get Carter was remade almost immediately in America as the excellent *Hit Man* (George Armitage, 1972), with Bernie Casey as the lead. It was a faithful recreation of the plot and fascinations, albeit shot through with the rage one associates with African-American cinema of the early 1970s. The ending, though, is different: Carter survives, arguably because, in the milieu of racial politics in which the story was now working, it would be inappropriate to have him die. Reviewed in the *New York Times* of 21 December 1972 by Roger Greenspan, it was called 'a kind of personality play of great resourcefulness and skill' with 'a fine sense of excitement'. It's a fine film, which acknowledges that which it is based on, and that picture's own predecessors, but finds its own path. Bernie Casey is brilliant in the title role. The later 2000 remake, starring Sylvester Stallone with a cameo by Caine, is so poor as to be unworthy of even commenting upon.

SEX/MONEY/DEATH: The trailer for *Get Carter* fetishes 'the cruel killer, the cool lover' but at no point does the film ever do this. Caine's punctilious, precise performance is a thoroughly repellent portrayal of a man of extremes, a man who throws money at any problem hoping that this will make it go away. Sexually potent? Yes. Emotionally crippled? Certainly. Skilled in the use of violence? Absolutely. Admirable? Clearly not. There's absolutely nothing but irony in Carter reading Raymond Chandler's *Farewell, My Lovely* on the train: this man may walk down mean streets but he is himself utterly mean. There's a single-minded sociopathy to Carter's quest to avenge his brother's death, which spirals even more out of control after his discovery of the porn film *Teacher's Pet*, which features his niece (daughter?) Doreen.

The question of Doreen's paternity is brought up time and again in relation to *Get Carter*; but it's questioned directly only once in the picture itself, when young Keith is shouting at the retreating Carter. That Jack Carter slept with Frank Carter's wife and that the only child of his marriage may actually be Jack's adds subtextual worry to many scenes, particularly when Jack inadvertently finds himself watching said pornographic film. There is a slow freezing of the audience's collective gut as Carter watches the tacky, sordid, black-and-white images projected on the wall. But he doesn't turn it off: he watches it all with tears streaming down his face. Caine's performance is so powerful that it gets around the fact that the scene isn't terribly well edited together and has a lot of mismatched footage.

After this sequence, Carter isn't so much a man, more a force of nature. His arriving-in-a-strange-place-and-destroying-it-from-the-inside is a take on *Yojimbo* (Akira Kurosawa, 1960), but his terrible energy, utter ruthlessness (drugging a woman to death with heroin, then dumping her corpse where it will be found and Kinnear blamed for her death) and descent into madness (Caine's little chuckles and his sad dead eyes) make Jack Carter out as a new and special case. Viewers also specifically see that a young girl is in the car when Carter throws Brumby to his death and see that a young girl is being traumatised by his actions. It's another visual indication of Jack Carter's hypocrisy, his debasement of all of life.

Get Carter is not only the hangover from *The Italian Job*: it's the film that says that the sixties are dead, and that they weren't all that good anyway, now you come to think of it. It was released in the year that a bloated Sean Connery, slick with hair dye and wearing a pink tie with a white suit, made his first unsatisfactory appearance as James Bond (in *Diamonds Are Forever*).

The world of *Get Carter* – not merely the Newcastle but the *world* – is unbearably dour and grim. The colours are muted and dark, it's dull in *hue*. The decorations are bland, the food is slop, the people are ugly and the 'entertainment' in the pubs consists of fat old women singing standards. It's all just a bit *crap*, a sad and sorry world through which dreadful people slowly move, and in which a truly evil and possibly insane man is the closest thing we have to a hero, to a dispenser of justice. In the end, even he's gone, his corpse lapped at by foul brown water on a coal- and rubble-strewn beach.

THE VERDICT: That a film as dark and condemning, as crisp and clever, as *Get Carter* should have been co-opted by 'Cool Britannia' is repellent. *Get Carter* isn't cool, it's cold, but there is power and intoxication in that coldness and it's in that that the picture finds its own considerable power.

The Godfather (1972/1974/1990)

(175 minutes; *Part II* 200 minutes; *Part III* (theatrical)
162 minutes, (VHS) 169 minutes)

Paramount Pictures Presents
Mario Puzo's *The Godfather*
An Albert S Ruddy Production
Music Scored by Nino Rota
Screenplay by Mario Puzo and Francis Ford Coppola
Based on Mario Puzo's novel *The Godfather*
Produced by Albert S Ruddy
Edited by Walter Murch
Directed by Francis Ford Coppola

Paramount Pictures Presents
Francis Ford Coppola's Production
Mario Puzo's *The Godfather Part II*
Music Scored by Nino Rota
Conducted by Carmine Coppola
Screenplay by Francis Ford Coppola and Mario Puzo
Based on the novel *The Godfather* by Mario Puzo
Co-Producers: Gray Frederickson and Fred Roos
Edited by Walter Murch
Produced and Directed by Francis Ford Coppola

Paramount Pictures Presents
Mario Puzo's *The Godfather Part III*
Original Music by Carmine Coppola
Film Edited by Barry Malkin, Lisa Fruchtman and
Walter Murch
Written by Mario Puzo and Francis Ford Coppola
Produced and Directed by Francis Ford Coppola

PRINCIPAL CAST: Marlon Brando (Vito Corleone), Al Pacino (Michael Corleone), James Caan (Sonny Corleone), Richard S Castellano (Peter Clemenza), Robert Duvall (Tom Hagen), Sterling Hayden (Captain McCluskey), John Marley

(Jack Woltz), Richard Conte (Barzini), Al Lettieri (Sollozzo), Diane Keaton (Kay Adams/Corleone), Abe Vigoda (Sal Tessio) Talia Shire (Connie Corleone/Rizzi), Gianni Russo (Carlo Rizzi), John Cazale (Fredo Corleone), Rudy Bond (Cuneo), Al Martino (Johnny Fontane), Morgana King (Mama Corleone), Lenny Montana (Luca Brasi), John Martino (Paulie Gatto), Salvatore Corsitto (Bonasera), Richard Bright (Al Neri), Alex Rocco (Moe Greene), Tony Giorgio (Bruno Tattaglia), Vito Scotti (Nazorine), Tere Livrano (Theresa Hagen), Victor Rendina (Philip Tattaglia), Jeannie Linero (Lucy Mancini), Julie Gregg (Sandra Corleone), Ardell Sheridan (Mrs Clemenza), Simonetta Stefanelli (Apollonia), Angelo Infanti (Fabrizio), Corrado Gaipa (Don Tommasino), Franco Citti (Calo), Saro Urzì (Vitelli)

PART II: Al Pacino (Michael Corleone), Robert Duvall (Tom Hagen), Diane Keaton (Kay Corleone), Robert De Niro (Vito Corleone), John Cazale (Fredo Corleone), Talia Shire (Connie Corleone), Lee Strasberg (Hyman Roth), Michael V Gazzo (Frankie Pentangeli), G D Spradlin (Senator Pat Geary), Richard Bright (Al Neri), Gaston Moschin (Don Fanucci), Tom Rosqui (Rocco Lampone), Bruno Kirby (Peter Clemenza), Frank Sivero (Genco Abbandando), Francesca De Sapio (Young Mama Corleone), Morgana King (Mama Corleone), Marianna Hill (Deanna Dunn), Leopoldo Trieste (Signor Roberto), Dominic Chianese (Johnny Ola), Amerigo Tot (Busetta), Troy Donahue (Merle Johnson), John Aprea (Young Sal Tessio), Joe Spinell (Willie Cicci), Abe Vigoda (Sal Tessio), Tere Livrano (Theresa Hagen), Gianni Russo (Carlo Rizzi), Maria Carta (Vito's Mother), Oreste Baldini (Young Vito Corleone), Giuseppe Sillato (Don Francesco Ciccio), Mario Cotone (Don Tommasino), James Gounaris (Anthony Vito Corleone), Fay Spain (Marcia Roth)

PART III: Al Pacino (Michael Corleone), Diane Keaton (Kay Adams), Talia Shire (Connie Corleone), Andy Garcia

(Vincent Mancini), Eli Wallach (Don Altobello), Joe
Mantegna (Joey Zasa), George Hamilton (B J Harrison),
Bridget Fonda (Grace Hamilton), Sofia Coppola (Mary
Corleone), Raf Vallone (Cardinal Lamberto), Franc
D'Ambrosio (Anthony Corleone), Donal Donnelly
(Archbishop Gilday), Richard Bright (Al Neri), Helmut
Berger (Frederick Keinszig), Don Novello (Dominic
Abbandando), John Savage (Father Andrew Hagen), Franco
Citti (Calo), Mario Donatone (Mosca), Vittorio Duse (Don
Tommasino)

SUMMARY: It is 1946. An Italian American war hero,
Michael Corleone, takes his girlfriend, Kay Adams, to meet
his parents on the day of his sister's wedding. His father,
Vito Corleone, is known as 'the Godfather' and is the head
of the largest crime family/syndicate on the East Coast of the
United States. Following an assassination attempt on the old
man (Vito has refused to involve his criminal empire in drug
trafficking, which he despises) Michael's elder brother
Sonny, assisted by his middle brother Fredo and adopted
brother Tom Hagen, takes charge of the family. Despite
never having wanted anything to do with the family's
'business', Michael volunteers to murder the corrupt police
captain and his associate, a rival gangster, who plotted his
father's death.

In order to avoid arrest, he flees to Sicily, eventually
returning to take over the family himself. Sonny has been
murdered at the climax of a gang war that resulted from the
police captain's killing, and their father is too old and ill to
take direct control. Michael tries to run the family for a
short time, and he and Kay are reunited and married. Vito
dies of old age and, shortly afterwards, Michael organises a
spectacular bloodbath, timed to coincide with his son's
christening, in which he settles the Corleones' disputes with
rival families. They become ever more powerful as a result.
To Kay's increasing horror, the family proclaim Michael
Don Corleone and his father's true heir.

PART II: It is 1948. Michael attempts to legitimise his family business by making a deal, which includes the Jewish gangster Hyman Roth, with the government of Cuba. Somebody attempts to assassinate Michael, and it soon becomes clear that an old New York associate of Frankie Pentangeli is responsible, backed up by Roth and provided, unwittingly, with information by Fredo. The Cuba deal collapses as a result of the Castro/Che revolution; Roth has betrayed them and has set up Frankie Pentangelis in New York.

Frankie has come to believe, as Roth intended him to, that a 'failed' bungled hit on him was organised by Michael Corleone. Frankie testifies to a grand jury investigation into Michael's business dealings that Michael is 'the Godfather' and deeply involved in organised crime. Frankie is convinced by the appearance of his brother at Michael's hearing that Michael did not attempt to have him killed, and changes his evidence. He later commits suicide in prison, after Tom Hagen has assured him his family will be cared for.

Sick of her life, Kay leaves Michael. One day, while he is out fishing, Fredo is murdered on Michael's orders for his part in the betrayal. In parallel with this, the story of young Don Vito, arriving in America as a child after the Mafia murder of his father in Sicily, is shown. These intercut and interconnected flashbacks show Don Vito's rise to power in New York, his return to Sicily to avenge his father and the establishment of his Mafia network, which functions, initially, simply as a system to protect Italian Americans, whom no one else is looking out for.

PART III: It is 1979. While attempting some sort of reconciliation with Kay and his estranged son Anthony (he has remained close to his daughter Mary), Michael tries, once and for all, to legitimise his family, by buying a company called Imobilare from the Vatican. Through this all the Corleone family's money will be laundered, and they will all become clean. Yet old mob contacts drag Michael back into the world he's trying to leave, and his ambitious illegitimate nephew Vincent Mancini both lays claim to being the heir to his criminal empire and begins an affair with Michael's daughter Mary, his cousin.

A stroke lays Michael low and Vincent runs much of the family in his absence. As he recovers, Michael takes back his empire, but offers Vincent the family name, Corleone, in return for his services. Besieged by old enemies and haunted by forces within the Vatican bank that have swindled him, Michael attends the operatic debut of Anthony, who, like his father before him, never wanted to be part of the family business. While Michael is at the opera the Pope himself is murdered by the very forces within the church that the Corleones were battling with; the assassination attempt on Michael fails, but Mary is killed. In a coda set in 1997 Michael dies, peacefully, in his garden in Sicily.

THE PLAYERS: The president of Paramount Pictures was convinced that Brando, former matinée idol, Oscar winner, graduate of the method school and reported out-and-out eccentric, would never accept the role of Vito Corleone. Moreover, he was determined that he should never be offered it, so unreliable did he consider the actor to be. Coppola was allowed to contact Brando on the condition that Brando would acquiesce to being screen-tested, something Paramount were sure he would never do. Coppola called the screen test a 'make-up test', and allowed the actor to improvise around themes and scenes, while giving him various make-up and hair options to play with. The process excited Brando, Paramount began to capitulate, and eventually the actor signed up for the defining role of his later career.

A Broadway actor with precious little movie experience, Al Pacino was always Coppola's choice for Michael Corleone. Paramount didn't agree and, despite the director's protestations that Pacino was the one, made Coppola screen-test dozens of actors of a similar age, including James Caan (already in the frame for Sonny in Coppola's mind) and Martin Sheen.

Pacino and Caan had, along with Robert Duvall and John Cazale, been called up by Francis and asked to American Zoetrope, Coppola's own production centre, to shoot tests and improvisations based on the characters they would all eventually play mere days after he'd signed his contract to direct the film. Coppola and Pacino have both publicly reflected on the waste of time and resources (so typical of Coppola's hated 'Old Hollywood') that the screen-testing process represented. At the end of the process, Coppola had the same list of four people he'd had at the beginning – four people of whom three (Pacino, Duvall and Caan) would be nominated for Academy Awards for their contributions to the finished picture.

James Caan's career has been varied. He impressed in Coppola's *The Rain People* (1968) as a man with brain damage, and came to the attention of mainstream America in the TV movie *Brian's Song* (Buzz Kulik, 1971) shortly before being cast in *The Godfather*. He turned down Coppola's *Apocalypse Now* (1979) and made his directorial debut with *Hide in Plain Sight* (1980), a compelling illustration of life in the Federal Witness Protection Program, which made virtually no money. He made a lot of bad films in the 1980s and, if not actually forgotten during that period, certainly disappeared from prominence despite an excellent performance in Coppola's *Gardens of Stone* (1987). However, his appearance in *Misery* (Rob Reiner, 1990), opposite an Oscar-winning Kathy Bates, put him back in the public eye and more and better films followed. He was hugely effective in *Honeymoon in Vegas* (Andrew Bergman, 1992). In more recent years, unapologetically middle-aged, he's taken to subverting his on-screen persona in comedies such as *Mickey Blue Eyes* (Kelly Makin, 1999) and *Elf* (Jon Favreau, 2003) with Will Ferrell.

'Whatever happened to John Cazale?' is a question that many, especially teenagers, find themselves asking when looking at the history of film. The answer is unbearably sad.

A handful of outstanding supporting performances in a small number of exceptional films (all of which were nominated for Best Picture at the Oscars) form the sum total of his on-screen work. As well as his appearances in *The Godfather* and *The Godfather Part II*, he is instantly recognisable to audiences as Stosh in *The Deer Hunter* (Michael Cimino, 1978), Sal in *Dog Day Afternoon* (Sidney Lumet, 1975) and Stan in *The Conversation* (Francis Ford Coppola, 1974). He died in 1978 after a long battle against cancer. He was 42.

Robert De Niro's first movie role was in *The Wedding Party* (Brian De Palma, 1969), and, before taking the role of the young Vito Corleone in *The Godfather Part II*, he had twice won the New York Film Critics Award for Best Actor, once for *Mean Streets* (Martin Scorsese, 1973) and once for *Bang the Drum Slowly*.

Before doing either of those pictures he had screen-tested for Sonny for *The Godfather* but his performance as the eldest Corleone son lacked the warmth and humour that James Caan brings to the part. De Niro's Sonny is more obviously psychotic, less humane, more aggressive. While there's no resemblance between De Niro's version of Sonny and his performance as Vito in *Part II*, Coppola presumably saw in the young actor something that would be of use to him.

Having played small parts on television and in film for years, Andy Garcia appeared as one of *The Untouchables* (Brian De Palma, 1987) opposite Sean Connery and Kevin Costner. *The Godfather Part III* soon followed, as did *Dead Again* (Kenneth Branagh, 1990), a ludicrously enjoyable faux noir in which his character linked two plots taking place decades apart and in which he was required to be smothered in ageing make up for half the time.

The highlight of Garcia's nineties career was *Things To Do in Denver When You're Dead* (Gary Fleder, 1995), but the early twenty-first century has seen him turn in radically different performances in two slick thrillers, *Ocean's Eleven*

(Steven Soderbergh, 2001, as a casino boss swindled by George Clooney) and *Confidence* (James Foley, 2003, as a seedy FBI agent named Gunther).

THE DIRECTOR: Born in 1939 in Detroit, Michigan, Francis Ford Coppola nevertheless grew up in New York City. He studied film at UCLA and worked as an assistant to 'schlock' filmmaker Roger Corman who latterly gave him his first directorial break on *Dementia 13* (1963), which was shot over three days. Coppola's final student project film for UCLA, *You're a Big Boy Now* (1966), clearly impressed someone at Warner Brothers. They distributed the film and asked Coppola to direct *Finian's Rainbow* (1968) starring Tommy Steele as a leprechaun. It was a disaster. He then directed the cheap, but impressive *The Rain People* (1969) starring James Caan but found more success as a screenwriter than a director. He won an Oscar for his screenplay for *Patton* (Franklin J Schaffner, 1970). About this time Coppola formed a production company American Zoetrope with friend George Lucas and used the facility to produce several films.

The job of directing *The Godfather* only came to him after many other directors, including Sergio Leone, turned it down. Throughout production, Paramount executives harried him and continually threatened to replace him. He responded by turning in an arguable masterpiece and gaining an Oscar nomination in the process. He was the producer of George Lucas's *American Graffiti* (1973, which resulted in another Oscar nomination for Coppola) and then went on to direct *The Godfather – Part II* and *The Conversation* in the same year. They are his best films and two of the best films ever made. He won Oscars as writer, director and producer for *Part II* and seemed an unstoppable creative and commercial giant. His next picture, an old project of John Milius and George Lucas's about Vietnam, *Apocalypse Now* (1979), took half a decade to complete and virtually bankrupted Zoetrope. A qualified artistic success, it did badly financially and Coppola's work has arguably never reached the same level since; it has been suggested the picture exhausted him artistically. He has certainly never regained his former powers.

Peggy Sue Got Married (1988) and *Tucker: The Man and His Dream* (1986, another Lucas collaboration) are the most satisfying of Coppola's post 70s works, with the single exception of *Part III*. This may have been produced due to commercial pressure, but is a worthy addition to its series. *Bram Stoker's Dracula* (1992) was visually sumptuous but overlong, pretentious and wrecked by atrocious performances from most of its cast, while 90s work-for-hire such as John Grisham potboiler *The Rainmaker* (1997) and *Jack* (1996) with Robin Williams as an idiot man-child are literally impossible to bear.

However, Coppola's place in history is assured and his indisputable talent is a sure reason never to dismiss a new project from this fallen genius until one has actually seen it.

VISUAL INTEREST: More has been written about *The Godfather* than any other 'series' of films. This is at least partly because there is no other film 'series' that can plausibly claim to rival *The Godfather*'s combination of sheer objective merit and audience popularity (although the status of George Lucas's *Star Wars* saga will remain, for many, a debatable point). So much has been written about Coppola's visual approach on these pictures that any praise for his restrained, reserved framing or the colour palette of sepias he uses risks being mocked as cliché. Such is the horror of commenting on something that has been so thoroughly deconstructed in public fora. This is especially true when one is commenting on something that has rarely, if ever, been found wanting.

Nevertheless, *The Godfather* is beautifully yet unobtrusively shot in a roving-camera style, filled with warm colours and beautiful production designs that both suggest opulence and create a sort of specific internal psychogeography. Compositionally, little is ever centred, nothing is ever straight on: it's a world of angles in the darkness. It's both literally and metaphorically a world of shadows through which Dons Vito and Michael Corleone move (especially when the audience are in the films' objective 'present') and Coppola diffuses his lighting. This is a world where the warmth and colour of family can become, with the movement of a character from one side of the frame to another, the cold yet cloying darkness from which men (and it is almost always men) wield the power to send other men to their deaths (see **SEX/MONEY/DEATH**).

Although the film has been noted for its violence (and censored for it on television showings), Coppola has himself repeatedly claimed not to like on-screen violence, either as a viewer or as an artist-involved-in-creation. Since he regards Akira Kurosawa as the father of all modern cinematic violence, it is unsurprising that Coppola should make the deaths in all instalments of *The Godfather* both so grandiose (almost operatic in their intensity) and so overtly symbolic. From the merely physically ludicrous (Moe Greene being shot through the eye, his blood pumping in gallons out of his cracked spectacle lens and his head slumping downward) to the insanely implausible (a trachea ripped open with the edge of a folded pair of glasses), the audience are usually seeing, in these movies, acts that strangely combine the literal, the symbolic and the demonstrative. The arterial sprays of dazzling bright red blood that accompany these killings (and indeed the 'puff', the cloud that floats upwards during Michael's killing of McCluskey) seem uniquely Catholic in their intensity. For a film that is as much about religion as it is about moral decay, organised crime and America, it's appropriate that there is something ritualistic as well as symbolic about the violence therein.

QUOTES:
Michael: 'If anything in this life is certain, if history's taught us *anything*, it's that you can kill anyone.'

Fredo: 'How do you say banana daiquiri?'
Michael: 'Banana daiquiri.'

Michael: 'Every family has bad memories.'

Michael: 'I spent my life protecting my son; I spent my life protecting my family!'

Kay: 'That's your big thing, isn't it? Reason. Backed up by murder.'

Michael: 'Friendship and money? Oil and water.'

Michael: 'Never hate your enemies: it affects your judgement.'

Tom: 'You want to wipe everybody out?'
Michael: 'I don't need to wipe everybody out, Tom, just my enemies.'

Michael: 'Just when I thought I was out, they pull me back in.'

Michael: 'I betrayed my wife. I betrayed myself. I killed men and I ordered men to be killed. I ordered the death of my brother. He injured me. I killed my mother's son. I killed my father's son.'

Michael: 'I command this family, right or wrong.'

Michael: 'If every drug pusher in this room were to drop dead, I would be the only one alive.'

SOURCES TO SCREEN: *The Godfather* is not a great novel. It is not, to be entirely fair, even a particularly good one. Although elaborately structured, readable and strongly and clearly characterised, it also has some more unfortunate elements, which are wisely exorcised in the screenplay(s). The violence and sex in the book are visceral to the point of being effectively pornographic. The film, although celebrated for its violent content by many, is altogether more subtle in its depiction of that violence and never descends to

the level of actually taking glee in its presentation of carnage
(see **VISUAL INTEREST**).

Puzo's novel's characterisation of its female characters is
clichéd and sexist to the point of verging on, to
contemporary eyes, outright misogyny. Lucy Mancini, a
woman who – owing to a defect of the pelvic bone – can be
satisfied only by the (repeatedly declared-to-be) massively
endowed Sonny Corleone, is wisely reduced to a cameo (it's
she whom he's having sex with upstairs at Connie's wedding
early in the film) and her, ahem, distinguishing feature, isn't
mentioned. Neither, wisely, is his. Her quest for plastic
surgery and emotional descent go unadapted.

There are also, inevitably, many details excised, mostly
wisely. For example, the movie mogul Woltz's enthusiastic
sexual abuse of a preteen Shirley Temple-esque movie starlet
is omitted, presumably for being both distasteful and
difficult to film without being exploitative. It is also too
traumatic an incident, and concept, to deal with so briefly as
to make it a minor detail relating to a minor character.

Lucy Mancini also features in the only major subplot from
the book that isn't utilised in either *The Godfather* or any of
its sequels. In this plotline, the activities of Moe Greene, a
Corleone associate who features in the first movie in a small
capacity (he runs the largely unseen Las Vegas end of the
family's operation, and is killed in Michael's grand massacre
at the film's end), are demonstrated at inordinate length.

The first film takes the essence of Chapters 1 to 11 of the
book (from the wedding party at the Don's to Michael's
escape to Sicily) in their entirety, skipping over only
incidental details and adapting the flow of events faithfully,
including keeping most of the dialogue intact, and making
only one significant change. This is to delete the character of
Genco Abbandando, Vito Corleone's first *consigliere*, who is
dying in hospital as the book begins. Removing Abbandando
and giving Tom Hagen this role from the opening scene (he
is merely 'acting *consigliere*' in the novel until Abbandando
dies) is a sensible act of economy, which also helps keep the

early part of the film focused. Coppola actually shot this scene and then deleted it from the film before release. Abbandando's scene is added to the version of the film recut by Coppola for US television transmission in 1976. The scene provides an endpoint for a character who features in the flashbacks of *The Godfather Part II* and which are incorporated, in chronological order, in that linear reworking of the film(s).

Other, minor, changes are of a similar nature: on the page, more people than the undertaker come to ask the Don for favours at the wedding; on the screen, the one, iconic, example is rightly considered enough. Amusingly, one of the removed minor plaintiffs goes by the name of Coppola.

The screenplay then skips over Chapters 12 and 13 (which are about the crooner Johnny Fontaine), Chapter 14 (which is Vito Corleone's backstory and childhood) and Chapter 15 (which is about Kay Adams's reaction to Michael's exile) and goes to Chapter 16 and the events leading to Sonny's murder. Interestingly, given the technique he would adopt when writing *Part II*, Coppola's screenplay straightens these events out into narrative sequence, whereas Puzo had, more ambitiously but perhaps slightly ineffectively, chosen to relate much of this portion of the story as a series of discontinuous flashbacks.

Chapter 21 tells the story of a young man who agrees to take the rap for Michael's murder of McCluskey and thus enables Michael to return from Sicily. This is removed, as is Chapter 22 (the aforementioned Lucy Mancini plotline). Chapters 23 and 24 contain more details of Michael's life in Sicily (again, not told chronologically) including some related incidents from Vito's past, which turn up in *The Godfather Part II*. Chapter 25 is Michael and Kay's reunion in America, Chapters 26 and 27 are about Johnny Fontaine and Lucy Mancini (although the Corleone brothers intrude a little) and Chapters 28 to 32 are the climax of the story as viewers of the film would recognise it.

In writing his screenplay, Coppola adopted an unusual technique. On his first reading of the novel he wrote many and elaborate notes in the margins of his large-format paperback copy. He then broke the back of the book, cut out all the pages and pasted them into the even larger pages of a sketchbook. However, he cut out the centre of the sketchbook's pages before pasting in the ones he had taken from the novel. By making holes like this, he could see both sides of the pasted-in pages. He then wrote further notes, progressing to dividing the storyline into individual scenes, each of which was then broken down into what he saw as its component categories – with titles such as 'Images', 'the Core', 'Synopsis', 'Pitfalls' and 'Themes'. From this vast notebook he then wrote up a full first draft screenplay, which he then rewrote in a full one-on-one collaboration with Puzo. Coppola has since opined that he could have shot the movie from the notebook, and seemingly regards the screenplay as an unnecessary object created largely to appease Paramount. What is certainly true is that Coppola had the notebook with him at all times on the set of the movie and has kept it among his papers to this day.

As an interesting aside, Paramount, aware of the potential cost of shooting the movie as a period piece, initially instructed Coppola to rewrite the plot to accommodate a then contemporary (i.e. early-1970s) setting. This pained Coppola, who had spent much of his reading of the book reflecting on how the story was so utterly of its own era. After much lobbying, he convinced the financiers of his point.

The screenplay for *Part II*, co-written again by Puzo and Coppola, utilises much of the material from Chapter 14, but expands and colours it, adding in detail in a way that is actually counterintuitive. You expect the events of a novel to be reduced in detail and complexity when they become screenplay, but Puzo and Coppola take the first paragraph of Chapter 14 and stretch it into the first twenty minutes of *Part II* without any difficulty at all. The 1950s section of *Part II* is entirely the invention of the screenwriting process, and has no basis in the novel at all except for the personalities of the characters who are carried over. This is equally true of *Part III*, although Andy Garcia's character, Vincent Mancini, is the son of Lucy Mancini, who was all but cut from the first film's script. (The relation of her further life in the novel actually makes it impossible for her to have borne Sonny's child, so it's her very omission from much of the first film that makes the existence of Vincent even possible. It's plausible, and pleasing, structurally speaking, that in terms of the film series the Sonny–Lucy sex scene near the beginning of *The Godfather* is actually Vincent's conception.)

CONTEMPORARY REACTION: Bewilderingly, *Variety* didn't think much of *The Godfather* when it first appeared, and neither did the *New York Times*. *Variety* (7 February 1972) felt the film had 'flashes of excitement' but was 'overlong' and while 'never so placid as to be boring' it was 'never so gripping as to be superior screen drama'. Overall *The Godfather* had 'one great performance [Pacino] . . . a lot of terrific mood' but achieved 'only half the job'. In the *New York Times* of 16 March 1972 Vincent Canby called the picture the 'most moving and brutal chronicle of American life' and both 'truly sorrowful' and 'truly exciting'. While acknowledging the source novel to possess 'more drive than genius', Canby found Brando 'magnificent' and Pacino 'an actor worthy to have Brando as his Father'. The screenplay lacked the 'false piety' of the 30s Warner Brothers gangster pictures and its paralleling of the Corleone family's lives of organised crime with the universal fascinations of the American immigrant experience was 'disturbing . . . so moving' and 'played havoc with the emotions'.

When it came to reviewing *Part II* over two years later *Variety* conveniently forgot its ambivalence towards the original picture and cheerfully informed readers that this was not an inappropriate cash-in sequel to the masterpiece of 1972. The sequel was an 'excellent, epochal drama' in its own right, one 'handsomely produced and superbly directed'. Unlike Canby two years before, the paper argued that the film avoided glamorising crime by making the central characters 'callous, selfish and undeserving of either pity or adulation', perhaps missing much of the movie's best material in the process.

That was only the start of course: there then came 28 Oscar nominations, translating into nine awards, two for Best Picture, Two for Best Screenplay, a Best Director for Coppola, acting honours for Brando and De Niro (uniquely as the same character), Art Direction (for *Part II* for Dean Tavoularis) and one for Nino Rota and Carmine Coppola for the music for *Part II*. Then came immortality.

When Coppola returned to the well for *Part III Variety* was, ironically, one of the papers that reviewed the film the most favourably (on 17 December 1990). 'Pacino is *magnificent*' it confided to its readership, and called the film 'a dramatic and commercial powerhouse that can easily stand on its own'. Coppola had come 'very close to completely succeeding' in creating a 'full equal' to his previous films in terms of 'narrative intensity, epic scope [and] physical beauty'.

TRIVIA: One of the most impressive and heart-rending scenes in the series, the slow and painful flashback to more innocent days prior to the events of the first film – which is shown at the end of *The Godfather Part II* (featuring James Caan, who appeared for free) – was originally also to have involved Marlon Brando. Brando, however, didn't turn up and the actors workshopped and improvised the scene of the family waiting for Don to return home for his surprise birthday party. Ironically, Brando's absence and the Don's existence as an off-screen presence make the character even more of a vast, mythic Titan than he would have been had he been there, and they echo the Don's empty chair, as seen in the second movie's very first scene. It's telling about the worldview of the second picture that, as Michael loses his way finally and completely succumbs to darkness, he can no longer remember the Don. It's a brilliant scene, which re-establishes and adds to the whole structure of the series in a few short moments. It's the first, and only, flashback in the series to show characters the audience already know played by the actors who were playing them when viewers first met them. It establishes Tom Hagen as Don Vito's confidant as early as 1941 and, in showing the moment when Michael told his family that he was going to go to war in the service of the United States (it takes place on Pearl Harbor day, 7 December 1941), it reinforces and re-establishes the relationships set up at the beginning of the first picture.

SEX/MONEY/DEATH: There is no insight, and little real merit, in saying that *The Godfather* is a brilliant series of films, but that fact (and it is a fact) remains true. *The Godfather* remains perhaps the only sacred cow of American culture that there has never been an even half-hearted attempt to slaughter. Held together by a fine ensemble cast, who are blessed to be working from an exquisite screenplay, it's arguably the finest work in the career of every single person involved. Al Pacino, given decades (in both fiction and fact) to work Michael Corleone into one of the most complex characters ever placed on screen, gives a performance that has been rightfully acclaimed.

That the Academy of Motion Picture Arts and Sciences had three opportunities to give Pacino an Oscar for playing Michael, and declined on every one of those occasions, borders on the unforgivable. It's certainly incomprehensible, especially in the case of *The Godfather Part II*. Pacino's slow moral and emotional *rotting* across the movie is extraordinary, culminating in the scene in which he stares blank-eyed, reptilian, chin cupped in his right hand, looking into the abyss. Even at the beginning of the movie, even as the audience see the reprise of a mafioso kissing his hand from the end of the first picture, there is still a shade of the Michael Corleone viewers first met at his sister's wedding. As the story progresses, the audience can still see chinks of this humanity, mostly expressed in his love for his family and in his reluctance to commit horrible acts unless he judges it *necessary* (although his definition of necessary and the audience's are not the same thing).

The final shot of *Part II* is the one and only moment in the three films where Michael is lost to the audience, where he no longer commands their sympathy and respect. Everyone from Pauline Kael to Robert McKee has observed that in the moral system of *Part II* Michael Corleone is principally, although not entirely, a bad man because he abandons his family. The most shocking acts he commits, the most shocking to both the audience and the other characters, are the murder of Fredo and the coldness of his abandonment of Kay. This is, time and again, deliberately contrasted with the warmth and humanity of Don Vito Corleone, as seen in flashback. If only Michael were more like his father, the film seems to say, he too would have been a great man. But this, though compelling and emotive, is nonsense. Michael Corleone's appalling behaviour towards his family is a *symptom* of his evil, not the cause of it.

When the audience first see Michael again in *Part III* the first words they hear from him are, 'My beloved children' – an attempt to claw back the audience's sympathy to Michael by invoking the spirit of family that Vito is said to embody. It works, but it also manages something else. Michael Corleone's age, his obvious remorse, his self-hatred, the very fact that his tone is confessional, not conspiratorial, all conspire to make the audience sympathise with him again. If this is not the case as the film starts, it's certainly true when, virtually on the hour, he suffers a stroke and – in agony – calls for Fredo. He is no longer the monster he was. The end of *Part II* is not, as it seemed to be for nearly two decades, the final moment of his descent into hell, it's the zenith on the inverted bell jar of his moral collapse.

This has been labelled irresponsible, even morally dubious in itself, in showing Michael emerging from total darkness, but the opposite is true. It rescues the series from the moral simplicity of 'good becomes bad' and allows audiences to be free of the strikingly harsh moral relativism that *Part II* practises. Moreover, it opens up the possibility that if Michael can mellow as he ages then perhaps Vito did too. The audience never see Vito Corleone at the very height of his power but they do see Michael Corleone at that point. *Part III* seems to know that the elder Don, too, must have had his own period of real darkness, and showing Michael's more humane older self ('Am I still the man that did those things?'), backed up by a performance from Pacino that deliberately echoes, and imitates, Brando's body language from the first film (watch the way he creases his hair with his hands, or the bearlike uncomfortable walk), is its way, I think, of letting the audience see that.

So, Part *III* does not live up to the awesome scope and sheer impact of *Part II*, but, then Coppola, New Hollywood and perhaps American film as a whole have now spent more than a quarter of a century not quite living up to that particular moment of apotheosis and it adds far more to the story of Michael Corleone than it takes away.

Those who come to *Part III* always having known of its existence will find their reactions far kinder than those of people who either had waited twenty years for another tale of Michael Corleone or were horrified that Coppola should be so crass as to return to the well once again. Another important factor in terms of the picture's long-term reputation, and there's no way to prove this one way or the other, is perhaps that the longer version of *Part III*, as released on home video and latterly on DVD, is a far stronger, more subtle picture than that released to cinemas. There are, admittedly, lots of short scenes and the sometimes erratic editing stands no comparison with the exquisite constructions and detours of *Part II*, but it builds to a climax of such horrifying beauty that it's surely impossible not to forgive Coppola the movie's earlier stumbles.

The picture also allows Coppola to indulge in further duplications and inversions of the kind that he employed in *Part II*.

All of the *Godfather* films begin with a party and end with a massacre; all feature a significant scene in a kitchen and a symbolic closing door. All of them also appropriate ceremonial scenes of Catholic significance as backdrops to acts of violence. There are obvious story parallels too: an obvious resemblance between Sonny in the first picture and Vincent in the third, and indeed in their respective plot roles; both *Part II* and *Part III* repeatedly compare and contrast Michael with his father; *Part III* even compares Vincent with the younger Vito as well, showing him as popular and trusted on the streets of New York City, admired by elderly women and trusted by neutral Italians – a far cry from Michael scheming in his compound or hiding in Sicily planning his next move.

The Godfather isn't really about sex or money or death. It has higher aims than that. In a way in which its source novel isn't, it's about the process of wielding power; and it knows both that power is corrupting and that there are times when it has to be wielded. The Italian community of the early twentieth century in *Part II* need Vito Corleone. They still need him in the immediately post-World War Two sequences in the first picture. The structure that he then creates in order to implement the process whereby he can both alleviate the pain of that need and profit from it then abhors a vacuum. The 'family' needs a Don Corleone, and so Michael becomes Don Corleone, forever pursuing the legitimate option, ever looking for a way to launder his money, clean his power base, cleanse his soul. There is a sense in which Michael Corleone sacrifices himself to the 'machine' of the family. He sublimates his humanity, his decency and all the things that made him his father's favourite son to fulfil his father's role. He throws away the things that made him go to college, go to war, romance the preppiest girl in the world (and she's played by Diane Keaton, who went on to win an Oscar as the eponymous *Annie Hall* (Woody Allen, 1977), the very definition of the 'whitebread' American female, not that anyone knew this at the time) and take her to his sister's wedding – in order to serve his father's memory. The tragedy of Michael Corleone has been called 'the tragedy of America'. It isn't. The Mafia is not a metaphor for United States society, either at the time the films were made or set or even now. It's something that operates inside that society and interacts with it, but it doesn't *represent* it. *The Godfather* isn't the Tragedy of America, but it is an American Tragedy. And it's the story of Michael Corleone.

When rumours suggested Coppola was floating, briefly, the notion of a *Part IV* in the late 1990s there were rumblings of discontent from every film critic and movie buff the world over. What *Part III* illustrates more clearly than either of the other two films is that the tragedy is a circular process, that history repeats itself. The audience know that Vincent, like Sonny, will never be a great don; they know that Anthony, like Michael before him, will be pulled in to save the family against his will and that the process of doing so will destroy him – unless he can escape the machine in the way his father never could. It doesn't have to be seen. It is entirely in the interests of American film that it never is.

THE VERDICT: Grandiose and eloquent as a unit, the individual films have different tones and different strengths and weaknesses. *Part III* is, of course, easily the weakest of the three, but it remains a five-star movie, worthy of the honours and awards it has been associated with. It's certainly the best movie nominated for Best Picture in its Oscar year. The first film is strikingly brilliant. Awesome in construction and epic in scope, it's simply both so powerful and so *entertaining* that it is always better, on repeat viewings, than you expect it to be. And that's when you expect it among the best films you've ever seen. *Part II* is simply the finest film ever made in America.

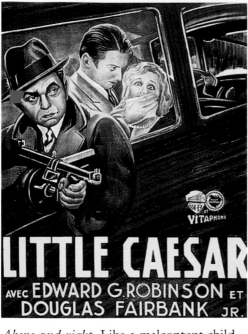

Above and right Like a malcontent child.
Edward G Robinson in *Little Caesar*

Scarface awaits his end

James Cagney and Jean Harlow in *The
Public Enemy*

Back from the trenches and forced into crime – *The Roaring Twenties*

Two icons form an uneasy alliance in *The Roaring Twenties*

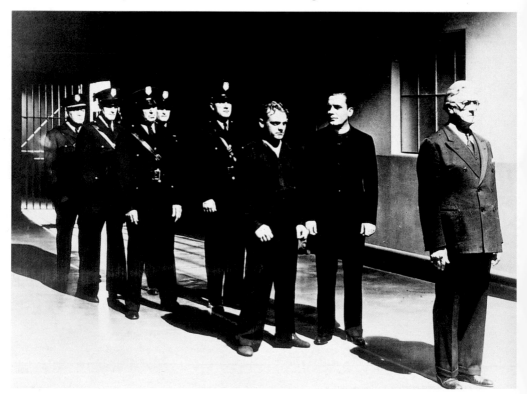

About to turn 'yellow'. Rocky redeems himself in *Angels with Dirty Faces*

'Top of the World!' in *White Heat*

Robin and the 7 Hoods: Frank, Bing and Dino indulge themselves

'A reasonable man.' Marlon Brando, magnificent in *The Godfather*

'The King is always alone.' Al Pacino as Michael in *The Godfather – Part II*

The Long Good Friday. 'You don't crucify someone outside a church! Not on Good Friday!' Caught up in events he doesn't understand Harold (Bob Hoskins) has a really bad day

Once Upon a Time in America: Has New York ever seemed more beautiful on film?

De Niro (under heavy make up) as the aged 'Noodles' in *Once Upon a Time in America*

And as Jimmy Conway, top-billed in a supporting role in *GoodFellas*

Bloody work. Vincent (John Travolta) and Jules (Samuel L Jackson) have a messy morning in *Pulp Fiction*

'We fucked up.' De Niro and Pesci reunite in *Casino*

'Tell me about Jenny!'
The 60s confronts itself in
The Limey

'Yes! yes! yes!' One last
job for Gal (Ray
Winstone) if Don (Ben
Kingsley) has his way

'My favourite axe.'
Genuinely sickening
violence in *Gangster No. 1*

Self-Mockery

With the notable exception of Al Pacino, most of the main players of *The Godfather* series have chosen to mock the films' earnestness and their personas from the pictures by making Mafia comedies. Marlon Brando got in first, making the ludicrous *The Freshman* (Andrew Bergman, 1990) in which his animal importer Carmine Sabatini (or Jimmy The Toucan) employs Matthew Broderick to look after a Komodo dragon for him. Brando's shambling, face-grabbing 'Toucan' is a pure parody of his Don Vito Corleone. In 1999 James Caan found himself mocking both his own Sonny Corleone and Brando's Don Vito as Frank Vital in *Mickey Blue Eyes* (Kelly Makin), an acceptable Hugh Grant vehicle in which Grant's stuttering, English art dealer falls for Vital's daughter (the luscious Jeanne Tripplehorn) and finds that not only is he trying to marry into the mob, but that his prospective father-in-law's associates want him to sell substandard paintings created by pretentious mobsters. Apart from a terrific scene in which Caan tries to teach Grant to say 'Forgeddabowdit' in a sufficiently 'New Yawk' accent, the film is only reasonably amusing. Far better is the year's other *Godfather*-baiting Mafia comedy *Analyze This* (Harold Ramis). Robert De Niro's Paul Vitti in that film and its sequel *Analyze That* (2002) is more Jimmy Conway (*GoodFellas*) or Ace Rothstein (*Casino*) than Vito Corleone however, although his performance hints at mockery of Brando on more than one occasion, especially in the latter film. Presumably the inevitable third film in the series will be called *Analyze The Other* and feature Paul analysing his analyst, Ben Sobel (Billy Crystal).

Black Caesar (1973)

(94 minutes)

American International
Music Composed and Performed by James Brown
A Larnco Production
Cinematography by Fenton Hamilton
Harlem Sequence Photographed by James Signorelli
Edited by George Folsey Jr
Executive Producer: Peter Sabiston
Associate Producer: James Dixon
Co-Producer: Janelle Cohen
Written, Produced and Directed by Larry Cohen

PRINCIPAL CAST: Fred Williamson (Tommy Gibbs), Gloria Hendry (Helen), Art Lund (McKinney), D'Urville Martin (Reverend Rufus), Julius Harris (Mr Gibbs), Minnie Gentry (Mama Gibbs), Philip Roye (Joe Washington), William Wellman Jr (Alfred Coleman), James Dixon (Bryant), Val Avery (Cardoza), Patrick McAllister (Grossfield), Don Pedro Colley (Crawdaddy), Myrna Hansen (Virginia Coleman), Omer Jeffrey (Tommy as a boy), Michael Jeffrey (Joe as a boy), Allan Bailey (Sport), Cecil Alonzo (Motor), Francisco De Gracia (Cab Driver), Larry Lurin (Carlos)

SUMMARY: Harlem, New York, 5 September 1953. A teenage shoeshine, boy Tommy Gibbs, has his leg broken by a corrupt cop, who insists that the payoff money Tommy has carried to him for a local gangster he runs errands for is $50 short and that Tommy must have taken it. On 23 October 1965 – after years in and out of jail on petty offences, and angry at the casually and savagely racist society in which he lives – Tommy plans to become the first black crime kingpin of New York city. He announces his presence by killing a man the Mafia have made known they want dead, and then showing that he's responsible.

He offers his services as a hit man to the mob, asking only one block of New York to control as his own rather than take a salary. He rises up through the mob hierarchy and gains a reputation for brutality, eventually killing his mob superiors and becoming the undisputed criminal master of New York. With the aid of stolen dossiers listing the financial criminality of various New York luminaries he buys himself police protection, and even co-operation, including from (now Captain) McKinney – the very cop who broke his leg twelve years before.

After a long reign at the top Tommy is betrayed by his former girlfriend, Helen, who has left him for his childhood friend Joey because she is afraid of the sexually violent monster he has become, and who is afraid that the police operation against Tommy will result in Joey's being sent to jail. Helen gives McKinney the dossiers, but in a final bloodbath Tommy kills McKinney before crawling back off home to the ruined tenement where he was born, to die. There he's beaten to death by a group of young black boys, who then steal his wallet. It's 20 August 1972.

THE PLAYERS: A writer/director as well as an actor, Fred 'The Hammer' Williamson is the kind of actor who is instantly recognisable to the average moviegoer while his name continues to elude them. He was Captain Jones in *M*A*S*H* (Robert Altman, 1970), Frost in *From Dusk Til Dawn* (Robert Rodriguez, 1996) and has been a constant presence on American television. His turn in the original *Star Trek* episode 'The Cloudminders' must, like most episodes of that series, be on somewhere in the world every day of the year. He was a huge star of African American produced cinema of the 1970s, and his talents have never truly been recognised by the mainstream.

A former model, the gorgeous Gloria Hendry was in the Bond epic *Live and Let Die* (Guy Hamilton, 1973) with Roger Moore and Yaphet Kotto, as was Julius Harris, who memorably played Kotto's hooked henchman Tee Hee.

THE DIRECTOR: New Yorker Larry Cohen (born 1938) created the cult US sci-fi TV series *The Invaders* (1967–8), and was a writer/producer on the legendary western pot-boiler *Branded* (1965–6), before becoming known as one of the more thoughtful and ambitious low-budget filmmakers of the 1970s. He was never afraid to shy away from political or philosophical content even in the context of what were, on paper, simplistic horror films.

Other films directed by him include *Maniac Cop* (1988) and *Wicked Stepmother* (1989), Bette Davis's last motion picture, in which she barely appears (she walked out days into production). Cohen continues to find success as a screenwriter in mainstream pictures, most recently penning Colin Farrell vehicle *Phone Booth* (Joel Schumacher, 2002).

VISUAL INTEREST: During the montage that shows Tommy's rise to power there are brief sequences of him slowly turning in front of camera while firing off a huge Tommy gun of a kind that was horrendously outdated at the time the movie was made and set. Tommy is also wearing anachronistic clothes and standing against a perfect black backdrop. The scene has no application to the contemporary reality of the film at all, and is a purely symbolic representation of Tommy's violent actions, as well as a clear attempt to place Tommy in the tradition of American gangster iconography.

Partially due to the cheapness of the film, there's a 'chop socky' vibrancy to the bright red blood that splurts across the screen every time there's a killing.

There's a very obvious pastiche of *The Godfather* 35 minutes or so in, when Gibbs organises a massacre of Sicilian Mafia chiefs so he can take over their territory. The music that initially plays over the scene is clearly intended as a pastiche of Nino Rota's famous 'Godfather Waltz', and this gradually gives way to the thwacking of soul guitars, and a heavy brass section. Visually, it's not exactly as if the cast of *Superfly* (Gordon Parks Jr, 1972) had turned up in the first scene of *The Godfather* and killed everyone, but it's as accurate an analogy as you're going to get. Incidentally, as Tommy staggers through the crowd, bleeding to death at the end of the movie, you can see a billboard in Times Square advertising that *The Godfather* is showing at that cinema.

QUOTES:
Cardoza: 'You do this to me after I gave you your big chance?'
Tommy: 'Who else am I gonna do it to?'

Cardoza: 'Since when do spades make as much as whites? Hey, listen, Shadow, you're lucky I'm still talking to you.'

Grossfield: 'Nobody likes to lose, like the Negroes.'

McKinney: 'They'd never accept a nigger into the syndicate.'
Tommy: 'Everybody's a liberal these days . . . Get with it.'

SOURCES TO SCREEN: Often talked about, thanks to the title, as if it were somehow a remake of *Little Caesar*, *Black Caesar* has far more in common with **The Public Enemy**. It shows two friends growing up together from petty adolescent crimes to murder and running gangs in adulthood. It uses jovial, inappropriate music – in this case a roaring James Brown track about living in New York – rather than 'I'm Forever Blowing Bubbles' to underscore its central character's rise and fall and it's also about another ethnic group gaining a foothold in an area usually dominated by Italians (in *The Public Enemy* it was the Chicago Irish; here it's New York African Americans).

Also, like Cagney in *The Public Enemy*, Tommy in this picture does much of what he does in order to impress and provide for a mother who worked hard for him in his youth, and for whom he wants better things. In the context of this argument, the presence of the actor son of the director of *The Public Enemy* in a minor role in this film just seems too good to be true. It's also worth noting that the subplot about the 'dossiers' that contain vital information about local corrupt individuals seems to have been drawn directly from **Angels With Dirty Faces**.

CONTEMPORARY REACTION: *Variety* appreciated the picture's commercial potential, saying it 'fits patly into current trend of violent "black" pix', but appreciated the 'remarkable photography' all the same. Gloria Hendry was picked out for specific praise. In the *New York Times* of 8 February 1973 A H Weiler liked the 'imposing, tough and unflappable' central performance from Williamson and approved of the 'black bad guys against white bad guys' moral ambiguity of the piece. What was less welcome to him was the way the plot hung together on 'contrivances that hinge mostly on action and bloodshed'.

TRIVIA: Star Fred Williamson later expressed a dislike of the term 'blaxploitation', which is often used to describe low-budget films of the early 1970s made predominantly to appeal to poor, urban black audiences and which used predominantly black talent both in front of and behind the camera. Hammer felt that the term, by the late nineties almost universally applied, was misleading. He argued that nobody involved in such films was exploited, that the actors and crews were being paid fairly for employment in their chosen profession and audiences were paying a reasonable price for a film that presented on screen things that they wanted to see.

The term 'blaxploitation' evolved out of the terminology of 'exploitation' filmmaking, and, while the exact origins of *that* term are difficult to define, it is probable that it refers to the exploitation of available resources (i.e. these films were made for minority audiences and were, therefore, regardless of content, always inexpensive) rather than the exploitation of human beings, or a group of human beings. Hammer, however, clearly has a point that, in the context of the historical treatment of black Americans, the term has certain other resonances and his complaint must be both respected and given some credence. For that reason the term has been avoided here.

SEX/MONEY/DEATH: The politics of the film's moral are interesting. Although this is partially a cry of rage and despair at the injustices of American society, it's also a critique of gangsterism and is ultimately a strongly moral tale. As Tommy rises to power it can be seen that, thanks to Joey, he is keen genuinely to protect the people of his neighbourhood and be socially responsible. Like the young Vito Corleone in *The Godfather Part II,* he's providing services and justice for those whom society neglects. 'We intend to do more than just organise the rackets in Harlem: we're going to see that black people get a fair shake, a chance to live better,' says Joey in their initial meeting with the lawyer Coleman, and there's talk of community centres and arranging for the rubbish to be collected in black neighbourhoods that are neglected by the city council.

Later on, though, Tommy loses interest in his social role, and becomes as coldly amoral as those he's replaced. In the film's own moral universe it is for shattering this compact that Gibbs is destroyed, not for killing Italians or running drugs – it's for not using the advantages he has gained to help the entire community that he dies. When he argues for the final time with Joey, Joey explains that the difference between them is that he 'never wanted to *own* anybody'. This makes a specific link between Tommy's behaviour and that of the history of slavery in America: Tommy is behaving like those freed nineteenth-century slaves who became slave owners themselves, in Joey's view, and that's why he attacks his former friend as a 'white nigger'.

Tommy's wider moral fall (which runs in parallel to his continued rise) is also counterpointed within the film by the collapse of his *personal* morality: he contemplates killing his father, he (at the very least) subjects his girlfriend to a serious sexual assault and he becomes physically violent with subordinates when they disobey him. He's becoming corrupted by the power he wields. It is, of course, Tommy's coldness and violence both towards Helen and other people that makes her prepared to betray him to protect Joey and their children.

Once Tommy has destroyed the unity of his community, as he does, it is easier for the forces of conformity and corruption, as represented by the spectacularly vile police captain, McKinney, to crush Tommy completely. Although the films mixes its messages a little (audiences are asked both to celebrate and to condemn Tommy, and not in a linear pattern of decline and fall or corruption and redemption), *Black Caesar* manages to be a powerful cry of rage at the injustices of the way black people were treated in sixties and seventies America. One is aware of the contradiction that often the only way to survive is to emulate your enemy,

141

prolonging your physical destruction in the process, but hastening your moral collapse.

The racist language used in the picture, especially (though not exclusively) when spat out by white characters, is shocking by today's standards. Whereas the work of Quentin Tarantino and Spike Lee has adjusted even the most mainstream audiences to the notion of 'reclaiming' racist language in order to drain it of any power, that's happening only half of the time in a film like *Black Caesar*. The other half of the time it's using racist language to *be* racist, using language as a tool of oppression rather than self-expression.

THE VERDICT: Slickly done, and filled with a sense of righteous rage, *Black Caesar* is a lot smarter than its critics might think, and a great deal more seriously minded than the clichéd perceptions of its genre might suggest.

Hell Up In Harlem (1973)

The sequel to this movie reunited writer/director Larry Cohen with Fred Williamson, Gloria Hendry, Julius Harris and D'Urville Martin in a less political story, which either ignores the ending of *Black Caesar* or subverts it, or it is set in the middle of it, depending on how you want to see it. Relying more on action than *Black Caesar*, it's entertaining but very much a lesser film – suffering, perhaps, because both Williamson and Cohen were working on other projects while making it (some of the stand-in doubling for Williamson is really *very* bad).

The Long Good Friday (1980)

(114 minutes)

Handmade Films Present
Music Composed by Francis Monkham
Director of Photography: Phil Meheux
Associate Producer: Chris Griffin

Art Director: Vic Symonds
Editor: Mike Taylor
Written by Barrie Keeffe
Produced by Barry Hanson
Directed by John Mackenzie

PRINCIPAL CAST: Bob Hoskins (Harold), Helen Mirren (Victoria), Dave King (Parky), Bryan Marshall (Harris), Derek Thompson (Jeff), Eddie Constantine (Charlie), Paul Freeman (Colin), Leo Dolan (Phil), Kevin McNally (Irish Youth), Patti Love (Carol), P H Moriarty (Razors), Ruby Head (Harold's Mother), Charles Cork (Eric), Olivier Pierre (Chef), Pierce Brosnan (First Irishman), Daragh O'Malley (Second Irishman), Karl Howman (David), Brian Hall (Alan), Alan Ford (Jack), Dave Ould (Don), Paul Kember (Ginger), Bill Moody (Boston), Alan Devlin (Priest), Stephen Davies (Tony), Bruce Alexander (Mac), Nigel Humphreys (Dave), Brian Hayes (Pool Attendant), Georgie Phillips (Eugene), Mary Sheen (Lil), Pauline Melville (Dora), Trevor Laird (Boy Under Car), Paul Barber (Erroll), Dexter Fletcher (Kid), Billy Cornelius (Pete), Ryan Michael (Waiter Ricardo), Robert Walker Jr (Jimmy), Nick Stringer (Billy), Gillian Taylforth (Sherry), Robert Hamilton (Flynn), James Ottaway (Commissionaire), Roy Alon (Captain Death), Tony Rohr (O'Flaherty), George Coulouris (Gus)

SUMMARY: Big-time London gangster Harold is wining and dining American business contacts in order to secure a deal that will make them all rich. The contract they are discussing involves the building of facilities for use in London's projected 1988 staging of the Olympic Games. He has it all: there's been peace among London's gangsters for ten years; the police do what he tells them; he has a beautiful mistress and several legitimate business interests. Then his men start dying. One is knifed in a public baths, his chauffeur is blown up while taking his mother to church and an unexploded bomb is found in his casino. Then, one of his pubs is blown up and, as the day spirals out of control, Harold, who is initially convinced that someone has initiated a gang war, realises that he is being targeted by the IRA.

Harris, a corrupt councilman, has used, with Harold's deputy's blessing but without Harold's knowledge, Harold's men to carry payoffs to Republican terrorists in Belfast. On the night of the payment three IRA men were killed and the terrorists assume that he is responsible and are set to destroy him. Refusing to be cowed, Harold has the IRA's representatives in London killed while pretending to broker a peace deal. Happy with his lot, he tries to make his deal with the Americans, but they pull out, unconvinced that London is safe or that Harold is competent. He is exiting a hotel when IRA men kidnap him and his wife.

THE PLAYERS: Born in Bury St Edmunds, Suffolk, on 26 October 1942 – where his pregnant Londoner mother had been evacuated due to the heavy bombing of the capital by the Luftwaffe – Bob Hoskins left school at fifteen and remains an entirely self-taught actor. Singing, dancing and emoting his way to public attention in Dennis Potter's *Pennies From Heaven* (1978) for the BBC, he soon found himself much in demand on television and in the (collapsing) British film industry. He was a viscerally evil Iago in *Othello* (1981) for the BBC and the band's fictional manager in *Pink Floyd: The Wall* (Alan Parker, 1982).

He impressed as Spoor in *Brazil* (Terry Gilliam, 1985) and his ability to do accents saw him play the American gumshoe lead in *Who Framed Roger Rabbit?* (Robert Zemeckis, 1987). The same year would have seen him play Al Capone opposite Kevin Costner's Elliot Ness in Brian De Palma's dull film of *The Untouchables*, but Robert De Niro was available at the last moment. Hoskins was paid for playing a role he didn't ultimately perform, and later asked De Palma if there were any other movies he wanted him not to be in.

Films he might prefer not to have been in include *Hook* (Steven Spielberg, 1991), as Dustin Hoffman's swarthy sidekick, and *Super Mario Bros* (Annabel Jankel, Rocky Morton, 1993), a failed and inexplicable attempt to turn the justly popular computer-game characters into movie stars. He lent his star power to *twentyfourseven* (Shane Meadows, 1998) in order to get the low-budget boxing flick made, and returned to television to play De Flores in a superb 1994 production of Thomas Middleton's 1618 play (published in 1623) *The Changeling*. He gained an Oscar nomination in 1987 for his role in Neil Jordan's *Mona Lisa*.

Born Ilynea Lydia Mironoff on 26 July 1943 to Russian émigré parents in London, Helen Mirren found acclaim with the National Youth Theatre, National Theatre and Royal Shakespeare Company before becoming better known for film and television, although she has never abandoned the stage. Never one to shy away from controversial or difficult roles, she was Caesonia, the mother of Caligula's child, in *Caligula* (Tinito Brass, 1978) and doubled up as both Gertrude and Ophelia opposite a prince portrayed by twins in a production of *Hamlet* (Celestino Coronado, 1976), which remains easily the most daring committed to film. She was outstanding opposite Michael Gambon in *The Cook, The Thief, His Wife and Her Lover* (Peter Greenaway, 1987) and as Harrison Ford's wife in *The Mosquito Coast* (Peter Weir, 1986). She was nominated for an Oscar for her triumph as Queen Charlotte in *The Madness of King George* (Nicholas Hytner, 1994). She is best known for her starring role as Jane Tennison in *Prime Suspect* (1991–2003), ITV's uncompromising police-procedural drama, which is perhaps that network's most impressive television series ever.

As in many a British film of recent times, the supporting cast are filled out with people recognisable from major television or minor film – in this instance even the occasional future star. Paul Freeman was the villainous French archaeologist Belloc in *Raiders of the Lost Ark* (Steven Spielberg, 1981). Gillian Taylforth became a television, and tabloid, staple in *EastEnders*. Derek Thompson became known for his mono-expression on TV's *Casualty*. The much-underrated Kevin McNally was Castor in *I, Claudius* (1976) and Drake Carne in *Poldark* (second series only 1977), both for the BBC. He has a major supporting role in *Pirates of the Caribbean: The Curse of The Black Pearl* (Gore Verbinski, 2003). Paul Barber was Denzil in *Only Fools and Horses*. The future James Bond, Pierce Brosnan, turns up twice as an implicitly homosexual IRA man.

In the minor role of Gus is George Coulouris, a British actor of Greek descent who has one of the most interesting and varied careers imaginable. Born in Manchester in 1903, he worked at the National Theatre in London as a young man, and was summoned to America by an admiring Orson Welles to be a part of his Mercury Theatre Company. He was Thatcher in Welles's *Citizen Kane* (1941) and appeared in every conceivable type of production for an actor, from that cinematic groundbreaker to an episode of *Hancock's Half Hour* and a guest appearance in *Doctor Who* (in the very first series in 1964 with William Hartnell). He was notable as Dr Chatal in *Papillon* (Franklin J Schaffner, 1973), opposite Steve McQueen. He died in 1989.

THE DIRECTOR: John Mackenzie worked under Ken Loach on such important TV plays as *Cathy Come Home* (1967) before graduating to directing his own entries in *Play For Today*. These included *Double Dare* (1976), a stimulating Dennis Potter play in which a writer and an actress become confused as to whether they are themselves or the characters he is writing into a play. An entirely satisfying experiment in the nature of fiction, it anticipates Potter's own *The Singing Detective* (1987) in its concerns. After *The Long Good Friday*, Mackenzie's films varied from the outright ludicrous (*The Fourth Protocol*, 1987, about as far politically as it's possible to get from Loach's work while remaining within the British mainstream) to the thoughtful (*Ruby*, 1991, an intelligent study of the assassin of JFK's assassin, Jack Ruby). *Looking After JoJo* (1998), starring Robert Carlyle as a Glaswegian drug dealer, for BBC2, showed that the more detailed canvas of television is where his talents for energy and earnestness could be best utilised.

VISUAL INTEREST: Much of the film's style and appeal comes from its frequent dialogue-free scenes. Black cars slink sinisterly along roads in funeral processions. Women spit on young men for reasons that won't become apparent for over an hour. The opening is really striking as unexplained and seemingly unconnected events (a street killing, and altercation in a car park) take place without context.

Later, Colin is stalked around a public swimming baths to the sound of jarring electro-mood music (and it's disturbing *before* he gets a knife in the guts) and a coffin is seen, again silently, from above in a manner that makes it difficult to work out exactly what it is. The camera slides past the sight of Thameside in the midst of redevelopment, marking the time and place of the story so securely that the visuals don't so much seem *dated*: they seem *period* already. The story and imagery are so clearly, unapologetically part of the early Thatcher era that only twenty or so years on this is a film that could never be considered even faintly contemporary.

Hoskins's performance visibly references Edward G Robinson in *Little Caesar*. The two men are of similar build and Hoskins clearly and deliberately points and shrugs in a way that's reminiscent of the earlier performance and adopts the other actor's frenzied squinting look at times, although this is quite subtly done.

Everywhere the camera finds greys and dull colours, managing to shoot building sites and construction projects in a way that makes them appear to be symbols of desperation, not regeneration or hope. This is harder than it sounds, and is achieved by subtle lighting and camerawork that would normally be designed to 'show off' what's being looked at. Instead, it merely demonstrates the blandness of the 'vision' extolled by Harold (and by implication the decade as a whole).

The style of the film, initially loose and full of long and wide shots, high shots, low shots and just about any kind of angle available to liven up the pictures, tightens up as the day/film goes on, becoming more restrained, with sharper cuts and tighter and tighter frames. This reaches a peak with the extreme close-up of Harold's sweaty face as he's carried off in the IRA's car at the very end of the film.

QUOTES:

Harold: 'You don't crucify someone outside a church on Good Friday!'

Harold: 'The Yanks love it. They know they've arrived in England when the upper classes start treating 'em like shit.'

Harold: 'I've heard of a sleeping partner, but you're in a fucking coma.'

Harold: 'We're looking for people who can contribute to what England has given the world! Culture! Genius! Sophistication! Bit more than an 'ot dog, know what I mean?'

Harold: 'It's Good Friday. Have a Bloody Mary.'

Harold: 'The Mafia? I shit 'em!'

CONTEMPORARY REACTION: In the *New York Times* of 2 April 1982 Janet Maslin was appreciative of this 'swift, sharp edged . . . unexpectedly captivating' British picture with its ''30s Chicago style' and 'plenty of flair'. Yes, it had 'no shortage of loose ends', but this was 'not the drawback it sounds like'. A week or so later on 11 April the same paper's Vincent Canby took up the film's cause also calling it as 'satisfactory as it is scary' with its 'topical underpinnings' a 'genuine surprise' after all the genre trappings of the preceding film despite it seeming, in retrospect, 'too intelligent, too vividly realized' to be purely about gang warfare.

SEX/MONEY/DEATH: Suggestions that Harold is positively portrayed are severely misplaced: while he demonstrates a dislike of drugs and those who deal them and has a strong sense that anyone who has 'served' him should be compensated financially for any losses they incur in that service, he's also a colossal racist, intrinsically nostalgic in a destructive way and has no qualms about using violence to get his own way. He has a man tortured for little reason, hangs his rivals from meathooks and kills a man with a broken bottle for betraying him. His twin flaws of sentimentality and an inability to keep his temper find their clearest expression in the scene in which he attacks, and then cries on, his mistress Victoria. This is the classic pattern of violence and emotional collapse within a physically and emotionally abusive relationship.

He's also consumed by self-importance, smug and reckless. What the picture does is create some sympathy for this character by ranging him against forces that are incomprehensible to him (and indeed, largely, to the audience) in the shape of the Irish Republican terrorists whom he has unwittingly crossed. The selection of this group as his opponents is appropriate, since their idealism/fanaticism contrasts utterly with his amoral pragmatism. Money matters little to their cause (or at least that's what the other characters believe, and that, in context, is all that matters) but it's *everything* to him. They also represent a harsh intrusion by reality into a cosy world.

Harold may talk up London's, England's (and even occasionally the whole of Britain's) importance to world history and its place in contemporary reality, but he's a small-time hood, xenophobic and crass, who can't cope when faced with a situation as complex as the politics of the province. His solution – to have some people killed – is about as successful as you might expect it to be.

Harold's bar, incidentally, is called the Lion and Unicorn, two medieval symbols of England, further indication that he should be seen as an indicative figure rather than simply a character. (Helen Mirren's Sue Lawley-like wittering indicates that she too is grasping for a universality related to the era in her characterisation.) Harold's material crassness is an obviously Thatcherite element to his character and his talk of 'this decade' (the one that is just beginning) is very much of the period.

The film's dislike of Harold's *noveau riche* tendencies is less defensible, objectively, but the picture exhibits a very real despair at the spirit of its times. Harold is England, parochial, aggressive, limited and needlessly proud. More importantly, he's incapable of dealing with anything complex without retreating into his own clichés.

There's a religiosity that runs through this picture that marks it out as an heir to *Brighton Rock*, and it goes further than that film in its appropriation of the furniture of the American gangster picture by actually bringing in American characters who represent that. The religious thread is obvious (from the title, the day of its setting, from Harold's mother's very un-English Catholicism, from much of the dialogue) even before Harold becomes embroiled in a conflict that is partially *about* religion, even before one of his men is found crucified. The film seems to see Harold's kind of Englishness as under siege but, unlike most films about a perception of national identity under siege, it doesn't seem to have any time at all for the kind of person that its protagonist is.

THE VERDICT: A spectacular collision of gangster clichés and harsh reality, bitingly critical of its characters and the time of its production, *The Long Good Friday* does not perhaps develop all of its elements as fully as it might, but it has a terrific momentum and a snarling central performance from Hoskins that dominates everyone around him.

Once Upon a Time in America (1984)

(220 minutes)

Arnon Milchan Presents
A Sergio Leone Film
Music Composer: Ennio Morricone
Executive Producer: Claudio Mancini
Screenplay by Leonardo Benvenuti, Piero De Bernardi,
Enrico Medioli, Franco Arcalli, Franco Ferrini, Sergio Leone
Produced by Arnon Milchan
Directed by Sergio Leone

PRINCIPAL CAST: Robert De Niro (Noodles), James Woods (Max), Elizabeth McGovern (Deborah), Treat Williams (James Conway O'Donnell), Tuesday Weld (Carol), Joe Pesci (Frankie Minaldi), Burt Young (Joe Minaldi), Danny Aiello (Police Chief Vincent Aiello), William Forsythe (Philip 'Cockeye' Stein), James Hayden (Patrick 'Patsy' Goldberg), Darlanne Fluegel (Eve), Larry Rapp ('Fat' Moe Gelly), Dutch Miller (Van Linden), Robert Harper (Sharkey), Richard Bright (Chicken Joe), Gerard Murphy (Crowning), Amy Ryder (Peggy), Olga Karlatos (Woman in the Puppet Theatre), Mario Brega (Mandy), Ray Dittrich (Trigger), Frank Gio (Beefy), Karen Shallo (Lucy Aiello), Angelo Florio (Willie the Ape), Scott Tiler (Young Noodles), Rusty Jacobs (Young Max/David Bailey), Brian Bloom (Young Patsy), Adrian Curran (Young Cockeye), Mike Monetti (Young 'Fat' Moe), Noah Moazezi (Dominic), James Russo (Bugsy), Frankie Caserta (Bugsy's Gang), Joey Marzella (Bugsy's Gang), Clem Caserta (Al Capuano), Frank Sisto (Fred Capuano), Jerry Strivelli (Johnny Capuano), Julie Cohen (Young Peggy), Marvin Scott (Marvin Brentley), Mike Gendel (Irving Gold), Paul Herman (Monkey), Ann Neville (Girl in Coffin), Joey Faye (Old Man Beside The Hearse), Linda Ipanema (Nurse

Thompson), Tandy Cronyn (Reporter #1), Richard Zobel
(Reporter #2), Baxter Harris (Reporter #3), Arnon Milchan
(Limousine Chauffeur), Bruno Iannone (Thug), Marty Licata
(Cemetery Caretaker), Marcia Jean Kurtz (Max's Mother),
Estelle Harris (Peggy's Mother), Richard Foronji (Officer
'Fartface' Whitey), Gerritt Debeer (Drunk), Jennifer
Connelly (Young Deborah), Margherita Pace (Body Double
for Jennifer Connelly), Alexander Godfrey (Newstand
Proprietor), Cliff Cudney (Mounted Policeman), Paul
Farentino (Second Mounted Policeman), Bruce Bahrenburg
(Sergeant P Halloran), Mort Freeman (Street Singer), Sandra
Solberg (Friend of Young Deborah), Jay Zeely (Foreman),
Massimo Liti (Macrò)

SUMMARY: In 1933, fleeing betrayal and the death of his
friends, Jewish gangster David 'Noodles' Aronson leaves
New York City, pausing only to smoke opium in a local den.
In 1968, having received a letter warning him that the bodies
of several dead friends are going to be moved when a
cemetery is dug out to be built upon, Noodles returns to
New York, and reacquaints himself with his childhood
friend Fat Moe.

Noodles reminisces about his childhood in the early part
of the century, being sent down for murdering a local
criminal who killed another boyhood pal, and emerging
from prison to become, with his friend Max, a prime mover
in Prohibition-era bootlegging. His reminiscences over,
Noodles visits Secretary Bailey, a scandal-plagued member
of the government, who, it transpires, is actually Max, who
faked his own death on the night Noodles ran away. And
then, well, something very strange happens (see **VISUAL
INTEREST** and **SEX/MONEY/DEATH**).

THE PLAYERS: Since his Oscar triumph for *The Godfather
Part II*, De Niro had been nominated a further three times,
for *Taxi Driver* (Martin Scorsese, 1976), *The Deer Hunter*
(Michael Cimino, 1978) and *Raging Bull* (Martin Scorsese,

1980), the last of which saw him also take home the statue. Born in 1943 in New York to a mother and father who were both artists, the intensely private De Niro discovered a love of acting at school (playing the cowardly lion in *The Wizard of Oz* at age ten). He studied under Lee Strasberg at the Method School and worked in on- and off-Broadway theatrical productions before breaking into films. His first headline role was in *The Last Tycoon*, Elia Kazan's 1975 adaptation of F Scott Fitzgerald's novel. He has been one of America's most respected actors ever since.

Following *Once Upon a Time in America* he would continue his partnership with Scorsese in *The King of Comedy* (1983), shot after this picture but released before, and be devastatingly brilliant as a man with a broken mind in *Jackknife* (David High Jones, 1989).

Over six foot tall, with an IQ (180) as imposing as his height, James Woods attended MIT, studying political science, but left to pursue his acting career shortly before graduation. Impressive roles include one as one of a pair of cop killers in *The Onion Field* (Harold Becker, 1979), one in David Cronenberg's *Videodrome* (1984) and (Oscar-nominated) as the journalist playing both sides against each other in Oliver Stone's *Salvador* (1986).

Arguably, though, it is in television where, *Once Upon a Time in America* aside, he has done his best work. He won an Emmy as James Garner's schizophrenic, epileptic, alcoholic brother in *Promise* (Glenn Jordan, 1986) and another in the title role of *My Name Is Bill W* (Daniel Petrie, 1989), playing the founder of Alcoholics Anonymous. Both were potentially clichéd and sentimental roles, which Woods brought to multifaceted life in a manner that was seemingly effortless.

Born the same year as his friend and frequent collaborator Robert De Niro, Joe Pesci started as a singer/guitarist. His first on-screen role was in such a capacity in *Hey! Let's Twist!* (Greg Garrison, 1961). De Niro and Martin Scorsese saw Pesci in his only other film appearance in *The Death*

Collector (Ralph DeVito, 1975) and tracked him down to the New York City club in which he was performing, begging him to play De Niro's brother in the then planned *Raging Bull*. He was rewarded for his efforts with an Oscar nomination.

THE DIRECTOR: Sergio Leone was the son of the Italian film pioneer Vincenzo Leone. His father gained him a series of small jobs in the film industry, and he worked his way up to being a screenwriter. He took over as director on *Gli Ultimi giorni di Pompeii* (*The Last Day of Pompeii*) (1959), when the original director, Mario Bonnard, fell ill, and his handling of that was sufficiently assured for him to be given *Il Colosso di Rodi* (*The Colossus of Rhodes*) (1961) to handle solo. His next film, *Per un pugno di dollari* (*A Fistful of Dollars*) (1964), popularised, even if it didn't create, the notion of the 'spaghetti western' (movies set in the American West, shot cheaply in Spain using Italian talent) and was an entirely self-aware clone of Akira Kurosawa's samurai film *Yojimbo* (1961) relocated to Spaghetti Western Land. It also made its lead actor, Clint Eastwood, until then a minor TV actor, a star. A conceptual, if not actual, sequel followed: *Per qualche dollaro in più* (1965) (*For a Few Dollars More*), with Eastwood as a near-identical character. The 'trilogy', as it became known, was completed with *Il Buono, Il Brutto, Il Cattivo* (*The Good, the Bad and the Ugly*) (1966).

Leone then made the vast, expensive and sprawling *Once Upon A Time in the West* (1967) with Henry Fonda and a cast of thousands. It was his first film made with American audiences in mind and his first whose primary title was in English. After this he turned down the opportunity to direct *The Godfather* and instead made his worst film *Giù la testa* (*A Fistful of Dynamite*) (1971).

Once Upon a Time in America was his dream project, and he laboured over it for more than a decade. It was also his last picture. He died in 1989.

VISUAL INTEREST: A film that largely exists in a world where only browns, maroons and sepia exist as colours, *Once Upon a Time* is the only one of Leone's mature works not shot in his beloved screen ratio of 2.35:1. This picture is about twice that in terms of depth, but Leone turns this to his advantage. Rather than create compositions that lack the width of his frames for the *Dollars* trilogy or *Once Upon a Time in the West*, Leone somehow makes them just as wide and as deep again.

Has New York ever seemed so tall on screen before or since? Has it ever reached so compellingly from the gutter to the stars all in one shot, with people visible real and moving within that reach? Assuredly not.

There are so many lengthy dialogue-free, or near-dialogue-free, sequences in this movie, in which Leone lets his camera do all of the talking for his characters: the comical, quizzical march when the characters-as-boys first place their savings in the deposit box; the deeply sinister sequence in which the elderly Noodles walks through the New York night, a suitcase containing a fortune clasped in his nervous hands; the famous image of the boys, in vast long shot, moving briskly through New York, shortly before the youngest, most innocent one of their number is shot dead in terrible, painful slow motion by their rival. One of the most effective shots is the earliest, as the old Noodles conducts a silent telephone conversation with Fat Moe. The use of a close-up on De Niro's eyes to indicate extreme sadness at one point is an appropriation by Leone of his own extreme close-up technique for an entirely different effect from the intimidation it captures in, say, *The Good, the Bad and the Ugly*.

The voodoo funeral given for Prohibition in Noodles and Max's speakeasy is spectacular and rich in imagery. The scene also marks the death of their friendship, the end of their business arrangements, and is also virtually the last moment in which Noodles believes that Max is alive for decades.

The slow zoom into David Bailey's face, when Noodles and the audience realise that Max and Secretary Bailey genuinely are one and the same person – and that Max named his son after Noodles – is extraordinarily powerful for simple slow zoom. The next but one shot, of James Woods opening a door and allowing the audience to see that this really is the case, is spine-chillingly impressive.

According to James Woods, the controversial moment in which Max/Secretary Bailey may or may not commit suicide by throwing himself into the dumper truck (and it's difficult to comprehend what else may have happened to the figure outside the door in that moment if not that, unless someone else, unseen, threw him in) was not acted by him. It was a body double, not Woods, who walked the short way from the gate and then disappeared, as Leone wanted as much ambiguity as possible in that scene.

That Deborah looks little different after 35 years is entirely deliberate, as the dialogue comparing her to Cleopatra exists to make clear. That some people have failed to grasp this is odder than the film's, admittedly peculiar, decision on this front (and McGovern is, after all, made up to be older, just to a lesser extent than De Niro and Woods are).

The moment when antique cars swing out of the fog in the 1968 sections and – for a moment – the audience believe that the film has dipped back into flashback is strangely affecting. After the best part of four hours of being pushed, gently and without confusion, backwards and forwards in time, the audience are tricked – by use of the film's own grammar – into thinking it has happened again when it hasn't. Transitions between past and present in the film are often handled by the repetition of images, such as Noodles driving the car into the river in the 1930s, reflecting a car being dragged out of the same river in the 1960s. The change from the red tail lights of the dumper truck to the white headlights of the automobiles seems to be an example of this, and it isn't. The audience are almost immediately then pushed back into flashback again, this time without any warning from such devices, and back into the past they willingly go.

The final moment, of De Niro's beatific smiling face, is one of the most memorable last shots in film (see **SEX/MONEY/DEATH**) and asks many questions.

QUOTES:

Noodles: 'You can always tell the winners at the starting gate.'

Fat Moe: 'What have you been doing all these years?'
Noodles: 'Been going to bed early.'

Noodles: 'It wasn't my choice.'
Deborah: 'It was. It still is'.

Max: 'You'll carry the stink of the streets all your life.'
Noodles: 'I like the stink of the streets on me. It opens up my lungs.'

SOURCES TO SCREEN: Upon completing *Once Upon a Time in the West* (1968), Sergio Leone became fascinated with the semiautobiographical novel *The Hoods* by Harry Grey and resolved to adapt it into a film. Pausing only to make *A Fistful of Dynamite* (1971), he devoted the rest of his life to pursuing the picture. It has been fatuously claimed that Leone spent eleven years on a balcony in Rome waiting for someone to walk up to him and offer him funding for the picture, but it's certainly true that he spent that amount of time searching for such funding and that funding arrived only when he was approached on that balcony by the producer Arnon Milchan, who did just that.

The screenplay for the picture has six credited writers, including Leone himself, and it was Leone who began writing it, turning the novel into a two-hundred-page outline without dialogue but with elaborate shot descriptions. Leone's conception for the picture was so precise that he was able to describe the picture's camera setups in detail years before he had a hope of lensing a frame of it. His ideas for the music were so clearly advanced that most of it was recorded before the film was shot, and the actors had it played to them during certain scenes.

Uncredited writers also contributed to the screenplay during its long gestation, including Stuart Kaminutesky and the novelist Norman Mailer.

Noodles's reply to Moe's query about what he's been doing all these years (see QUOTES) indicates a familiarity on the part of the character (and by extension the screenwriter) with Marcel Proust, whose *A la Recherche du temps perdu* contains this line very near the beginning. The implication may be that Noodles has spent the 35 years the film omits from his life reading this famously lengthy, weighty tome.

CONTEMPORARY REACTION: The 140-minute original American release prepared by, according to movie legend, the editor, the director or the assistant editor of *Police Academy* (no interviewee can agree, and the man responsible presumably won't step forward himself), reordered the picture into chronological order, so it begins in a pre-World War One world and moves through the story as it unfolds. All of the essential plot scenes are retained, but much of the subtlety and nuance of the picture is lost: a lot of the long, lingering shots are gone; lines of dialogue are gone; and Leone's subtle evocation of scenes from before/after the scenes the viewer is watching, via similar camera movements around now-changed architecture, are gone. Instead, the audience watching this film gets establishing shots of buildings and sets they've long been familiar with – despite having been initially confused by them – several hours into the picture. This edition is a travesty of Leone's intentions and friends of the director, including James Coburn, have claimed that the experience of seeing the film he had worked on for so long mutilated in this way had a pronounced negative effect on the director's health. In the *New York Times* (1 June 1984) Vincent Canby reviewed this version saying that Leone had 'made some weird movies in his day but nothing to match' this one. He called it 'lazily hallucinatory', seemingly unaware that the editing had altered the structure and apparently thinking that footage had simply been removed rather than re-ordered. He noted that it 'seems endless, possibly because whatever internal structure it might have had no longer exists'. The film as a whole was 'vivid but unfathomable'.

Variety of 23 May 1984 had earlier reviewed the full version of the film so, unlike Canby, really has no excuse for its opinions: 'Surprisingly deficient in clarity and purpose,' it said although 'The basic material [was] potent enough.' The paper thought the characters were 'brutal' and 'unsympathetic' but at least the 'slow film' was 'never exactly boring'. This review is, scandalously, largely typical. As a whole *Once Upon A Time In America* got less favourable reviews than *Star Trek III: The Search For Spock* (Leonard Nimoy, 1984), which opened the same week in much of the United States.

Once Upon A Time In America cost around $30 million, but didn't make a tenth of that in the United States. This financial failure was not the only way in which the negative reviews and the controversy and chaos that surrounded the film's release took a negative toll. The picture was nominated for no Academy Awards, but it did pick up BAFTAs for music (Ennio Morricone) and costumes (Gabirella Pescucci) and won Silver Ribbons for Score, Design, Effects, Photography and Direction in Leone's native Italy.

Fortunately, the film's fortunes, both critically and financially, have constantly improved over the last twenty years. It is available in a lavish, successful DVD edition utilising Leone's favoured cut, and was released to universally acclamatory reviews. The picture is now rightly regarded as a tightly controlled and subtle epic, blending mood and character together with moments of refreshing ambiguity and an impressive total control over both the audience's emotions and the complex structure. It is a very, very beautiful film.

TRIVIA: The bar in which the young gangsters debate, before Max joins them, whether or not to accept the dollar the bartender offers them is McSorley's Alehouse at 15th East and 7th Street in New York. Opened for business in 1854, it's the oldest still open bar in the United States.

SEX/MONEY/DEATH: It's clear that the desperation brought about by poverty and boredom – the twin evils of growing up as the Depression began to bite – forces the boys audiences see into lives of increasingly less petty crime. While the dialogue of the screenplay is often clumsy, the action of it very clearly and successfully portrays this period in the life of New York City with frankness and a lack of nostalgia. By laying bare the ablutions of this time (we see metal baths and shared bathrooms, shabby kitchens and wooden, broken stairways and corridors), Leone's camera immerses the viewer in the dark and dreary world the characters have to live in. Alternately brazenly carnal and casually sentimental, the environment reflects the adolescent predilections of ambitious, ill-educated young men who don't have enough to eat. Noodles's casual, ultimately violent, misogyny and an inability to comprehend or confront women as human beings is clearly a product of this time. He has a Madonna/whore complex that results from an adolescence so nascent it's still virtually childhood. His fascination is split between the charming innocence of Fat Moe's sister Deborah and the chortling comfort of the already-whoring-herself-for-money Peggy. It's a fairly straightforward division of available and confident sexuality and unavailable 'perfection'.

It's arguable that Noodles, who goes into prison at a young age and emerges largely unchanged mentally, is stuck in this adolescent world for most of his life – despite his protestation that he's 'not that kind of guy', when Carol suggests that he, Max and she indulge in a 'threesome' he obviously is. When Deborah makes clear that she is unobtainable, and will always remain 'unobtained' (she's leaving for a career in Hollywood), he somehow feels the need to drag his Madonna down to the level at which he perceives other women as operating. By introducing violence to her the moment she openly invokes her sexuality to him (she kisses him, and he then violently sexually assaults her), he proves he's incapable of coping with the concept of a woman being simultaneously both sexual and a human being. It's this concept at the centre of Noodles (an emotionally debased character with an amusingly incongruous nickname, a man who is presented for all of the film as the protagonist and with whom it is demanded the audience sympathise, if not empathise) that has created problems with this picture for some people. This is entirely understandable. The presentation of sexually violent crimes in filmed fiction in any context – even the explicitly condemnatory, even as the actions of a disturbed person – raises serious questions about the exploitation of such events for titillation.

Whether or not Leone's film goes far enough in its condemnation of Noodles's sexual sociopathy is for the individual filmgoer and/or critic to decide. It is worth pointing out, however, that the mere fact that Noodles is a double rapist (he assaults Carol earlier in the film) could be seen as a confirmation of his aberrant nature, that these acts arise out of his psychology, his emotional problems. *He* enjoys it and this makes him, for want of a better word, essentially evil. Were it not for this duplication, condemned by some as further exploitation, it would be easier for viewers to attempt to construct a case explaining Noodles's attack on Deborah as a (still appalling) aberration brought on by short-term emotional collapse. In the finished film it's clearly part of a long-term pattern of (to put it mildly) vilely unacceptable behaviour on Noodles's part.

The oft-made suggestion that the whole film is an opium dream isn't one I'm drawn to. It seems to be a needlessly 'clever-clever' way of rationalising the peculiarity of what happens to Secretary Bailey at the end, or a blandly orthodox way of refusing to see that Noodles's losing sight of Max once more – his eyes again too full of tears to see that it may not be him at all – is a purely metaphorical act in a film that seems to have been building towards such a thoroughly un-western (pun intended) denouement. While seeing the film as a dream does make 'sense' of a picture whose sensibilities blur realism, surrealism and magic realism into one immaculately comprehensible whole, it also demands that one believe that Noodles is capable of imagining, in his opium dream, the whole of the cultural shift from 1933 to 1968. This would include composing the melody to Paul McCartney's 'Yesterday' (although, given that the melody came to McCartney himself in a dream, this choice of music may be entirely deliberate on this front) and all the changes to New York City's architecture. This is a little too much to stomach. If the dream is precognitive rather merely fantasy, however, there's more appeal in the notion. Certainly the 1968 sequences have a fanciful lack of reality to them, which makes them feel, to the viewer, more alien than the 1920s or 1930s sequences, despite their being more recognisably like the audience's contemporary reality. This is borne out by the outright oddness of the 1968 Penn Station or the huge marble edifice of the tomb in which the bodies of Noodles's gang are buried or the simple fact that Deborah doesn't seem to have aged very much in thirty years.

What seeing the film as a dream does, however, is rob the drama of one of its central pivots: that Max/Secretary Bailey wants Noodles to kill him because only Noodles has the right. The very Roman idea that Max/Bailey would accept death rather than the dishonour of having his political career collapse in public is also attractive and this is lost too if it becomes Noodles's fantasy. It also takes away the fascinating concept that Max could no longer bear being Max back in the 1930s, partly because he was afraid of dying in an insane asylum as his father had done, and that only by stopping being Max could he be free from 'being Max'.

These are, combined, too high a price to pay for the conscience salving that some may find if the picture's generally sympathetic portrayal of gangster/rapist Noodles is told from his own, self-justifying point of view. That all the characters become, then, reflections of Noodles in some way rather than people in themselves is also unsatisfying. It is more pleasing, surely, to see the final scene as the simple completion of a circle, the audience being allowed to depart at the point they came in (the point that the next audience, whether in the cinema or watching on video, television or DVD) will have to come in. All films are circular in that, having watched to the end, you find that there is nowhere to go but back to the beginning, and the last few moments of *Once Upon a Time in America* have always struck me as simple recognition of that. Noodles's blissed-out smile is merely the last moment of the (drug-induced) happiness of a broken man, his euphoria a reflection of the audience's as the last piece of a wholly satisfying motion picture clicks, with total assurance, into place. (There is, of course, the alternative though less popular notion that Noodles's whole life is a dream, that none of it is real and that everything is fantasy. What's unclear about this perception is why anyone should care if it's the case.)

THE VERDICT: A film about a life in America that could perhaps never have been made by an American, Leone's haunting final film marries his stylistic predilections with an atmosphere of waste, of mistakes, of stupidity, of misunderstandings and of regret that is almost funereal. It's vast, it's elegant and, oddly for a project on which so much time and energy was expended, it doesn't feel particularly personal or self-justifying (just another reason to reject the style as a deliberate evocation of Noodles's own dreamlike state). This is a filmmaker lost in his art, not lost in himself, and what art it is that results from that absorption.

GoodFellas (1990)

(139 minutes)

Warner Bros Presents
An Irwin Winkler Production
A Martin Scorsese Picture
This film is based on a true story
Executive Producer Barbara De Fina
Based on the Book *Wiseguy* by Nicholas Pileggi
Screenplay by Nicholas Pileggi & Martin Scorsese
Produced by Irwin Winkler
Directed by Martin Scorsese
Director of Photography: Michael Ballhaus, ASC
Production Designer: Kristi Zea
Film Editor: Thelma Schoonmaker, ACE
Associate Producer: Bruce Pustin
Title Design: Elaine and Saul Bass

PRINCIPAL CAST: Robert De Niro (Jimmy Conway), Ray Liotta (Henry Hill), Joe Pesci (Tommy DeVito), Lorraine Bracco (Karen Hill), Paul Sorvino (Paul Cicero), Frank Sivero (Frankie Carbone), Tony Darrow (Sonny Bunz), Mike Starr (Frenchy), Frank Vincent (Billy Batts), Chuck Low (Morrie), Frank DiLeo (Tutti Cicero) Henny Youngman (Himself), Gina Mastrogiacomo (Janice Rossi), Catherine Scorsese (Tommy's mother), Charles Scorsese (Vinnie), Suzanne Shepherd (Karen's mother), Debi Mazar (Sandy), Margo Winkler (Belle Kessler), Welker White (Lois Byrd), Jerry Vale (Himself), Julie Garfield (Mickey Conway), Christopher Serrone (Young Henry), Elaine Kagan (Henry's Mother), Beau Starr (Henry's Father), Kevin Corrigan (Michael Hill), Michael Imperioli (Spider), Robbie Vinton (Bobby Vinton), John Williams (Johnny Roastbeef), Nancy Ellen Cassaro (Joe Buddha's wife), Daniel P Conte (Dr Dan), Tony Conforti (Tony), Frank Pellegrino (Johnny Dio), Ronald Maccone (Ronnie), Tony Sirico (Tony Stacks), Joe D'Onofrio (Young Tommy), Samuel L Jackson (Stacks Edwards)

SUMMARY: This is the largely true story of the rise and fall and escape from justice of Henry Hill, who, all his life, wanted to be a gangster, and got his wish, moving slowly up in the New York mob under the command of Paulie Cicero, and working closely with Jimmy Conway, a skilled thief and enthusiastic murderer, and Tommy DeVito, a bona fide sociopath who is later killed by the mob for being such a loose cannon. Spanning decades, the story moves from childhood running for the mob to extortion, murder, mass robbery and embezzlement, taking in Henry's marriage to a nice Jewish girl, more than one spell in prison and his eventually turning state's evidence, turning in his erstwhile comrades, in order to avoid a lengthy prison sentence, and then entering the Witness Protection Program in order to avoid vengeance.

THE PLAYERS: Before *GoodFellas*, Ray Liotta had played minor roles in *Something Wild* (Jonathan Demme, 1986) and *Field of Dreams* (Phil Alden Robinson, 1989) and appeared on television. This remains his most impressive on-screen credit, although he is also known for providing the voice of the lead character in Rock Star's spectacularly amoral, ultra-hip computer game 'Grand Theft Auto: Vice City' (2002).

THE DIRECTOR: Like most of 'movie brat' generation of American filmmakers (Spielberg, Lucas, Milius, Murch), Scorsese studied film at university, graduating from NYU with a degree majoring in film in 1964. A native New Yorker of Italian/Sicilian heritage, Scorsese had previously considered becoming a priest, having been an altar boy in his youth at New York's St Patrick's Cathedral. Years later this building would become a popular movie location among his movie-making peers, appearing in *The Godfather* (Francis Ford Coppola, 1972), among other pictures.

His student films, *What's a Nice Girl Like You Doing in a Place Like This?* (1963), *It's Not Just You, Murray!* (1964), and *The Big Shave* (1967), and a stint as a film editor (including on *Woodstock* (Albert Maysles, David Maysles, Charlotte Zwerin, 1970)), caused Roger Corman to book him to direct the cheap exploitation flick *Boxcar Bertha* (1973). This led, somewhat indirectly (his friends criticised him for spending a year making a work-for-hire film of dubious artistic merit) to the far more personal *Mean Streets* (1973), a film that was also his first contact with an actor often considered his on-screen avatar, and even artistic, filmic muse: Robert De Niro.

It also established the more obvious fascinations of the Scorsese canon, often staggering violence, central characters struggling with enormous personal problems, New York City settings and characters whose activities and behaviour are so extreme that their motivations seem to the audience incomprehensible to the point whereby they come across as insane.

He followed this with *Alice Doesn't Live Here Anymore* (1974), perhaps his best film, and the rightly revered *Taxi Driver* (1976), a compelling study of an *über*-dark NYC and a lonely and depraved individual's almost messianic mission to clean up its streets. Nineteen seventy-seven's musical extravaganza *New York, New York* remains a misunderstood masterpiece, and 1980 saw Scorsese combine commercial, critical and artistic success completely with his Jake LaMotta biopic *Raging Bull*, starring a never-better Robert De Niro as the prizefighter throughout his life (the performance remains one of cinema's great on-screen transformations).

Throughout the 1980s Scorsese made more experimental (for him) pictures such as the disturbingly funny, blacker-than-black comedy *The King of Comedy* (1983) and *After Hours* (1985), although he also had a stab at the Hollywood sequel in *The Color of Money* (1986), a perhaps ill-advised return to the world of *The Hustler* (Robert Rossen, 1961), which nevertheless allowed Paul Newman to finally win an Oscar for playing Eddie Felson.

Scorsese saw the decade out with the controversial, yet magnificently human, *The Last Temptation of Christ* (1988), with Willem Dafoe utterly compelling as the Messiah, and a short but sharp contribution to *New York Stories* (1989), a portmanteau tribute to their city by Scorsese, Woody Allen and Francis Ford Coppola.

Although he is widely revered as a fierce independent filmmaker, Scorsese's pictures have largely been made by, or at least distributed through, the major studios of Old Hollywood, and he has dabbled in less prestigious forms such as the music video (Michael Jackson's appropriately entitled *Bad* in 1987), commercials for Giorgio Armani and an episode ('Mirror, Mirror') of the widely despised Spielberg-produced TV series *Amazing Stories*.

GoodFellas saw Scorsese open his fourth decade as a filmmaker with two Oscar nominations, one as director and another as co-writer, neither of which translated into a statuette on the night. He has, to date, somehow, never yet won an Academy Award.

VISUAL INTEREST: The very first shot is interesting as the camera swings from behind the car it is travelling along with in order to achieve a low-slung sideways look at the vehicle – a visual indication, perhaps, of the distorted and low, yet slick, moral universe the characters inhabit. *GoodFellas* is remembered by audiences primarily for its use of freeze-frames at moments of particular shock (such as when Tommy and Jimmy threaten to shove a man's head in an oven); and, while the technique is frequently utilised here, it never seems overused.

There's a rightly revered sequence where the camera follows Henry and Karen through the Copacabana nightclub. They enter through the staff door, past security and staff, passing through hallways and backrooms and kitchens until they emerge in the club. There a table is found and physically carried right to the very front of the audience for them, so that they come in front of and before all. It's a much-imitated, deliriously fluid piece of dextrous camera work, which demonstrates the ease with which Henry gets what he wants by doing something very difficult in a smooth and simple-seeming way. A gorgeous blend of form and content.

The final shot of the film, of Joe Pesci shooting towards the camera, is a straight lift from *The Great Train Robbery* (Edwin S Porter, 1903), which ends in exactly the same way. This, of course, explains Pesci's anachronistic clothes, gun and sudden appearance some time after his character's death.

It would be churlish, given the film's undoubted fine visual qualities, to harp on about the sheer number of anachronisms in it, but there are many. Particularly grievous is the close-up of a 747 (first flown in 1969) in a scene set in 1963, but there are other minor ones (for instance, Henry is arrested as a boy for selling cigarettes with barcodes on, when they hadn't been invented in the 1950s when the scene is set). I bring this up, though, only in passing, and as part of the observation that the general tone and scene setting of the movie are beautiful, from the use of music to the subtly shifting clothes and haircuts to the sensitively applied make-up, the passage of time and the feeling of eras – all superbly, sweepingly conveyed.

One of the film's biggest 'whoa' moments – one anyone writing about it is obliged to discuss – is the moment when Henry's narration and his physical presence in the movie fuse and Liotta's character becomes suddenly aware of his own fictionality, strolling away out of the witness box while talking to the camera. A perfect visual representation of the way that Henry Hill talked his way out of the dock (i.e. by becoming an informer) and his subsequent movement towards a media career, as a 'luxury shot' it has few equals in Scorsese's canon, for storytelling verisimilitude, shock value or technical bravura.

The lengthy sequence during which Henry's life finally spirals out of control, and which climaxes with his arrest, is a marvellously controlled portrayal of Henry's interior panic as he attempts to drive from one side of town to another, putting together a deal while hoping against hope that the food he's cooking won't burn and worrying about whether or not he's being shadowed by a helicopter. The swinging camera movements and sudden close-ups, the slow-motion and freeze-frames and steadily escalating panic of the voiceover push the audience's hearts into beating faster and faster. It's impressively visceral for something that features no violence, and even leaves one light-headed when it comes to its juddering finale.

It's a pleasing detail that at one point in the film Karen is seen watching *The Jazz Singer*, which is about a Jewish man failing to reconcile his lifestyle with his parents' beliefs – a neat commentary on her own situation.

QUOTES:

Henry: 'As far back as I could remember I always wanted to be a gangster.'

Henry: 'Anything I wanted was a phone call away. Free cars. The keys to a dozen hideout flats all over the city. I bet twenty, thirty grand over a weekend and then I'd either blow the winnings in a week or go to the sharks to pay back the bookies.'

Tommy: 'But, I'm funny how? Funny like a clown? I amuse you? I make you laugh? I'm here to fuckin' amuse you?'

SOURCES TO SCREEN: *GoodFellas* is based on the book *Wiseguy*, written by Nicholas Pileggi from conversations with Henry Hill, whose life story it purports to tell. The screenplay and picture follow events of the book fairly faithfully, and the book apparently follows Henry's perception of his own life to the letter. In essence, only the names have been changed. For Paul Cicero read Paul Vario; for Jimmy Conway read Jimmy Burke; for Timmy DeVito read Tommy DeSimone. Aside from that, even the dates and details are exact.

The screenplay by Pileggi and Scorsese combines the book and Hill's memories into a blueprint for a film that Roger Ebert in the *Chicago Sun-Times* felt contained 'so much information and feeling about the Mafia that finally it creates the same claustrophobic feeling Hill's wife talks about: The feeling that the mob world is the real world.' And, while this is undoubtedly true, I can't see it in quite the same positive light as he did (see **SEX/MONEY/DEATH**).

The further fates of the characters/people from Hill's life are covered in the picture's *American Graffiti* ending, but it's worth pointing out that Jimmy Burke died, in prison, of bronchial complications, in 1996.

CONTEMPORARY REACTION: Writing in the *Chicago Sun-Times* on 9 February 1990, Roger Ebert was impressed with Scorsese's epic, which he said dwelled with him for 48 hours after first viewing. 'Most films, even great ones, evaporate like mist once you've returned to the real world,' he said, claming *GoodFellas* as an exception. 'No finer film has ever been made about organised crime – Scorsese has never done a more compelling job of getting inside someone's head.'

Made for a budget of $25,000,000, *GoodFellas* opened in the USA on 21 September 1990 and made $6,368,901 in its first weekend, eventually totting up $46,836,394 domestically. It was nominated for Oscars for Directing, Editing, Writing (Screenplay Based on Material from Another Medium), Best Supporting Actress (Lorraine Bracco), Best Supporting Actor (Joe Pesci) and Best Picture. Only Pesci went home with Oscar on the night.

Pesci is brilliant in this picture. You have to go back to *Little Caesar* for such a compelling portrayal of a sick, twisted amoral child/monster/man. For me the only regret is that, if Pesci hadn't picked up the Academy Award for this picture, he might have been given it for *Casino* instead, in which he refines the performance he gives here and takes it to another level again.

TRIVIA: When Henry and Karen are negotiating to enter the Witness Protection Program, Edward McDonald plays himself. He was the government lawyer the real Hills spoke to.

The word 'fuck' (or one of its derivatives) is used approximately 250 times in the picture.

SEX/MONEY/DEATH: Aside from the spectacular precredits violence, the movie begins with Liotta's character telling the audience of his vast childhood admiration for the neighbourhood gangsters. The breathless cynicism of the faux-naïve little boy, who knows absolutely who Paulie is and what he does ('Every day I was learning to score' or 'It was all I wanted to do') is instantly absorbing; the problem is that it quickly becomes too engaging.

Early in his narration, Henry is keen to dismiss the core values of Americana ('pledge allegiance to the flag and all that bullshit'), and that kind anti-establishmentism is an easy way to get almost any audience on your side. He even goes through the motions of talking of the social value of the Mafia, claiming (as *The Godfather Part II* does) that it's really a system designed to protect and help people who can't go to the police. This, it becomes apparent as soon as viewers see some of Hill's actions, is manifestly untrue.

Henry Hill loudly and enthusiastically loves every petty advantage ever given to him by his life of crime, from never waiting for a table to getting served first in the bakery at all times. 'He knew what went on at that cab stand,' he sneers of his father early on, as if Hill Senior's anger at his son's calculated preparations for a life of crime is comically foolish.

The essential problem with *GoodFellas* is that it is too close to its subject matter: Henry Hill is keen both to aggrandise his own role with the New York mob and to avoid taking any blame for anything that the audience will find absolutely unconscionable. Because it's the 'authorised story' of Henry Hill, it has to take his word for who did what, when and how. It also means that Hill can't be seen to do anything not in his testimony, and that the other characters need to take the blame for any crime that Hill hasn't either been punished for or excused from. Thus, he talks of murder as being habitual for 'some of the guys' but the audience never see him commit murder himself. He approves of Jimmy's doing his first hit at the age of sixteen, but viewers never see Henry perform one. Ray Liotta's wide-eyed, faux-Bambi performance as Henry, gazing appalled at almost every act of violence and throwing up when confronted with a putrefying corpse, suggests that the actor has too much bought into Hill's own song of justification.

Either Hill was the Big Wiseguy he claims to have been, is proud of having been and regrets that he no longer is, or he was a flunkey. If he was that gangster, then he can't have known what he knew and seen what he did while keeping his hands and his sensibilities intact, which is what the movie goes out of its way to imply. If he was a flunkey, however, well, in his own words he was 'nobody'. This all evolves out of the 'striving for authenticity' committed to by basing the film on Pileggi's Hill-centric book. Once Scorsese did this he was committed to telling Henry's version of the story – any substantial deviation would be difficult to justify. This is why you get odd things like Henry's lack of involvement in the big airport heist. Henry knows all about it but he doesn't take part. Why not? And why does Jimmy let Henry live when he's killed off everybody else who could lead the cops to him?

GoodFellas arguably does not leave enough room for viewers to make up their own minds about Henry. There's not enough distance between the film and the character. In some senses, by the end the film has *become* the character, thanks to the voiceover and Scorsese's persuasive technique. Objectively, Henry Hill lies to his friends, cheats on his wife, is complicit (at least) in several murders, sells poison on the streets for a fortune and, ultimately, still wants to take the upside of being a gangster while ignoring the downside. For example: 'When I was broke, I'd go out and rob some more. We ran everything. We paid off cops. We paid off lawyers. We paid off judges. Everybody had their hands out. Everything was for the taking. And now it's all over.'

Scorsese showed in *Raging Bull* that he could take a sad, pathetic central character, like Jake LaMotta (whom surely no one can imagine liking) and make him into a compelling central character. *GoodFellas* falls at that last hurdle. Audiences almost inevitably come away thinking that Henry Hill was a swell guy. More than one friend of mine has referred to Hill's turning state's evidence as 'the only decent thing he ever did in his life' because this is how Hill, and the film, choose to present his act of cowardice. He's consistently smug and self-righteous throughout, in fact ('We did the right thing, we gave Paulie his tribute').

It is worth remembering that Henry's narration, which laces through and envelopes the film, is delivered, as far as the character is concerned, after the end. It is an ending that sees him entirely unrepentant, lest we forget. What are his last words in the movie? 'Today everything is different. There's no action. I have to wait around like everyone else. Can't even get decent food. Right after I got here I ordered some spaghetti with marinara sauce and I got egg noodles and ketchup. I'm an average nobody. I get to live the rest of my life like a schnook.'

Henry Hill isn't sorry for what he did, or the life he led: he's sorry he was caught. As even the film's own epilogue makes clear, he tried to return to crime after being granted immunity from prosecution for ratting on his old comrades. His regret when it all ends and he's got away scot-free is positively idiotic: he should be delighted. He continually attempts to be endearing and to paint himself as a victim. The ultimate example is when he, an arch betrayer, complains po-faced, 'Your murderers come with smiles, they come as your friends, the people who have cared for you all your life, and they always seem to come at a time when you're at your weakest and most in need of your help"

Roger Ebert, who knows Scorsese well, felt that the director identified very strongly with Henry Hill, another little boy from the Bronx who couldn't play sport, was tormented by his Catholicism and always knew what he wanted to do when he grew up. Maybe this fact is the element that capsizes the picture.

In light of this, it might have been more appropriate for Scorsese to tell Jimmy's story instead, using Pileggi's book as source rather than just adapting it wholesale. He could have made Henry a supporting character who ultimately betrays Jimmy. This would mean that Henry's activities could have remained more ambiguous, more off-screen and less self-justifying. It would also have allowed De Niro's restrained and lip-licking performance as Jimmy room to breathe. De Niro is so good in this movie that he eclipses Liotta (De Niro was nominated for a BAFTA for his scant screen time). There is always, thanks to De Niro's detailed performance, seemingly a more interesting story happening somewhere off-screen, particularly as Jimmy arranges the deaths of those involved in the Lufthansa job. Hell, the audience even somehow feels sorry when Tommy dies, despite his utterly monstrous nature, thanks to the overwhelmingly convincing nature of De Niro's own grief.

For a while there was a popular urban myth among movie buffs, which has since been discounted, that Jimmy Burke was so pleased to discover he was to be portrayed by Robert De Niro that he contacted the actor in an attempt to give him tips about playing him. Nicholas Pileggi has since discounted this, but the fact that it grew up at all is very telling about the atmosphere of this film.

THE VERDICT: Brilliant, but overrated, technically inspired but unselfconsciously morally bankrupt, *GoodFellas* is wrapped into its own hypnotic spiral with no way out and is both a little too in love with its subject matter, and a little too confused about the nature of that love, to achieve the greatness that it so clearly seeks and that many have bestowed on it.

The Krays (Peter Medak, 1990)

This British film telling of the lives of the Kray Twins (who, along with their less well-known third brother Charles Kray Jnr, ran organised crime in north London for decades) struggles to avoid glamorising the brothers, but is inhibited by the sad fact that these multiple-murderers and extortionists have become close to folk heroes to some in Britain. Wooden and non-compelling performances from brothers Gary and Martin Kemp (formerly of the pop band Spandau Ballet) fail to hold the attention, while Billie Whitelaw, who appears as their mother, doesn't do enough to make her own character's sociopathy clear. She even held to some of the mythmaking that surrounds the Krays when interviewed for the *Chicago Sun-Times* of 4 November 1990. She claimed 'They . . . only slashed, beat up and tortured . . . the gangs with which they were constantly warring. It has been said if the Krays were around today that they would clean up the drug scene, that they would have it under control.' It is this ambiguity of intent that really torpedoes the film's attempts to present a balanced portrait of the time. Screenwriter Philip Ridley is more interested in the supposed 'tension' that exists within characters like Ronnie and Reggie, who are capable of both loving their mother and yet being appallingly violent with others, but all this 'tension' in the screenplay implicitly excuses a lot of their actions by illustrating how happy their home life was. This leaves the viewer thinking, 'Well, they can't have been *that* bad'. Compare and contrast this with the complexities of White Heat. *The Krays* is cheaper than it needs to be as well: for example, the killing of Jack 'The Hat' McVitie is comical rather than horrifying because of the hopelessly unconvincing prosthetics used. The fall of the Krays' criminal empire and their subsequent trials and convictions are not portrayed at all leaving the portrait incomplete and unsatisfying.

Pulp Fiction (1994)

(148 minutes)

Miramax Films Presents
A Band Apart and Jersey Films Production

A Film by Quentin Tarantino
Pulp Fiction
Casting by Ronnie Yeskel, CSA, Gary M Zuckerbrod, CSA
Music Supervisor: Karyn Richtman
Costume Designer: Betsy Heimann
Production Designer: David Wasco
Editor: Sally Menke
Director of Photography: Andrzej Sekula
Co-Executive Producers: Bob Weinstein, Harvey Weinstein,
Richard N Gladstein
Executive Producers: Danny DeVito, Michael Shamberg,
Stacey Sher
Stories by Quentin Tarantino and Roger Avary
Produced by Lawrence Bender
Written and Directed by Quentin Tarantino

CAST (in order of appearance): Tim Roth (Pumpkin),
Amanda Plummer (Honey Bunny), Laura Lovelace
(Waitress), John Travolta (Vincent Vega), Samuel L Jackson
(Jules Winnfield), Phil LaMarr (Marvin), Frank Whaley
(Brett), Burr Steers (Roger), Bruce Willis (Butch Coolidge),
Ving Rhames (Marsellus Wallace), Paul Calderon (Paul),
Bronagh Gallagher (Trudi), Rosanna Arquette (Jody), Eric
Stoltz (Lance), Uma Thurman (Mia), Jerome Patrick Hoban
(Ed Sullivan), Michael Gilden (Phillip Morris Page), Gary
Shorelle (Ricky Nelson), Susan Griffiths (Marilyn Monroe),
Eric Clark (James Dean), Joseph Pilato (Dean Martin), Brad
Parker (Jerry Lewis), Steve Buscemi (Buddy Holly), Lorelei
Leslie (Mamie van Doren), Emil Sitka ('Hold Hands You
Lovebirds'), Brenda Hillhouse (Butch's Mother),
Christopher Walken (Captain Koons), Chandler Lindauer
(Young Butch), Sy Sher (Klondike), Robert Ruth
(Sportscaster #1), Rich Turner (Sportscaster #2), Angela
Jones (Esmarelda Villalobos), Don Blakely (Wilson's
Trainer), Carl Allen (Dead Floyd Wilson), Maria de
Medeiros (Fabienne), Karen Maruyama (Gawker #1), Kathy
Griffin (Herself), Venessia Valentino (Pedestrian/Bonnie),
Linda Kaye (Shot Woman), Duane Whitaker (Maynard),
Peter Greene (Zed), Stephen Hibbert (The Gimp), Alexis

Arquette (Man #4), Quentin Tarantino (Jimmie), Harvey Keitel (The Wolf), Julia Sweeney (Raquel), Lawrence Bender (Long-Hair Yuppie Scum)

SUMMARY (in chronological order): Hit man Vincent Vega and his partner Jules Winnfield have to clear up after Vincent accidentally kills a fellow employee of big-time gangster Marsellus Wallace while he's riding in their car. After being helped out of this tight spot by a 'problem solver' known as 'the Wolf', they go for breakfast, where Jules foils a robbery and announces that he's giving up his life of crime. Vincent later has to take Mrs Wallace out for dinner while Marsellus is not in town; she later overdoses on his heroin thinking it to be cocaine, and he fights to save her life. She goes home and they promise to never talk of the evening's events.

Butch Coolidge, a boxer, refuses to take a dive in the ring, and inadvertently kills his opponent in the process of winning the match. Fleeing, he kills Vincent, who has been sent after him, and is captured, along with Marsellus, by a pair of rednecks who plan to rape and murder both of them. Butch escapes, and then returns and rescues Wallace, unable to leave him to that fate. A grateful Marsellus cancels out the contract on Butch and relieves him of his debt on condition that he leave LA and never come back.

THE PLAYERS: John Travolta had once been the biggest movie star in the world (despite probably never having made a truly good film) and yet he had fallen slowly, yet spectacularly, from favour. By 1993 he had reached the point where he was appearing in the excruciating series of *Look Who's Talking* 'comedies' with Kirstie Alley. *Pulp Fiction* put Travolta back on the top of the Hollywood heap, winning him several awards and an Oscar nomination. He made the film for a salary of $100,000, below his fee even for that time, and despite reservations about playing a heroin user. It's the performance of his career.

Samuel L Jackson, a Morehouse College, Atlanta, graduate, had auditioned for *Reservoir Dogs* and appeared in a small role in the Tarantino-scripted *True Romance* (Tony Scott, 1992). An experienced stage and television actor, and former drug addict, he had beaten his problems to become a respected industry staple. The threatening manner in which he drinks a dixie cup of Sprite in this picture has to be seen and heard to be believed. He, too, is Oscar-nominated here.

Bruce Willis had come to public attention as wisecracking David Addison in the alarmingly self-aware TV series *Moonlighting* (1985–9) before breaking into leading movie roles with the romantic comedy *Blind Date* (Blake Edwards, 1987) and the action comedy *Die Hard* (John McTiernan, 1988). Superstar status seemed inevitable, but *Pulp Fiction* came at a point where Willis was actually failing to move into more serious roles and better movies than his recent projects, such as the execrable *Death Becomes Her* (Robert Zemeckis, 1992). *Pulp Fiction* came out in the same year as Willis's appearances in the far less impressive *North* (Rob Reiner, 1994) and *Color of Night* (Richard Rush, 1994).

A former shoe salesmen, soldier and court stenographer, Harvey Keitel has been Quentin Tarantino's favourite actor since the director was a child. Keitel has appeared in an extraordinary number of films in his career, including *Who's That Knocking At My Door?* (Martin Scorsese, 1968), *The Duellists* (Ridley Scott, 1977) and *Mean Streets* (Martin Scorsese, 1973).

Uma Thurman was immediately noticeable in *Henry and June* (Philip Kaufman, 1990) and *Dangerous Liaisons* (Stephen Frears, 1988) and played the planet Venus in *The Adventures of Baron Munchausen* (Terry Gilliam, 1988).

THE DIRECTOR: Quentin Tarantino is the King of the Movie Geeks and a self-described film junkie. It's hard for people of a certain generation to remember a time before he appeared, jabbering away on television and making not just films but the act of filmmaking into something cool in a way that they hadn't really been for a decade. His life is now as well known as his work.

He was born in Knoxville, Tennessee, is part Native American and used to work in a video store. An autodidact with a vast knowledge of popular culture and an intuitive understanding of film, he worked as a lowly script doctor (rewriting other people's screenplays for small sums of money and no credit) and sold some screenplays into development before securing funding to write/direct *Reservoir Dogs* (1992), the controversial, instant brilliance of which made him the first director since Orson Welles to leap into the critical, commercial and public A-lists with his first feature. (He had started directing an abortive self-financed movie, *My Best Friend's Birthday* (1987), while working at the video store, but it is incomplete and few have seen the cheaply shot, extant footage.) *Pulp Fiction* was his second. His third, the offensively underrated, emotionally complex and beautifully acted *Jackie Brown* (1998), was followed by a five-year silence in which Tarantino did acting work and seemed content to be famous for being famous. He was forbidden by the Directors' Guild of America (of which he is not a member) to direct an episode of the TV series *The X-Files* ('Never Again', written by Glen Morgan and James Wong) after he directed an episode of *ER* without compensating the union for, they argued, putting one of their members out of work. All four of his theatrically released pictures are extraordinary pieces of work and for many he has no equal among living film directors.

VISUAL INTEREST: Tarantino's virtuoso and versatile camera style uses the technique, influenced by Jean-Luc Godard, of parodying and subverting film conventions in order to draw attention to them. Mia Wallace's drawing a square (well, actually a rectangle) on the screen as she calls Vincent a 'square' and the use of deliberately bad back projection (a.k.a. 'process shots') to show the streets behind characters as they drive along in a car have been noted often.

What is less remarked upon is the constant shifts in how the camera is used, always tailored to the essential drama of the scene being shot but segued into the style of the preceding scene in such a way that there is little or no 'jolting' from one scene to another. It's the work of a master manipulator of his audience.

Early in the film there's a long tracking shot (over two and a half minutes) during which Vincent and Jules discuss massaging Mia Wallace's feet. Either side of this shot the conversation is shot in two-shots and in wide shots, emphasising the two men's closeness and the ease with which they work together (compare this with the conversation they have after Jules's 'moment of clarity', which is shot in profile; the two men don't get into the same shot, because they're no longer close). After the two decide not to enter the room just yet, the camera, which has stayed on the two constantly, refuses to follow them as they move away from the door and indulge in small talk. It's as if the camera were seeking to remind the characters that the door, the job, not the conversation, should be their focus.

When Vincent arrives at Lance's house begging for help with the overdosed Mia the scene is shot with a handheld camera and using merely 'available light' (rather than filmic light sources), which gives the scene the verisimilitude and pace of documentary footage. Later in the same scene the camera is unwilling to enter the room in which Lance is searching for his medical black book; this adds to the audience's fear that he won't find it, since they can't see him looking and don't know how likely he is to acquire it. It also means viewers don't get to look at the dying Mia for a long time, adding to the tension. A similar technique is used with completely different results in Butch's girlfriend's apartment, where having the camera lurk outside the bathroom in which she and Butch are getting ready for bed cunningly implying intimacy. The audience are made to feel as if they were eavesdropping through the door of the bathroom, penetrating a private world.

The camera initiates a slow, slow creeping into close-up as Butch realises that he doesn't have his watch, and asks his girlfriend if she's left it behind, a very subtle way of cranking up, almost imperceptibly, the tension in what is, in dialogue terms, an ordinary domestic scene.

The scene in which Christopher Walken cameos as Captain Koons giving the young Butch the above-mentioned watch isn't, as many recall it to be, one long take of Walken delivering the monologue. The camera actually cuts back and forth from Walken to the child several times. It is also handheld, though, and begins with a point-of-view shot (from Butch's perspective) into which Koons walks. It's reminiscent of several moments in *The Deer Hunter* (Michael Cimino, 1978), for which Walken won an Oscar for his performance as another Vietnam era serviceman. Walken performed the monologue three times, and the three, fairly long, close-ups of him reciting sections of it all come from different takes. Pleasingly, given the film's time-shifting narrative, this scene, chronologically the first thing that happens in the film, was the last piece of the picture shot.

As Butch, now an adult, sits being lectured by Marsellus Wallace on how he should throw his fight his face is horizontally bisected into areas of light and dark, reflecting his choice between right and wrong. The background around him is almost entirely red, reflecting equally on Marsellus's perhaps demonic nature.

Red is also used in the dizzyingly unpleasant sequence in which Vincent shoots up heroin. Slow, painful, mechanical, shot in close-ups with a black background so sinister that the scene almost becomes abstract, it's dreadful in the little-used sense of 'filled with dread'. The blood that fills the syringe is red, as is the light on Vincent's face as he smiles (an assured reference to the final shot of **Once Upon a Time in America**). If anyone seeing this scene thinks it's glorifying drug use, they don't have eyes. The horrific sight of Mia, dribbling, with blood pouring out of her right nostril a short while later should surely be enough to convince any doubters. The lingering close-up on her bloodied, drool-smeared face is enough to give anyone The Fear. Uma Thurman's commitment in this scene can't be praised enough.

Tarantino's use of a character looking into a mirror as he reflects on his possible choices and fates goes back at least as far as **Little Caesar** and seems to be an obvious reference to it.

Mr and Mrs Marsellus Wallace are both introduced without the audience seeing their faces for a long time. Effective in establishing his power and her sexual allure.

QUOTES:

Jules: 'Oh, I'm sorry, did I break your concentration?'

Jules: 'Y'know, like Cain in *Kung Fu*.'

Vincent: 'Goddam, that's a pretty fuckin' good shake. I don't know if it's worth five dollars, but it's pretty damn good.'

Vincent: You don't fuck with another man's vehicle; it's against the rules. [Beat] Mind if I shoot up here?'

Mia: 'Trying to forget anything as intriguing as this would be an exercise in futility.'

Jimmie: 'Did you notice a sign on the front of my house saying "Dead Nigger Storage"? . . . 'cos storing dead niggers ain't my business.'

Butch: 'This is America honey – names don't mean shit.'

Jules: 'My girlfriend's a vegetarian, which pretty much makes me a vegetarian too.'

Marsellus Wallace: 'This business is filled to the brim with unrealistic motherfuckers who thought their ass would age like wine. If you mean it turns to vinegar, it does; if you mean it gets better with age, it doesn't.'

Mia: 'I do believe Marsellus, my husband, your boss, told you to take me out and do whatever I wanted. Now, I wanna dance.'

Jules: 'Hamburgers, the cornerstone of any nutritious breakfast.'

Jules: 'Say what one more time. I dare you, I double-dare you, motherfucker!'

SOURCES TO SCREEN: In March 1992, having been given script-development money by Miramax to write his next picture, Quentin Tarantino hired an apartment in Amsterdam and began to work material devised by himself and his pal Roger Avary into a projected 'portmanteau' picture. The idea of a film containing several interconnected stories, perhaps linked with a framing sequence, had mostly been used for cheap horror movies in the past, but had lately garnered some critical respect with *New York Stories* (Woody Allen, Francis Ford Coppola, Martin Scorsese, 1989). Tarantino took as his model *Black Sabbath* (Mario Bava, 1963), an Italian horror film, and used the format to work in material reminiscent of the kind of story that had appeared in the magazine *Black Mask*. (Published between 1921 and 1951, *Black Mask* was a crime-fiction magazine notable for having characters such as Perry Mason, Sam Spade and Philip Marlowe all making their first appearances within its pages.) He was also keen to imitate the work of writers such as Elmore Leonard (whose novel *Rum Punch* he would film (as *Jackie Brown*) in 1998) and Bret Easton Ellis, both of whom had created elaborate fictional universes that all their characters inhabited. Events in one Ellis or Leonard book would connect, often only tangentially, to those in another and characters in one novel would be related to those in others. (Patrick Bateman, the eponymous antihero of Ellis's *American Psycho*, has a brother who is featured in *The Rules of Attraction*, for example.) Previous Tarantino scripts had done this, but with one directorial feature under his belt the process could begin in earnest. It was presumably with this in mind that Tarantino made his new script's lead, Vincent Vega, the brother of the torturer Vic Vega (a.k.a. Mr Blonde) from his previous hit *Reservoir Dogs*.

The shop in which Marsellus and Butch are assaulted is named Mason-Dixon. Mason-Dixon were stenographers who mapped the route of a railroad in the early nineteenth century. The route of the line became known as the boundary (though it wasn't exact) between the states that permitted the owning of human slaves and those that didn't both before and during the American Civil War. Here this information is used to clue the audience into the fact that these people are rednecks, straight out of *Deliverance* (John Boorman, 1972) and *The Texas Chainsaw Massacre* (Tobe Hooper, 1974).

Mia's haircut is that of Louise Brooks in G W Pabst's *Pandora's Box* (1928). If you haven't seen that film, by the way, do so.

The moment where Butch, waiting at the crossroads in his car, has his path crossed by Marsellus Wallace is a direct borrowing of the moment in *Psycho* (Alfred Hitchcock, 1960) when Marion Crane (Janet Leigh) sees her boss walk in front of her car while she is fleeing from him, having stolen $40,000. Tarantino is, incidentally, an outspoken defender of the remake of *Psycho* (Gus Van Sant, 1998), and good for him.

Although it is never mentioned, it's fair to assume that Jules is named after the great black actor Paul Winfield.

Jules's habit of reciting pieces of the Bible is reminiscent of the Robert Mitchum character's habit of doing just that in *Night of the Hunter* (Charles Laughton, 1955). It's also indebted to the homilies delivered by Sonny Chiba in his *Shadow Warriors* TV series (see **Kill Bill – Volume One**).

The fighter Butch is meant to lose to is Floyd Wilson, the same fighter who is fighting an opponent paid to take a dive in *On the Waterfront* (Elia Kazan, 1954).

Jules's being friends with Jimmie is a nod to François Truffaut's *Jules et Jim* (1962).

The fighters on the billboard outside the club where Butch has unexpectedly won his fight have two wildly different precedents. Vossler and Martinez were two guys who worked with Tarantino in his days in the video-rental trade. Wilson and Coolidge were two US presidents, Woodrow Wilson (4 March 1913–3 March 1921) and Calvin Coolidge (3 August 1923–3 March, 1929), albeit two who never actually 'fought' by contesting the same presidential election.

CONTEMPORARY REACTION: Part of the *Pulp Fiction* legend is that during its very first screening at the New York Film Festival a man collapsed and had a seizure during the scene in which Mia Wallace has adrenaline injected into her heart. It was nominated for seven Oscars including Best Picture, Best Actor (John Travolta), Best Supporting Actor (Samuel L Jackson), Best Supporting Actress (Uma Thurman), Best Film Editing (Sally Menke) and Best Screenplay (Quentin Tarantino and Roger Avary), of which only the last was converted into an actual statue on the night.

The film received many other awards, of which the most significant was the Palm D'Or from the Cannes Film Festival. Best Picture and Best Director awards came from the Los Angeles, New York and National Board of Review Critics' Circles and the film won four Independent Spirit Awards, including Best Picture.

As with anything that seems to arrive on a wave of hyperbole, there were many naysayers, including some people obviously merely reacting against what they perceived as received wisdom, but reviews were generally, overwhelmingly positive.

Janet Maslin, writing in the *New York Times* of 23 September 1994, admitted that she had found the level of excitement surrounding the movie 'suspect' but that, once she had seen the picture, the 'proof is on the screen'. 'You don't . . . enter a theater to see *Pulp Fiction*, you go down a rabbit hole,' she opined, calling the film a 'stunning vision of destiny, choice and spiritual possibility' that was 'surprisingly tender'.

SEX/MONEY/DEATH: Given that every character in the film is intimately connected to organised crime, you could call *Pulp Fiction* the purest gangster movie ever made, but it's so much more than that. What unites all of Tarantino's pre-*Kill Bill* features is their deliberate collision between the clichés of film storytelling and the awkwardness of real life. Tarantino himself has said that the essence of his moviemaking technique is the idea of a man hi-jacking a car as he runs away from a crime scene, only to discover that the car is a manual-stick-shift vehicle, and he knows only how to drive an automatic. What *Pulp Fiction* does is to take this technique of collision to its obvious extreme, contrasting three of the most obvious and hackneyed plotlines conceivable (the hit man who mustn't fool around with his boss's wife, the boxer who should have thrown a fight and didn't and the pair of gunmen sent to retrieve a MacGuffin) with a chaos and random messiness that should be almost anti-dramatic. It combines this by attempting to reach the, equally extreme, logical conclusion of its title. It turns *Pulp Fiction* into a pun. The film pulps fiction, takes as many separate elements as it can and crushes them into one mass so dense it seems likely to become a gravitational endpoint.

It also pulps *time*. That's why the plot is non-linear to the point whereby some ordinary moviegoers have claimed it doesn't make sense; why so many of the clocks in the picture are set to the same time (4.20); why the Wolf is at a cocktail party that is clearly being held in the evening when called by Jules and Vincent in the morning (and he can't be in a different time zone: he arrives to visit them in minutes); and why almost all of the picture takes place on the same day and before breakfast. It's also why the film ends where it began – in the diner with Pumpkin and Honey Bunny. That's why Lance is eating a brand of cereal that hasn't been made since 1983 and why Mia Wallace has only a record player and a reel-to-reel tape machine rather than a CD player and a tape deck. That's why Vincent can go to a retro fifties diner and meet someone (Butch) who is later seen treating a

1940s taxi cab as if it were a contemporary object. That's why Butch watches a television set that is both visibly a very old-fashioned model and clearly very new. There are many other examples of this temporal twisting in the film.

Too much time and effort has been devoted to the MacGuffin of what is in the briefcase that Jules and Vincent are sent to retrieve, but, since that's what a MacGuffin is meant to do, I suppose one can't complain too much. Most people's favourite theory is that it contains Marsellus Wallace's soul, which he has sold to the devil (hence the glowing light and the fact that the combination is 666). Also seen to back this up is the plaster on Marsellus Wallace's neck. Apparently, mythologically speaking, it is possible to extract someone's soul through the back of his or her neck, though no exponent of this theory has ever identified which myths state this. Other, less eccentric, explanations include that it's a suitcase full of gold or of stolen Academy Award statues or that it contains a gold lamé suit. It doesn't, of course, really matter.

Although much criticised for its violence, there's very little on screen. All the characters are gangsters, yes, but Jules and Butch are redeemed and Vincent is punished while Marsellus Wallace is seen to be an unrepentantly bad man. Butch puts his life on the line for an enemy because it is morally the right thing to do. Jules saves the lives of countless people in the coffee shop for the same reason. More lives are saved than taken during the course of the picture.

While none of the characters are shown descending into a life of crime, it's clear that none really want to be there. Money does seem to solve problems, but this late in the twentieth century how can this be any of the characters' faults?

TRIVIA: The roaring 'Theme From Pulp Fiction' (actually 'Misirlou' by Dick Dale and the Del Tones) was picked by Tarantino as his movie theme because it struck him as being a piece of music on a comparable scale to the themes for *Ben-Hur* and *The Good, the Bad and the Ugly*.

Stabbing someone directly in the heart with a syringe full of heroin will not save the life of someone with life-threatening amounts of heroin in their system. Even assuming that the needle goes through the breastbone (which is hugely unlikely, no matter how sharp the needle, and which is also unnecessary, the heart being accessible from the side), injecting adrenaline into the heart won't alleviate the symptoms of heroin overdose. The scene was written by Tarantino, with assistance from Roger Avary, with dramatic impact rather than medicine as the paramount concern.

THE VERDICT: Intelligent, consistently stylish (yet resolutely unglamorous, a difficult amalgam to pull off) involving and morally complex, this is another film that is probably the best work in the career of everyone involved. It's also easily the best film of the 1990s and among the best dozen American movies ever.

'You're 'avin' a laugh!'

If the nineties in America is characterised by a combination of Quentin Tarantino's gleeful, yet considered, approach to the gangster picture and Martin Scorsese's struggles with the underlying character of organised crime, in the UK only one voice really counted: Guy Ritchie. Ritche's two pictures, *Lock, Stock and Two Smoking Barrels* (1996) and *Snatch* (1999), filtered *The Italian Job* through the British nineties habit of middle-class people pretending to be working-class and produced two joyless, violent, patronising comedies that were enormously successful. Less engaged with the ideas and issues surrounding the genre than any other example of it, *Lock, Stock* spun off into an unpopular TV series and had a derogatory effect on popular culture generally. *Snatch*, with its juvenile title and Brad Pitt cameo was the same again, but worse.

Although they are worth mentioning because of their popularity, there is nothing else to say about these films. The more contemplative British gangster film of the end of the decade would ignore them entirely or reject their stylings without even referencing them. They were a cultural and cinematic dead end built on an inappropriate, lazy reading of *Get Carter* and fuelled by the mid-nineties craze for the memoirs of 'reformed' gangland figures.

Casino (1995)

(178 minutes)

Universal
An MCA Company
Universal Pictures and Syalis DA & Legende Enterprises
Present
A De Fina/Cappa Production
Adapted From A True Story
A Martin Scorsese Picture
Casting by Ellen Lewis
Costume Designers: Rita Ryack and John Dunn
Title Sequence: Elaine & Saul Bass
Edited by Thelma Schoonmaker
Production Designed by Dante Ferretti
Director of Photography: Robert Richardson, ASC
Based on the book by Nicholas Pileggi
Screenplay by Nicholas Pileggi & Martin Scorsese
Produced by Barabara De Fina
Directed by Martin Scorsese

PRINCIPAL CAST: Robert De Niro (Sam Rothstein), Sharon Stone (Ginger McKenna), Joe Pesci (Nicky Santoro), James Woods (Lester Diamond), Don Rickles (Billy Sherbert), Alan King (Andy Stone), Kevin Pollak (Phillip Green), L Q Jones (Pat Webb), Dick Smothers (Senator), Frank Vincent (Frank Marino), John Bloom (Don Ward), Pasquale Cajano (Remo Gaggi), Melissa Prophet (Jennifer Santoro), Bill Allison (John Nance), Vinny Vella (Artie Piscano), Oscar Goodman (Himself), Catherine Scorsese (Piscano's Mother), Phillip Suriano (Dominick Santoro), Erika von Tagen (Older Amy), Frankie Avalon (Himself), Steve Allen (Himself), Jayne Meadows (Herself), Jerry Vale (Himself), Joseph Rigano (Vincent Borelli), Gene Ruffini (Vinny Forlano), Dominick Grieco (Americo Capelli), Richard Amalfitano (Casino Executive), Richard F Strafella (Casino Executive)

SUMMARY: Summoned to Las Vegas by the mob bosses of Kansas City, sports betting specialist Sam 'Ace' Rothstein is put in charge of four casinos in the city, and his vision and attention to detail transform them into moneymaking enterprises on a scale unprecedented, with profits both legitimate and illegitimate being scammed, creamed off and sent away to his masters. Ace's empire is ruined by the tensions among him, his friend Nicky and his wife, ex-hooker Ginger.

THE PLAYERS: Since *GoodFellas*, Robert De Niro had, perhaps, largely made unfortunate film choices. With the exception of his Oscar nomination for Scorsese's *Cape Fear*, he had largely appeared in undistinguished pictures such as *Backdraft* (Ron Howard, 1991), an insipid fire-fighting drama with little to recommend it beyond a slumming-it cast, and had played the Monster in Kenneth Branagh's unwieldy, grotesque attempt at making an 'accurate' film of *Mary Shelley's Frankenstein* (1994).

Joe Pesci, too, had not been through the best phase of his career since he last worked with Scorsese. An impressive role in Oliver Stone's startlingly paranoid *JFK* (1993) and a cunning turn as *My Cousin Vinny* (Jonathan Lynn, 1992, opposite an Oscar-winning Marisa Tomei) aside, he'd mostly worked in formula comedies, such as the high-grossing but appalling *Home Alone* (Chris Columbus, 1993) and its sequel, and the truly dire *Lethal Weapon 3* (Richard Donner, 1992).

Sharon Stone leaped to public attention in *Basic Instinct* (Paul Verhoeven, 1992), the Swedish auteur's densely plotted soft-core-pornographic, postmodern noir. She followed that up with the less-well-plotted, and far less entertaining, but equally soft-core-mainstream 'thriller', *Sliver* (Phillip Noyce, 1993), which was, frankly, rubbish. Having successfully established herself in the film industry, and become a sex symbol (by the somewhat direct route of appearing naked and in lengthy sex scenes in those two pictures), she seemed to embark upon a search for material with which she could prove her abilities as an actress. She had long worked in semi-obscurity and has admitted that taking the controversial role in *Basic Instinct* was a calculated risk that paid off.

Ginger, a role Scorsese also considered Madonna for, could be said to be the first truly convincing demonstration of her talents on screen. She was nominated for an Academy Award for her performance – one that many critics, this one included, thought her incapable of giving. She lost out on Oscar night to Susan Sarandon, although a Golden Globe win may have been some compensation.

THE DIRECTOR: Since *GoodFellas*, Scorsese had remade *Cape Fear* (J Lee Thompson, 1961), replacing Gregory Peck with Nick Nolte, although the film overall was more successful than *that* makes it sound, chiefly due to a dynamite performance by Robert De Niro. Other projects had included a documentary short on, and interview with, Giorgio Armani (*Made in Milan*, 1991) and the Edith Wharton adaptation *The Age of Innocence* (1993), a deliriously wonderful film, much praised by critics but ignored by audiences, and a stark contrast to Scorsese's 'signature' works that nevertheless bears his stylistic hallmarks and carries over many of his obsessions.

VISUAL INTEREST: *Casino* was filmed entirely in the Las Vegas Valley. The Riviera Hotel stood in, mostly, for the fictional Tangiers. Exteriors, though, were shot outside the Landmark casino, which had then recently closed. The Landmark was destroyed, with controlled explosives, in 1995. The event was captured by Tim Burton's camera crew and he went on to include the footage in the Las Vegas massacre scenes in his own *Mars Attacks!* (1997).

Scorsese's crew shot for six weeks, four nights a week, taking over a section of the Casino between midnight and ten in the morning. Gaming continued around and behind them, with more punters than was perhaps normal for that time of night (the Casino had erected a huge sign outside, which informed potential customers that De Niro, Scorsese, Pesci and Stone were making a movie inside).

A lot of the film is shot using a Steadicam operated by Garret Brown. This was an experimental model roughly half the width of what was then the industry-standard Steadicam. This miniaturisation allows Garret's camera to bob and weave in and out of intimate situations, to move through doors and even change direction on a dime. The audience's eyes consequently drift up and down, smoothly moving in ellipses through its immaculately rendered real/unreal fantasy world of opulence and money. The effect is to totally immerse the audience in Ace's world. The long, long tracking scene that details how money makes its way from the punters' pockets, through the casino, to the Kansas City mob bosses is fascinating, information being released in an easily comprehensible and entirely visual way – the kind of thing Scorsese is best at.

The introduction of Ginger, via a long montage that shows what she does (accompanied by a voiceover from Ace, which makes it clear he always knew what she did) and the way this is crashed into the freeze-frame that accompanies Ace's falling in love with her is jaw-dropping. The way this is followed by further short scenes, run together quickly, all of which give the audience more information about Ginger, is another example of Scorsese's ability to release huge amounts of detail to the audience quickly, effectively, almost subliminally.

Scorsese the showman is really able to go for it in presenting Las Vegas. Oddly, given the director's lifelong devotion to portraying his home city of New York on screen, Vegas seems the natural home for his spinning cameras, sudden freeze-frames and unexpected close-ups. Also impressive is the almost symbolic table around which the crime bosses (largely absent from the rest of the film) gather shrouded in a darkness which is largely metaphorical.

There's also a car journey around Vegas during which the camera stays on Nicky and Ace and the audience observe the colours of Vegas only as reflections in the glass and across their faces. There are so many moments of technical inspiration in this picture; so many shots that bear down from the ceiling; so many unexpected close-ups to pick out details; so many long pulls back away from a small detail to reveal a vast panoply; so may shots up from inside suitcases or boxes and even times when a character bends his neck in one direction as the camera twists in another. You never know what the camera is going to do next. You can't take your eyes off the screen for a moment.

The colour scheme is packed with greens, reds and dark browns – colours that suggest opulence without taste. This is carried over into the authentically seventies costumes: riots of clashing pastels and tones and materials. The suits aren't easy on the eye, less easy, even, than the violence, and *Casino* is, even for a Scorsese picture, even for a gangland epic, spectacularly violent. Scorsese has stated publicly on more than one occasion that the now infamous scene in which Nicky puts a man's head in a vice, and then crushes him to death, was included partially to draw attention away from violence contained elsewhere in the picture. He was always prepared to cut it in its entirety, but the censors wanted only trims, so the scene stayed in. (It's worth pointing out, incidentally, that while the scene in which Nicky murders a man in cold blood with a pen is more horrific than any moment of violence in *GoodFellas*, the man whom Nicky kills *is* being unreasonable. Not *so* unreasonable that he deserves to die, obviously, but more deserving of ire than the people that Pesci randomly offs in *GoodFellas* (see **SEX/MONEY/DEATH**).)

The film's narrative is almost entirely nonlinear in its presentation, and profoundly novelistic. Prose fiction is capable of moving from the specific to the general and back again. This is very difficult to achieve on screen. A series of short scenes cut together, or even long and short scenes pasted together, usually seem broken up and indistinct, lacking in pace and coherence. But here Scorsese and editor Thelma Schoonmaker can go from the specifics of Nicky's first arrival in Vegas, via a diamond-smuggling anecdote that may take place before or after it (and it doesn't matter which it is), to Nicky's children in school and at play months after they've been in Las Vegas, while the narrator talks still of Nicky's earliest times in Vegas.

Cause and effect are all jumbled up: Ace's stories of how he first stamped his authority on the Tangiers are interlarded with moments that must come long after in terms of the central dynamic between the characters. Ace asks Ginger to marry him after knowing her for three months, and the audience see their wedding as the very next scene. But at the wedding they have a baby because, as Nicky tells the viewer, Ace wanted to make sure they had a child before they married, to 'cover his bets'. And despite these unorthodoxies, these seemingly bizarre sequential choices and juxtaposing sequences, it all makes sense, *all* of the time. The audience always know how the characters relate to one another and how it all hangs together. Editorially, *Casino* is a triumph.

QUOTES:

Ace: 'Running a casino is like robbing a bank. With no cops around.'

Nicky: 'This guy could fuck up a cup of coffee.'

Ace: 'Even the coppers aren't afraid to bury a guy in the desert out here.'

Ace: 'I had it down so good, I ran paradise on earth.'

Nicky: 'So, in other words, I'm fucked?'
Ace: 'In so many words? Yes.'

Ace: 'There are three ways of doing things around here: the right way, the wrong way and the way I do things.'

Ace: '[Nicky] had a scheme, it wasn't very scientific. When he won he collected, when he lost he told the bookies to go and fuck themselves.'

SOURCES TO SCREEN: Like that for *GoodFellas*, the screenplay for *Casino* is a collaboration between Martin Scorsese and Nicholas Pileggi. Something else it has in common with *GoodFellas* is that it's largely based on the life of one individual, in this case Chicago-born Frank 'Lefty' Rosenthal, who becomes Sam 'Ace' Rothstein for the purposes of the film (presumably named for Al Rothstein, often quoted as the man who fixed the World Series in 1919 as mentioned in F Scott Fitzgerald's novel *The Great Gatsby*).

During the seventies and very early eighties, Rosenthal ran four casinos (the Stardust, the Fremont, the Hacienda and the Marina) in Las Vegas and is credited as the man who introduced the concept of betting on sports to Las Vegas. He's also often credited with coming up with the aesthetic (neon, bright lights, glitz) of the Las Vegas casino that people are familiar with. The essential facts of Rosenthal's life are utilised, without much embellishment, for Pileggi and Scorsese's screenplay. Rosenthal's wife Geri is the basis for Ginger, and Rosenthal's childhood friend and enforcer, Tony 'The Ant' Spilotro, is the basis for Pesci's Nicky Santoro. Tony really was beaten to death and buried in a cornfield in 1986. Rosenthal really did host a TV show from his casino, too. These days he runs a gambling website.

Other minor characters are also drawn from real life. K K Ichikawa, the film's Japanese gambler, is based on Akio Kashiwagi, who, in the seventies and eighties, often played the tables in Vegas. He was murdered by gangsters in his own country in 1992. There's even more verisimilitude in the fact that Oscar Goodman, the real-life lawyer who has defended alleged gangsters in Las Vegas on numerous occasions, plays Ace's lawyer in the film. (At the time of writing, incidentally, Goodman is the elected mayor of Las Vegas.)

One difference between the Pileggi/Scorsese screenplay for this picture and their previous collaboration is that the *Casino* screenplay was written in parallel with, and in some instances before, the book upon which the credits claim the script is based. Pileggi began researching his book about Las Vegas during postproduction on *GoodFellas* and found himself, five years later, in the position where he felt able to begin writing the book. Almost as soon as he had begun, however, Scorsese called him and asked him if he instead wanted to collaborate with him on turning this research into a screenplay. Pileggi recalled, in interviews, the process of writing the screenplay as being much harder than it had been on *GoodFellas*, because this time they were adapting notes, not a finished book, into a script – pulling the narrative out of the research rather than simply transposing the already visible structure of a book into script form.

CONTEMPORARY REACTION: 'Scorsese tries to weave visual poetry out of warped ambitions,' claimed Peter Travers in *Rolling Stone* (14 December 1995), opining that the director played his mobster story as 'Shakespearean tragedy with Ace as an Othello so driven by jealousy and pride that he loses his wife and his fiefdom'; a character ultimately motivated by one sad thing: he 'wants the dream back' because the reality of life isn't enough. Roger Ebert (in the *Chicago-Sun Times* of 22 November 1995) felt that the film, like *The Godfather* before it 'makes us feel like eavesdroppers in a secret place' telling its story with the 'energy and pacing' Scorsese is famous for. The picture's appeal lay in the 'wealth of little details' and how Scorsese got 'the feel, the mood, almost the smell of the city just right'.

In the *New York Times* of 22 November 1995 Janet Maslin thought that the real world looked 'shockingly impoverished by comparison' with *Casino*. While much of its technique was 'staunchly journalistic' there was fascination for the audience in how it 'luxuriantly explores the anatomy of America's playground'. That same audience though would soon, she felt, get bored with the way the picture 'overloads [our] capacity to absorb arcane schemes or fiscal data'.

Casino cost $52 million. It was a prestigious picture with a respected director and cast, and, while it wasn't expensive (especially considering the length), it wasn't cheap either. That length also counted against the film in cinemas, meaning that fewer showings could be squeezed into one screening day. However, *Casino* took more than $42 million during its US domestic release, which, even allowing for the sharing of profits with cinemas and filmmakers, means the movie must have long ago made back its budget for the studio thanks to foreign markets (it made nearly $4 million in the UK and another $1 million in France) and television, VHS and DVD sales.

As well as Sharon Stone's Oscar nod and Golden Globe, the film was also nominated for an Eddie (editing prize) for Thelma Schoonmaker, while Scorsese was also up for a Golden Globe for directing. None of them won.

SEX/MONEY/DEATH: Peter Travers may not have liked how *Casino* distanced its audiences from its characters, but it's by doing this that the movie grasps the authority that *GoodFellas* lacks. There are times when *Casino* seems like a documentary, so scrupulously does the film explain *exactly* how things work in a mob-run gambling house (compare it, for example, with the genuinely incomprehensible deal struck in the Cuba sequences in **The Godfather – Part II**), but this is a strength of the picture, not a weakness. *Casino* is a 'world-building exercise', as critics have liked to call later films that demonstrate an entire environment. It's as much concerned with the creation and presentation of the world in which its plot takes place as it is in detailing that plot; and it's as much about the institution of the casino (which is, after all, the title) as it is about its ostensible lead characters.

While the plot sprawls, it sprawls with some elegance, and

justifies every foot of film, every elaborate frame. With *Casino*, the audience need the time and space devoted to the description of the world, and then to the introduction of the characters, in order to appreciate how being placed at the centre of that world affects those characters. Some audiences, sadly, don't have the patience. Whereas *GoodFellas* was about the people, *Casino* is about the people's world. And that's how it avoids becoming the hymn of hubris that *GoodFellas* descends into.

Ace is a compelling lead character from the beginning. Endowed by De Niro with a twitchy body language and perpetually crossed arms, he goes to Vegas seeking some kind of absolution or redemption (he speaks of the operation as a 'morality car wash' and claims 'Las Vegas washes away your sins') and this is a far more comprehensible initial motivation than Henry Hill's childhood wish fulfilment (*GoodFellas*), while Ace's creed – that he likes to gamble, he likes to win and he likes his luxuries – is not only much more comprehensible than Henry Hill's pathological desire to be like a character in a gangster movie, but also more morally and socially acceptable. Whereas Henry Hill's obsessions seem to be with power, Ace's seem to be with *thrills*, and the fairly innocent ones of playing games at that.

Also, as with a character in a Warner Bros gangster film of the thirties, it's his nearest and dearest who threaten him and bring him down. It's his inability to say no when Tony virtually demands he be allowed to come to Vegas to hustle that leads to virtually the whole chain of events that leads to the explosive attempt to kill him in his car. It's his absolute love for Ginger, and inability to believe badly of her, and to act when he knows she's working against him, that leads to her disintegration and his own exile.

Although there is a sense that Nicky, Ginger and Ace are all victims of some kind of *über*-Vegas, a person-crushing machine, the first part of the picture leaves audiences in no doubt that Ace helped create this machine and that he's used it both to enrich himself and to crush others.

De Niro's still, eye-of-the-storm Ace is a reincarnation of
Jimmy Conway, here placed centre stage as perhaps he
should always have been. Pesci's Nicky is, as people are keen
to point out, in some respects just Tommy DeVito by
another name; but there are other, more important, respects
in which he's a very different character. What makes Tommy
in *GoodFellas* so terrifying is that he's barely a recognisable
human being at all. Nicky has the same manic bursts of
violence, the same studied amorality and the same almost
insane lust for power and prestige but, and this is important,
he *evolves*. He shifts and changes, he's far less of a cartoon.
He's still vile, but you get to see the process whereby he
becomes as vile as he does. You get to see him with his
children. You get to see him display affection. Of Ray Liotta
there is no sign at all, but is there really anyone on earth who
would rather watch Liotta on screen than De Niro? Really?

More importantly, though, *Casino* merely illustrates a life
as it describes a world; it doesn't aggrandise (or even
particularly condemn) it and it certainly doesn't go on and
on about how great it all was while pretending to apologise
for it as *GoodFellas* does. Even *Casino*'s multiple-person
voiceover spares audiences the self-pity that smothers too
much of *GoodFellas* and surely it must be a reaction to just
that. The narration-switching allows moments where the
audience are clearly having it demonstrated to them that a
character is an unreliable narrator. *GoodFellas* contains no
such moments, and it contains nothing close to the
pleasurable insanity of Nicky, still narrating, being beaten to
death on screen while his narration begins to yelp little
'Ows!'

Casino doesn't feel like an 'authorised story', either, and it
is neither smug nor self-justifying. The characters, all the
characters, accept a degree of personal responsibility that
Henry Hill wouldn't even recognise if he fell over it. Even
Nicky, psychotic little Nicky, knows who to blame for the
end of their Camelot: 'We fucked up,' he says. '*We* fucked
up.'

Casino has been sarcastically referred to as '*GoodFellas* again', and maybe it is. But would Scorsese, who moves from diverse project to diverse project throughout his career, have really made *Casino* at all if he rated *GoodFellas* as highly as others do? This is purely speculative, but I think not. The very existence of *Casino* at all implies Scorsese's unhappiness at the way the earlier film turned out; perhaps for some of the reasons I've outlined here and in the picture's own chapter. If he thought *GoodFellas* had worked, why did he decide to do it all again? The most plausible answer is that he wanted to do it again so that he could do it right.

THE VERDICT: *Casino* is *Goodfellas* done properly. Is there a moment as heart-stopping, as magnificently human, as Ace's first sight of Ginger in *GoodFellas*? Are the relationships anything like as complex? Is anywhere near as much information conveyed? Is it half as much *fun*? Is it a third as smart? *Casino* surpasses its sainted predecessor on every level and in virtually every scene.

The Limey (1999)

(88 minutes)

Artisan Entertainment present
Terence Stamp in
The Limey
Casting by Debra Zane CSA
Music by Cliff Martinez
Costume Design by Louise Frogley
Edited by Sarah Flack
Production Design by Gary Frutkoff
Photography by Ed Lachman ASC
Produced by John Hardy and Scott Kramer
Written by Lem Dobbs
Directed by Steven Soderbergh

PRINCIPAL CAST: Terence Stamp (Wilson), Lesley Anne Warren (Elaine), Luis Guzman (Ed), Barry Newman (Avery), Joe Dallessandro (Uncle John), Nicky Katt (Stacy), Peter Fonda (Valentine), Amelia Heinle (Adhara), Melissa George (Jennifer), William Lucking (Warehouse Foreman), Matthew Kimbourh (Tom), John Robotham (Rick), Steven Heinze (Larry), Nancy Lenehan (Lady on Plane), Wayne Pere (Pool Hall Creep), John Cothran Jr, Ousan Elam, Dwayne McGee, Brian Bennet (DEA Guys), Allan Graf (Gordon), Carl Ciarflo, George Ruge, Lincoln Simmons (Warehouse Thugs), Rainbow Borden (Warehouse Sweeper), Michaela Gallo (Young Jennifer), Jose Perez, Alex Perez (Teen Gun Dealers), Brandon Keener (Excited Guy), Jim Jenkins (Party Guy), Mark Gerschwin (Party Guy #2), Johnny Sanchez (Valet), Brook Marie Bridges (Child Actress), Randy Lowell (Director), Eva Rodriguez (Ed's Sister), James Earl Olmedo (Ed's Nephew), Jamie Lin Olmedo (Ed's Niece), Clement E Blake (Pool Hall Bartender), Tom Pardoe (Party Bartender)

SUMMARY: North Londoner and ex-con Wilson arrives in America looking for answers relating to the death of his daughter Jenny. After visiting Ed, the man who wrote to him to tell him about his daughter's death, he follows the trail, via Jenny's acting teacher, to the record producer/promoter and sixties icon Terry Valentine, whom his daughter dated for five years. Killing three men who worked for Valentine as a warning, he gatecrashes a party at the rich American's house, with Ed in tow, where he throws one of Valentine's lieutenants to his death from Valentine's raised swimming pool.

Between them Valentine and his lieutenant arrange for some local hoods to kill Wilson, but the Englishman is rescued by the Drug Enforcement Agency, who inform Wilson that Valentine is laundering money from drug deals for a tidy profit. Wilson makes an assault on Valentine's house, killing much of his security force, before trapping him on a beach, and demanding he be told the truth about his daughter's death.

THE PLAYERS: Born in London in 1939, the marvellous, soulful Terence Stamp, here given his best role in more than a decade, was an *enfant terrible* of the 1960s whose early career was not so much 'filled with promise' as 'beyond compare'. His screen debut, in Peter Ustinov's magnificent Herman Melville adaptation *Billy Budd*, won him an Oscar nomination; he went on to work with Fellini (*Histoires Extraordinaires*, 1968) Passolini (*Teorema*, also 1968) and won the Best Actor award at Cannes for *The Butterfly Collector* (William Wyler, 1965).

As if sensing that this momentum couldn't be sustained, Stamp went into spiritual semi-retreat in India for the best part of a decade, emerging as a more mature-looking actor, content to play character roles. Good parts for him in this renewed period of his life include the ex-con drama *The Hit* (Stephen Frears, 1984) and an outstanding cameo in *Wall Street* (Oliver Stone, 1987). Less effective movies given some small dignity by Stamp's involvement include the rock-and-roll western *Young Guns* (Christopher Cain, 1988) (which featured most of Hollywood's then prominent Brat Packers and even more prominent guitars by Jon Bon Jovi) and *Alien Nation* (Graham Baker, 1988), a bizarre cop/buddy movie/cross-cultural comedy/science-fiction thriller, which spawned a TV series sequel in which Stamp didn't participate. In 1994 he exploded back into public notice with, and received a second Oscar nomination for, his proud and glorious portrayal of the eponymous heroine/hero of *The Adventures of Priscilla, Queen of the Desert* (Stephen Elliot, 1994).

In 1999, the year of *The Limey*, he cameoed as Supreme Chancellor Valorum (in effect the president of the entire universe) in George Lucas's criminally underappreciated *Star Wars: Episode I – The Phantom Menace* (1999), where his personal dignity added depth and status to a character who appeared in only a mere two scenes. The actor later expressed a great dislike of the process of filming the SFX-heavy adventure, something he had experience of, having played General Zod in *Superman – The Movie* (Richard Donner, 1978) and *Superman II* (Richard Donner/Richard Lester, 1980), Zod being the nemesis of both Superman and his Father Jor-El (Marlon Brando). Neither film is up to much, despite enormous box office, but Stamp makes the most of his iconic line 'Kal, Son of Jor-El! Kneel before Zod!' In 2002 Stamp completed another circle of sorts, by taking the recurring role of Jor-El himself in the Superman prequel TV series *Smallville* for the WB.

Peter Fonda is another sixties icon, albeit from the other end of the decade and the other side of the Atlantic. Everyone over fifteen must have seen and embraced *Easy Rider* (1969) which Fonda co-wrote as well starred in. Hollywood royalty and part of a vast acting dynasty that includes his father, the legendary Henry Fonda, he first came to notice in films such as *Tammy and the Doctor* (Harry Keller, 1963, with Sandra Dee) having done some television work (such as episodes of *Wagon Train* and *Arrest & Trial*). He also appeared in *Histoires Extraordinaires*, like Stamp, but was in a different segment under a different director, and the two never shared any scenes. *Easy Rider* seemed, for decades, set to remain his single great accomplishment in cinema, but in 1997 he was arguably robbed of an Academy Award for his frankly astounding performance in *Ulee's Gold* (Victor Nunez, 1987). The film, a contemporary adaptation of the *Odyssey* for which he won many other awards, saw him give a performance in which, for perhaps the first time in his career, he resembled his late father. In 2000 he won an Emmy for his performance in the TV Movie *The Passion of Ayn Rand* (Christopher Menaul, 1999), in which he played opposite Helen Mirren.

THE DIRECTOR: Steven Soderbergh remains one of the very late twentieth century's most talented, versatile and consistently impressive directors. He directed the breakthrough indie hit *sex, lies and videotape* (1989), which saw Soderbergh pick up his first Oscar nomination (for the screenplay) and, less fortunately, temporarily convinced the film industry that Andie MacDowell could be a star.

He followed up with a series of fascinating, but hardly commercially or critically lauded pictures. These included *Kafka* (1991), a semi-portrait of the writer, featuring an impressive cast (Alec Guinness, Jeremy Irons, Joel Grey, Ian Holm) and stunning cinematography, and *King of the Hill* (1993) an adaptation of A E Hotchner's novel of the trials of a child whose mother is in a sanatorium. Across the mid-nineties, Soderbergh made increasingly obscure, cheap and unprofitable films climaxing in (the brilliant) *Schizopolis* (1997), a defiantly, and self-declaredly, impossible-to-summarise picture. The only place to go after that was back to the mainstream, where Soderbergh arrived with a vengeance shooting Elmore Leonard's adaptation *Out of Sight* (1998), which initiated his longstanding creative partnership with George Clooney and effectively launched the screen career of Jennifer Lopez.

It is a slick, hugely sexy thriller in which Lopez is so good it's hard to believe, looking back, that it's her. A spin-off series, *Karen Sisco*, with Carla Gugino in the Lopez role, was made for American television in 2003. *The Limey* followed for Soderbergh, as did *Erin Brockovich* and *Traffic*, two masterful pictures shot and released in the same year. Soderbergh's workaholism saw him competing against himself for Best Director at the Oscars, having been nominated twice, once for each film. *Traffic* deservedly delivered him the statue.

Next up was *Ocean's Eleven* (2001), a zingily enjoyable remake of the Rat Pack caper, again with Clooney, and then *Full Frontal* (2002), a perilously onanistic jeer at celebrity culture saved by the performances of the vast ensemble cast. A very cheap film, it was shot on digital video and seemed to many to be Soderbergh reminding everyone of his Indie roots. *Solaris*, a remake of the 1974 existential Soviet science-fiction film was, unfairly, less well received.

VISUAL INTEREST: Soderbergh's editing into *The Limey* of pieces of Stamp's earlier movie *Poor Cow* (Ken Loach, 1967) was one of the most remarked-upon aspects of the film on its original release. There are, of course, precedents for the essence of the technique, most obviously *Sunset Boulevard* (Billy Wilder, 1950), in which Norma Desmond (played by the silent-movie star Gloria Swanson) watches Swanson's own *Queen Kelly* (Von Stronheim, 1929) as she reminisces about her past. Other examples of this technique include *Whatever Happened to Baby Jane?* (Robert Aldrich, 1962), which uses pieces of Bette Davis's and Joan Crawford's earlier pictures to show their younger days.

Something that has been less remarked upon than the obvious facts is the way that Soderbergh and the editor Sarah Flack somehow avoid this being a mere conceit and make it part of an all-embracing visual style. After beginning, the film spends less than a minute with Wilson as he lurks outside the airport and travels in the car. He arrives at his rental home, unpacks and moves to Ed's in less than two minutes and fifteen seconds. During this the film moves back in time to his plane journey, to England and Wilson's first reading of the letter about Jenny's death, to Jenny's childhood, back to the plane, to scattered fragments of life in England, the journey to America and more moments of Jenny's childhood, before arriving back outside Ed's for the same piece of footage (and mispronunciation), a mere three minutes and forty seconds after the audience first saw him. It's an incredibly detailed, amazingly swift emotional journey.

At other moments in the film this visual pattern is used in the service of other aspects of the presentation of the character of Wilson. At 24 minutes, for example, the audience sees sequences depicting Jenny's death. This, it's later learned, isn't what actually happened at all. They're Wilson's imaginings of what might have happened and are thus emphatically not flashbacks. Thirty-six minutes in, the film drifts from flashback and counterpoint to vivid fantasy, as Wilson imagines, no fewer than three times, brutally gunning Valentine down in a variety of shocking ways.

If Soderbergh's many and disparate films have one consistent element, it is their director's interest in film grammar. Soderbergh has spoken of *The Limey* as an experiment in 'releasing information'. Early on, Soderbergh made the decision to challenge traditional filmic assumptions that it was impossible to show a character thinking on film – and the frequent crosscutting and mismatching of sound and vision, the constant 'layering' of information within the film, is a hugely effective method of conveying enormous amounts of both atmosphere and characterisation. Throughout *The Limey*, the audience are more or less constantly interiorised inside Wilson's perceptions of events. The film is about him and his reactions more than it is about the events in which he is participating. This is a film in which viewers don't really see anything other than a character thinking. Only rarely does the observer move out of Wilson-vision, and when this happens it's all the more effective for it. One wonderful example is the famous sequence where Wilson throws one of Valentine's henchmen to his death from the pool deck outside his hillside home. The camera observes this shocking act from inside Valentine's sanctuary. The audience view the murder through the window, literally over Valentine's shoulder as he laughs and schmoozes in what appears to him to be total safety, never noticing the violence behind him.

The Limey is fluidly shot, almost, if not actually, entirely handheld. Its washed-out colours and bleached cinematography recall the pale beauty of *Billy Budd*, Stamp's first feature. Soderbergh adopted a policy of shooting with 'all available light' for the film, avoiding using artificial light sources outside of those already present on location, and allowing the light to flare into the camera whenever it happened naturally (traditionally, such 'mistakes' would be cut out or around). There's an energy in the film that comes from this kind of 'naturalism'.

One of the most interestingly edited sequences in the movie is the 'walk and talk' Stamp conducts with Lesley Anne Warren. If you watch this carefully it makes no literal sense. The point of view jumps from one location to another, and back, backwards and forwards in time, between different times of the night and day, as the conversation simply slides inexorably forward. This was a deliberate experiment on Soderbergh's part, the director feeling that if one were looking back over a long conversation that had taken place over several hours and in several locations one would not necessarily remember which parts of the conversation occurred in which location and when. Memory would conflate events. It's a brilliantly unorthodox cinematic presentation of a common real-life phenomenon rarely glimpsed on screen.

SOURCES TO SCREEN: As well as the *Poor Cow* (Ken Loach, 1967) connection (see **VISUAL INTEREST**), *The Limey* is packed with external references, being almost furiously and semiotically thick with many moments of allusion. Here are a few of them.

The opening credits run over the song 'The Seeker' by the Who, managed during their sixties heyday by Terence Stamp's brother, Chris.

Valentine first appears to the sound of 'King Midas', written by Allan Clarke, Tony Hicks and Graham Nash, which contains a reference to an 'Easy Rider'.

Peter Fonda tearing along the road to a Steppenwolf song (in this case 'Magic Carpet Ride') surely can't fail to remind *anyone* of Fonda's antics to the band's 'Born to Be Wild' in his own *Easy Rider*.

Soderbergh also allows a moment from his own personal legend to infect the film: Valentine is seen watching George Clooney, a Soderbergh business partner and star of his then most recent picture *Out of Sight* (1998) (see **THE DIRECTOR**).

The relationship between Wilson and Ed echoes the relationship between the literary characters of Don Quixote de la Mancha and Sancho Panza as seen in Cervantes' novel *Don Quixote*. Just to hammer the point home Wilson at one point calls Ed 'Sancho'.

The dialogue combines a bizarre naturalism with utterly inconsequential, clearly Tarantino-influenced comic 'character' jabbering, especially an argument about throwing the nutshells back into the nut bowl with all the uneaten nuts.

The later part of the film clearly recalls *Straw Dogs* (Sam Peckinpah, 1971), when Wilson and Ed lay siege, in wild-west style, to a contemporary dwelling.

The ending of the film, as Wilson approaches the camera while being fired at repeatedly but with no bullets ever visibly striking him, is clearly evocative of a similar scene in *Point Blank* (John Boorman, 1967) – although Soderbergh has emphatically denied that that movie is as big an influence on this one as some have suggested.

Throughout the movie Ed (Luis Guzman) is seen wearing shirts with famous political figures on them. At the beginning it is Ayatollah Khomeini, in the middle it is Che, and towards the end it is Mao Tse Tung.

In terms of plot structure, the film draws on Japanese *Ronin* or *Jojimbo* tales, which tell of the outsider walking in and causing a situation/society to self-destruct by using his wits, presence and more than a smattering of violence. These have, of course, been a massive influence on Western cinema, from *The Good, the Bad and the Ugly* (Sergio Leone, 1967) to the James Bond film *Licence to Kill* (John Glen, 1989). (Speaking of Bond, Wilson's comment, when physical action is demanded of him, that he is 'not James Bond' seems to deliberately echo Stamp's publicly expressed regret that he never got to play the character in the Eon Films series.)

Wilson's dialogue is delightfully exact for the part of north London he's said to come from; he even uses 'chap' to describe people, which sounds instinctively wrong for his hardboiled language, but is in fact exactly right for his (and my) part of London. The fact that his immediate reference point for a rich and important man is 'the Marquis of Fucking Tavistock', principal landowner of much of north London, is another amusing subtlety.

Barry Newman was the lead in *Vanishing Point* (Richard C Sarafian, 1971). Casting him as Valentine's henchman backs up the atmosphere created by casting Fonda as a counterculture icon gone to seed. It's worth noting that both Valentine and Captain America are profiting from drugs.

When Wilson throws a man off a high building to his death, the source is clearly **Get Carter** as, indeed, is the basic theme of a career criminal looking for revenge. (Terence Stamp was, incidentally, Michael Caine's flatmate through the 1960s.) All in all, it has to be said that, thematically and in terms of its effectiveness, *The Limey* is an infinitely better American remake of *Get Carter* than the appalling effort (also called *Get Carter*) by Stephen T Kay (2000), starring Sylvester Stallone.

Even the title refers to antiquated colonial slang for an English sailor, an obvious nod to Stamp's first film role.

CONTEMPORARY REACTION: In the *New York Times* of 8 October 1999 Janet Maslin seemed slightly infatuated by *The Limey*, calling Stamp's character a 'walking Proustian reaction' and commenting on how the visual orthodoxies 'ought to be terribly distracting' but somehow weren't. She admired how they seemed to convey successfully 'every possible angle' and 'every possible perspective' on the material – an approach that suited its 'hard distant tone'.

TRIVIA: Ann-Margret shot scenes as Terry Valentine's ex-wife. These weren't included, despite the very brief running time of the picture, presumably because they took the focus of the picture too much away from Wilson, although it has been suggested online that the scenes were designed to establish the general sleaziness of Valentine, and that Fonda's powerhouse performance elsewhere in the film made such exact embellishment redundant.

The song Stamp is seen singing is 'Colours', written by Donovan for *Poor Cow*.

SEX/MONEY/DEATH: What the fractured and beautiful *The Limey* achieves is, somehow, a form of nostalgia that lacks sentimentality. There's so much looking back, and so much regret in the movie that the audience come to understand that it's the fact that these things are gone that make them important, not what they were. It's a simple story told in a complex way, and as such it has enormous room for its visual presentation of the inside of one man's mind (see **VISUAL INTEREST**).

Wilson is so far past his prime, and so beyond his criminal career, that the only thing that matters to him is his dead daughter. This stands in sharp contrast to the rich, successful, amusing, human but deeply sleazy Terry Valentine. Valentine is still working a debased version of late-sixties California chic. He's not above having a sexual relationship with a much younger woman whose parents, the script explicitly tells us, he knew before she was born, when he advised them on suitable names for her. There's really no way such a relationship can be seen as anything other than an abuse of power, although it is also a symbolic reflection of the sixties generation's refusal to cede power to their inheritors. Wilson, of course, has had his inheritors taken from him by Valentine's actions.

Wilson and Valentine thus stand at opposite extremes: both are sixties career criminals, one has nothing – in a materialist, consuming sense – and the other (in that same limited sense) has everything; one has answers, the other has questions. When Wilson confronts Valentine on the beach, and Valentine explains to him that Jenny died as a result of an accident after she threatened to report him to the police by phone, Wilson knows – because she used to threaten to do the same to him – that the story is true. This tiny detail gives Valentine's alibi credibility, and Wilson knows that, whatever else Valentine may be, his daughter loved him too.

Somehow, this tiny moment is one of extraordinary catharsis for both character and audience. The audience are freed from Wilson-world and move on and out of the film. Seemingly, he is freed, too, joking deadpan on the plane at the film's end, the anger gone from his eyes. No longer swimming in the past, he has a future.

THE VERDICT: If Alan Resnias had made *Get Carter* . . .

Poor Cow

Most 'facts' trotted out about *Poor Cow* are wrong. It doesn't 'star' Stamp (he's billed sixteenth) as a career criminal called Wilson (he's a petty louche called Dave), and he isn't put in prison, and thus separated from his wife and daughter. He abandons his wife and baby son out of choice. There is no sense in which *The Limey* is a sequel to, or even particularly derivative of, *Poor Cow*, which is an earnest kitchen-sink melodrama with, as the title implies, a female protagonist whose path through life is somewhat unfortunate. Soderbergh makes very creative use of the limited footage he does use from Loach's picture, often using reaction shots of Stamp looking at one thing, and combining them with newly shot footage that is used to make him look at something else entirely.

Sexy Beast (2000)

(88 minutes)

Recorded Picture Company and Film Four Present
In association with Fox Searchlight Pictures and
Kanzman SA
A Jeremy Thomas Production
A Jonathan Glazer Film
Music Composed by Roque Banos
Costume Designer: Louise Stjernsward
Editors: John Scott, Sam Sneade
Production Designer: Jan Houllevigue
Director of Photography: Ivan Bird
Written by Louis Mellis and David Scinto

Co-Produced by Denise O'Dell
Produced by Jeremy Thomas
Directed by Jonathan Glazer

PRINCIPAL CAST: Ray Winstone (Gal), Ben Kingsley (Don), Ian McShane (Teddy Bass), Amanda Redman (Deedee), James Fox (Harry), Cavan Kendall (Aitch), Julianne White (Jackie), Álvaro Monje (Enrique), Robert Atiko (Andy), Nieves del Amo Oruet (Air Hostess), Enrique Alemán Fabrega (Pilot), Gérard Barray (Spanish Official)

SUMMARY: Living in retirement in Spain, former London gangster Gal is visited by a former colleague, Don Logan, who asks him to do one final job for an old acquaintance known to both of them, Teddy Bass. Gal refuses: he's happy with his wife and friends, he doesn't need the money and he risks nine years in prison for breaking his parole and taking part in a crime in Britain. Don refuses to take no for an answer, and, in a struggle with Gal and his wife, is killed.

Reasoning that the only way to draw suspicion away from himself is to go and do the job, Gal does so – the raid (on a vault accessed via a water-filled pipe) is a success but Teddy clearly knows that Gal is responsible for Don's 'disappearance'. He sends Gal on his way, aware that Don was chronically unstable and that his death will be partially a result of his extreme methods. He warns Gal never to return to London, and refuses to pay him his share of the heist. Happy to be alive, Gal leaves for Spain and his beloved wife.

THE PLAYERS: The journey from amateur boxer to internationally respected actor was a long one for Ray Winstone, a facially mobile, charismatic and ever-interesting screen performer. Born in 1957, he made his screen debut in the banned 1977 TV version of *Scum* (Roy Minton, 1977) playing the leading tough boy Carlin, a role he reprised when the piece was remade, with virtually the same cast and crew, as a cinema film two years later. That year he also made a memorable appearance in *Quadrophenia* (Franc Roddam, 1979), but the decline of the British film industry meant that Winstone's work would, for many years, be dominated by television.

He played the younger, boxing brother in ITV's *Fox* (1980), and a series of memorable television guest shots (including on Roddam's *Auf Wiedersehen, Pet* (1983–)) led to the regular role of Will Scarlet in Richard Carpenter's HTV-funded *Robin of Sherwood* (1984–86), a part Winstone made entirely his own. It was his genuinely terrifying performance as an alcoholic father in *Nil By Mouth* (Tim Roth, 1997) that saw him gain international recognition. Large amounts of film work, initially in middle-aged character roles, then increasingly as the lead, began to be offered to him.

Film work of recent years includes *Martha Meet Frank, Daniel and Lawrence* (Nick Hamm, 1988), *Face* (Antonia Bird, 1997), *Last Orders* (Fred Schepisi, 2001), with Michael Caine and Bill Nighy, and another portrayal of a (this time sexually) abusive father in Gary Oldman's *The War Zone* (1999), an intelligent adaptation of Alexander Stuart's voyeuristic, and perhaps irresponsible, novel. He also appeared with John Malkovich in *Ripley's Game* (Liliana Cavani, 2003) and later that same year played the title role of *King Henry VIII* in a sadly lacklustre mini-series for British television.

Ben Kinglsey will for ever be best known for his Oscar-winning performance as Mahatma Ghandi in Richard Attenborough's film of the revered leader's life and work (1982). Nothing in his subsequent career has really equalled the impact and power of that role, which was built on a fine reputation in British theatre, although that of clerk Izthak Stern in Steven Spielberg's *Schindler's List* (1993) perhaps came closest. A memorable comic role for Kinglsey was in *Without a Clue* (Thom Eberhardt, 1988), in which he played a very different Dr Watson opposite Michael Caine's imbecilic Sherlock Holmes.

His pyrotechnic, profanity-laden performance in *Sexy Beast* saw him nominated for another Oscar, this time as Best Supporting Actor. Although he didn't win, the Academy's obvious desperation to find a suitable clip of his performance to use at the ceremony (he genuinely doesn't have one line of dialogue that isn't riddled with obscenities) was a real highlight of the 2002 ceremony. The Academy eventually used a clip in which Kingsley stood silently by as other actors talked. He has claimed, incidentally, that Don Logan is largely based on his maternal grandmother, an aggressive and openly racist woman who worked in the East End rag trade in London. Kingsley professes to have loathed her.

He was latterly knighted for services to the acting profession.

Ian McShane will always be, to British television audiences at least, the antique dealer Lovejoy in the enjoyably whimsical BBC TV series of that name – scripted by Dick Clement/Ian La Frenais – which he headlined between 1986 and 1994. To the world at large he's better remembered as a genuinely tortured Judas Iscariot in *Jesus of Nazareth* (1977). A popular guest actor on British and American television, he has appeared in *The West Wing* and *Babylon 5*.

James Fox is a member of the vast acting clan that includes his brother Edward, mother Angela, son Laurence and niece Emilia. His best-known role remains that in *Performance* (Nicolas Roeg, 1970), after which he gave up acting for a decade to concentrate on charitable work, mostly in India. He then returned to acting – mostly in cameos and never in as high-profile roles as before – giving many excellent performances on radio.

Amanda Redman, warm and effective here as Gal's wife, is recognisable from vast amounts of below-par, heavily formulaic British television, including *Dangerfield* (1995), *At Home with the Braithwaites* (2000–3) and *New Tricks* (2003).

THE DIRECTOR: *Sexy Beast* was the first feature work of Jonathan Glazer, a respected director of commercials and pop-music promos, who had won plaudits for his 'horses surfing' Guinness ad, and worked with Radiohead and Massive Attack. Since helming the picture, Glazer has returned to commercials (including an inspired comic short for Stella Artois featuring a prisoner trying to drink his pilfered beer in peace) and directed the 2004 feature *Birth*, which is about a woman who becomes obsessed with the idea that a ten-year-old boy is the reincarnation of her dead husband (featuring Nicole Kidman and Lauren Bacall). At the time of writing, his next project is scheduled to be *Chaos*, one of Hollywood's current slew of Hideo Nakata remakes, in this instance of the Japanese wunderkind's kidnap thriller *Kaosu* (1999).

VISUAL INTEREST: Like *The Limey*, *Sexy Beast* could be called a deconstructionist gangster picture, one that draws on a variety of British and American movies, their clichés and tropes, to produce something that is as much a commentary on its genre as an addition to it. Also, like *The Limey*, it could be considered a simple story, excessively told, and the level of visual invention and trickery on display here surpasses even that of Soderbergh's movie, and makes the earlier picture seem almost restrained.

Glazer gives the audience internalised dream sequences (with a hallucinated rabbit/critter that pesters Winstone, occasionally with firearms) but doesn't restrain his directorial theatricality to unreality. The party that Teddy attends with Harry (the one with all the 'wanking, spanking, fucking . . . cocaine and camcorders') is shot with dreamy camera moves and harsh red filters, which hint at the Hellfire Club via Fox's own *Performance* (Nicolas Roeg, 1968) plus *Caligula* (Tinto Brass, 1979) and *Eyes Wide Shut* (Stanley Kubrick, 1999) for good measure. Glazer and the script are also smart enough to know that the exact nature of the heist for which Gal has been pulled out of retirement is irrelevant (it's a Hitchcockian MacGuffin, not the story after all) and so he contrives a visually arresting, if nearly nonsensically, seminaked underwater robbery that keeps the audience's eyes amused while acting as a perfect visual metaphor for Gal's sinking both back into his old life and into a situation over which he has no control.

Sexy Beast achieves a rare unity between style and content, so much so that they seem to fuse to the point where it's impossible talk about one without running into the other. Having become known for slow-moving cameras and strong symbols in his work in commercials, Glazer constructs a picture that, while not long (88 minutes), could never be described as fast, and one that is rich with imagery, symbolism and outright abstraction.

The most obvious moments of abstraction occur during the aforementioned 'dream sequences' (there were more, but they were cut from the finished film), in which the audience see Gal's imaginings. These, such as the vision of Teddy holding a gun in a twisted, feral, hirsute arm, are not always actual dreams, but are just as often a glimpse into Gal's interior view. He sees Teddy as a monster, so the audience, too, briefly see Teddy as a monster. Gal imagines the dead Don ranting beneath his repaired swimming pool, where he's been buried, and so viewers see this entirely nonliteral image, and even hear words that Gal imagines Don would say.

The burying of Don beneath the swimming pool is, it goes without saying, a superb literal/metaphorical burying of Gal's own past, just as the rolling boulder that descends on Gal, but misses him, is a symbol not only of the way his past is bearing down on him, but also of how he will ultimately escape unscathed, albeit more by luck than judgement.

As the film begins, with the aforementioned tumbling boulder, the colours are overtly reminiscent of the Technicolor process (or, in Winstone's words in contemporary publicity, 'like an Elvis movie'): the sun is bright, the water is a vibrant blue and all appears like some sort of earthly paradise, a paradise about to be invaded by the snake that is Don Logan. This blatant Biblicalism begins to run riot later on, when Teddy Bass is referred to as 'Mr Black Magic himself'; and the goat that watches Don and Gal on the road is implied to be some kind of Satanic familiar of, or representation of, Bass himself. Note also how the light loses its lustre and the shadows lengthen and darken as Gal returns to a London seemingly trapped in permanent rain and perpetual night. The darkness that passes across his face as he walks down a corridor to do the job is a predictable, but entirely appropriate, touch.

QUOTES:

Don: 'I know a bloke, who knows a bloke, who knows a bloke; now you know this bloke. This is a bloke you know.'

Don: 'It's a piece of piss, a monkey could do it, that's why I thought of you . . .'

Don (taking exception to Gal's suntan): 'Suntan? Like leather. Like a leatherman, your skin. Make a fucking suitcase out of you. Fucking holdall. You look like a crocodile. Fat crocodile. Fat bastard. Look like Idi Amin, know what I mean?'

Gal (to Dee): 'I love you, like a rose loves rainwater.'

CONTEMPORARY REACTION: Contemporary reviews for Glazer's film were pretty much universally positive, buoyed by the accessible nature of the story, the then current popularity of British films in America, Kingsley's undoubted celebrity and the impressive visuals. In the *New York Times* of 13 June 2001, A O Scott spoke of Kingsley's performance as jolting 'the movie like an exposed high-voltage wire' and opined that Don Logan was the opposite of Gandhi, 'a sociopath who radiates menace', one whom audiences would find funny and terrifying in roughly equal measure. The film overall had 'stylish, eye-popping' visuals and, in plot terms, 'the haunting indirection of a Pinter play'. Thanks to the subtlety of Ray Winstone and the convincing middle-aged romance of him and Redman, he felt *Sexy Beast* delivered 'not only sensation but also, more remarkably, feeling'.

In the *Chicago Sun-Times* of 22 June 2001, Roger Ebert was also impressed with Kingsley's dynamism. 'Who would have guessed that the most savage mad-dog frothing gangster in recent movies would be played by Ben Kingsley?' he staggered. Seeing the movie as part of a tradition that contained *The Long Good Friday* and *The Limey*, he responded to what he saw as the movie's love of its protagonists and that tradition: 'These are hard men. They could have the Sopranos for dinner, throw up and have them again,' he finished with some admiration.

In *Rolling Stone* (15 June 2001) Peter Travers thought Glazer was 'trafficking in substance as well as style' with 'flashy brilliance'. He thought the movie was 'dynamite' although he dwelled on little but the picture's immediate entertainment value.

Released on 14 January 2001 in the UK and 17 June the same year in the US, *Sexy Beast* made around half a million pounds in the UK domestic market, and nearly seven million dollars in the States.

SEX/MONEY/DEATH: The traditional gangster film dichotomy between business (usually represented as a kind of masculinity, with 'the boys' and their adolescent-influenced behaviour) and life and humanity (as usually shown through a more positive character's actions towards women, or more particularly *a* woman) is played out superbly here. The division is between the emotionally stunted, adolescent, aggressive, petulant, uncontrolled Don Logan – somewhere between the physicality of Gianluca Vialli and the personality of Mephistopheles – and the warm and mature Gal.

Don, in essence, stands for a certain kind of perceived masculinity, and Gal, with his odd outbursts of poetry ('I know you love me, 'cos I feel strong'), responsible attitude and humanity is more 'feminine'. The diminutive of his proper name, Gary, sounds more like a corruption of 'girl' than anything else. While Logan deliberately urinates on Gal's carpet like a dog marking his territory, has no regard for anyone but himself and stares endlessly at his own rough visage in the mirror, Gal blows smoke hearts towards the wife he spends every possible moment looking lovingly towards, is persecuted by his conscience and is kind to children and animals. It could barely be a more clear-cut battle between good and evil, calm and aggression, love and hate. Logan is motivated by money, Gal by a desire for happiness – a happiness he's already found away from the world he and Logan once shared.

'I won't let you be happy – why should I?' screams Don at one point, and there's no reason why he should: he hasn't, unlike Gal, experienced the redemptive power of real love. Don's last words are, with brutal irony, 'I love you . . .' directed to a woman, Jackie, with whom the audience know he once had sex, but whom he has spent every possible minute since insulting, again like an emotionally recalcitrant, attack-is-the-best-form-of-defence teenage thug.

THE VERDICT: Continually surprising, subtly acted and invigorated with a freight-train performance from Kinglsey, *Sexy Beast* sets out to do something very different with familiar things, and succeeds.

Gangster No. 1 (2000)

(105 minutes)

Film Four Presents
A Pagoda Film Production
In Association with Road Movies Filmproduktion
With the Participation of British Screen,
BSkyB and Filmboard Berlin-Brandenburg

A Paul McGuigan Film
Casting by Jina Jay
Costume Designer: Jany Tamime
Hair and Make-Up Design: Jenny Shircore
Production Design: Richard Bridgland
Executive Producer: Peter Bowles
Music Composed by John Dankworth
Sound Designs by Simon Fisher Turner
Editor: Andrew Hulme
Director of Photography: Peter Sova ASC
Based on Louis Mellis' and David Scinto's play
Screenplay Adapted by Johnny Ferguson
Directed by Paul McGuigan

PRINCIPAL CAST: Malcolm McDowell (Gangster), David Thewlis (Freddie Mays), Paul Bettany (Young Gangster), Saffron Burrows (Karen), Kenneth Cranham (Tommy), Jamie Foreman (Lennie Taylor), Eddie Marsan (Eddie Miller), Andrew Lincoln (Maxie King), Doug Allen (Mad John), Razaaq Adoti (Roland), Cavan Clerkin (Billy), David Kennedy (Fat Charlie), Johnny Harris (Derek), Anton Valensi (Trevor), Alex McSweeney (Bloke in Tailor's), Martin Wimbush (Judge), Binky Baker (Dodgy Geezer), Martyn Read (Rough Diamond), Johnnie Guld (Scarey), Don McCorkindale (Smashing Bloke), Ralph Collis (Stocky), Charles Anderson (Brute), Arthur Nightingale (Toilet Attendant), Jack Pierce (Jack the Lad), Emma Griffiths Malin (Julie), Gary McCormack (Giggler Bennett), Sean Chapman (Bent Cop), Georgina Bull (Fat Charlie's Girl), Jo-Anne Nighy (Roland's Girl #1), Simone Bowkett (Roland's Girl #2), Caroline Pegg (Flo), Mark Montgomerie (Thug Car #1), Dave Ould (Eric), Lisa Ellis (Waitress), Simon Marc (Freddie's Attacker), Tony Denham (Club Manager), Nadine Leonard (Mel), Jo McInnes (Lesley), Lorraine Stanley (Attacker's Friend), Wayne Matthews (Youth 1), Tony Bowers (Youth 2), Danny Webster (Youth 3)

SUMMARY: Gangster, a violent and cocksure young man, is co-opted in Freddie Mays's criminal gang. It's 1969 and

Gangster is soon earning enormous amounts of money for the era, spending time indulging his vices and spending time in clubs with Freddie, on whom he clearly very quickly develops an obvious crush. He affects to despise Karen, a young woman with whom Freddie falls in love, because he is clearly jealous of her position in Freddie's life. Gangster discovers a plot to kill Freddie and, knowing this is his chance to take over the gang, doesn't tell his mentor about it. The assassination fails, but both Freddie and Karen are seriously injured. Gangster kills Lennie and allows the incapacitated Freddie to take the rap for it.

Freddie goes down for thirty years, during which Gangster takes over his flat and his empire, expands it into a hugely profitable business, running not just clubs but casinos, and dealing drugs. In 1999 Freddie is released. Karen has waited for him all these years and they arrange to get married. Gangster and Freddie meet, and Gangster asks Freddie to kill him – Freddie refuses and walks away. Enraged, Gangster seems to suffer a nervous breakdown, and torches his flat, standing on the roof of his building screaming into the night about his achievements and importance.

THE PLAYERS: Malcolm McDowell's varied career has seen him mix great art with truly appalling filmmaking, and vast commercial success with box-office poison. Most impressive among his performances remain those for Lindsay Anderson, such as in *If . . .* (1968) and *O Lucky Man!* (1973) and his rightly acclaimed portrayal of Alex in Stanley Kubrick's eternally controversial *A Clockwork Orange* (1971). Less impressive, in terms of both performance and prestige, are his turns in *Tank Girl* (Rachel Talalay, 1995) and *Caligula* (Tinto Brass, 1979) – arguably two of the worst films ever made.

For the most part, however, McDowell's career has consisted of enjoyable performances in enjoyably daft potboilers such as *Blue Thunder* (John Badham, 1983) and *Star Trek: Generations* (David Carson, 1994), in which he perhaps sealed his pop-culture immortality by becoming the man to kill, once and for all, Captain James T Kirk (William Shatner).

David Thewlis remains best known for *Naked* (Mike Leigh, 1993), although an unrecognisable, uproarious cameo in *The Big Lebowski* (Joel Coen, 1998) should be sought out by all. Like, it seems, almost all British actors, he has appeared in one of the *Harry Potter* series of overlong children's pictures.

Paul Bettany, much reported (like all British actors of marriageable age) as a possible future James Bond, is most familiar to audiences for performances given in films made after this one – playing Geoffrey Chaucer in *A Knight's Tale* (Brian Helgeland, 2001), Charles Herman in *A Beautiful Mind* (Ron Howard, 2001) and as the ship's surgeon in the hugely exciting, if exhaustingly entitled, *Master and Commander: The Far Side of the World* (Peter Weir, 2003), the last two opposite Russell Crowe.

Saffron Burrows is most recognisable from her role in Dennis Potter's final two television series, *Cold Lazarus* and *Karaoke*, with Albert Finney.

Andrew Lincoln was Egg in *This Life* (1996–7) and Simon in *Teachers* (2001–3), the two best British television series of the last ten years. His performance here is unrecognisable as him, indicating a range his headlining TV work has barely hinted at.

THE DIRECTOR: Paul McGuigan's debut feature was the disappointing Irvine Welsh portmanteau *The Acid House* (1998), backed by Channel 4, which was actually artificially constructed out of short films previously transmitted on television, combined to make a theatrically releasable product. Since *Gangster No. 1*, he has completed *Wicker Park* with Josh Hartnett (an American remake of *L'Appartement* (Gilles Mimouni, 1996)) and *Morality Play*, again with Paul Bettany, about a group of travelling actors dealing with a murder among their number that is reflected in the play they are about to perform. *Morality Play* is available on video and DVD in much of mainland Europe, despite never having received a domestic cinema release, and *Wicker Park* is scheduled to be released in America in 2004.

VISUAL INTEREST: A consistently visually impressive film from the Scottish director Paul McGuigan, *Gangster No. 1* seems to use every technique available (within its £4 million budget, that is) in the pursuit of its portrayal of a sick world ripped apart by an even sicker individual. Despite a wealth of flashbacks, flash-forwards, jump cuts, slow-motion sequences, split screen, fractured images and repeated shots, the audience are ever aware of what is going on, and where and when characters are and how and why they are there.

The movie's sixties setting is beautifully recreated. It's not nostalgic or heedlessly grim and it captures the hand-me-down griminess of a world not as postwar as it now seems with extraordinary skill. The contrast of the worn carpets, blue chipboard cupboards and orange linen curtains of an earlier, supposedly more innocent, era with some of the most appallingly brutal violence ever seen on a cinema screen has an incendiary effect.

The largely mobile visuals were created using cameras tied to bungee ropes (McGuigan dislikes Steadicam and this was judged an acceptable alternative), and there is much good use made of light: demonic red filters, white slashes across Gangster's eyes, light diffused by smoke and light shot down the lens until it flares – which, as always, adds some verisimilitude to the scenes in which it happens.

One particularly interesting and innovative technique is the use of a split-screen lens (usually used to allow an actor to appear on screen with him- or herself) to create scenes in which the centre of the screen is out of focus. Viewers' eyes are unavoidably drawn, consequently, to the far edges of the screen, a cunning way of directing their view, particularly in the opening scene at the boxing club.

There are more interesting screen games than this, however. There are moments when the screen breaks into shards and flakes; reminiscent of the shattered glass from the table under which Gangster kills Lennie, perhaps, and certainly an on-screen representation of Gangster's destructive influence.

The fire that billows around Gangster is as surefooted a representation of his pseudo-demonic nature as are the silent screams Bettany occasionally gives whereby, according to the director, 'the beast possesses him' (metaphorically speaking) and he becomes entirely monstrous.

Twenty-seven minutes in, there's a scene in which Gangster is reflected on to Freddie, with the young gangster's (Bettany's) face essentially projected on to the back of Freddie's head. The audience sees them mixed together, sees how similar they are physically, but it's also a splendid visual representation of Gangster's desire to possess Freddie in every possible sense of the word. The homoerotic undercurrents that are such a strong part of the young Gangster's relationship with Freddie are given other visual outlets, such as in the car, when, accompanied by a throbbing soundtrack, Gangster inspects Freddie, the loud pumping of his blood, of his heart, nearly deafening the audience as they are also nearly blinded by the light slashing across Gangster's eyes as he stares, silenced and open-mouthed, at the object of his desire.

'Who'd want to be Freddie Mays?' Gangster tries to taunt later, and the visual games McGuigan plays are what enable the audience to see just how powerfully ironic those words are.

The wobbling visuals in the scene where Gangster murders Lennie were achieved by using a cheap camera fixed to the actor Jamie Foreman's head. It's something that should become as famous as Kubrick's destruction of a cheap camera to achieve Alex's suicidal fall at the end of *A Clockwork Orange*. The effect is to make the audience feel that it is *they* who are being violated. As Lennie drifts in and out of consciousness the light ebbs and grows. The audience has little idea what exactly is going on, but always has a very good idea how it should be feeling, as Gangster, ironically backlit with a halo that makes the young Gangster, with his blond hair and blue eyes, look ever more angelic, charges towards the camera waving an axe.

All this technical legerdemain is used entirely to the benefit of the film's story and character; the visual restraint shown later, during the extraordinarily strong verbal, physical, moral duel between Freddie and Gangster, is entirely appropriate. A few jump cuts aside, it's played in near enough real time. With no technical tricks required, the two actors are given enough room to breathe and the result is one of the picture's stand-out moments.

Far from a case of style over content (see **SEX/MONEY/ DEATH**), here style and content merge beautifully to create a coherent reality and a coherent moral whole – the image of a machete dripping blood on to the floor of the shower is an arresting image that lurks in the mind of the viewer long after the film has ended.

QUOTES:

Gangster 55 (to camera): 'What do you take me for? A cunt?'

Miller: 'What's that?'
Gangster: 'It's my favourite axe.'

Gangster: 'You ever kill anyone?'
Miller: 'How'd you mean?'
Gangster: 'Kill 'em.'
Miller: 'Dead?'
Gangster: 'Yeah.'

Gangster: 'Love makes you fat.'

Gangster: 'You let a bird into your life, the next thing you know the walls are poof pink, there's potpourri all over the bog and knickers in your cornflakes.'

CONTEMPORARY REACTION: In his *Chicago Sun-Times* column of 19 July 2003 Roger Ebert praised

MacDowell for playing 'a man who has lost all joy, retaining only venom' with integrity and called the sequence of Gangster's murder of Lennie 'one of the most brutal and, it must be said, successfully filmed acts of violence I have seen'. He found the film as whole to be an impressive portrayal of its subject matter but felt that the final scene, the conclusion, was 'too pat to be satisfying, but the film has a kind of hard, cold effect'.

Writing in *Sight and Sound* (July 2000), Mark Kermode found himself opining that the movie was 'surprisingly discreet in its choice of what to show in all its gory glory, and what to leave to the imaginings of the audience' and wondered why the suggestions that the movie might be banned had been made at all. 'It's a handsomely ugly affair,' he concluded, 'well dressed enough to make a few friends, but tough enough to make just as many enemies.'

In the *New York Times* of 19 July 2003, Elvis Mitchell called the film 'crisp, tart and often infuriating', while praising all the performances and complimenting the 'charged emotional atmosphere' caused by the 'dizzying unspoken feelings between the two men' that made the picture seem like a 'perverse drawing-room comedy'.

Rolling Stone's Peter Travers (4 July 2000) found the movie 'a potently in-your-face crime drama' of 'energy and danger and depraved wit' and reserved special praise for Bettany. Like Mitchell, he noted the young actor's obvious range. Travers also absolutely grasped the psychosexual nature of Gangster's desire for and desire to be Freddie.

SEX/MONEY/DEATH: Not so much a gangster movie as an anti-gangster-movie movie, this is clearly another stab at a deconstructionist film, one arriving a little too late to be a clear example of the prevalent trend of the mid-nineties for sixties retro.

It's very clearly indebted to *Get Carter* for its portrayal of a psychotic individual, but not so much indebted to that as it is to *A Clockwork Orange*. This is not merely to do with the presence of McDowell (and in Bettany a substitute for the younger McDowell), but also to do with the utterly unflinching, entirely noncelebratory attitude the film demonstrates towards its protagonist and the violence and damage he inflicts on the world. In fact, Film Four even went to the trouble of producing a specifically *Clockwork Orange* referencing trailer to be shown before screenings of the rerelease of the picture, so keen were they to emphasise the link. ('See it while you can,' it demands, implying that, like *A Clockwork Orange*, the movie will be withdrawn from release due to violence.) This is however essentially a trick – inviting people to watch *Gangster No. 1* in order to get kicks from the violence is disingenuous at best, but ties in perfectly to the movie's own agenda of deconstruction.

Gangster is, like Alex in *A Clockwork Orange*, really more a statement of a principle than a character per se. When the viewer sees his home it's sparse and empty. He doesn't seem to have any interests or friends outside those connected with his work. When he takes Freddie's home he doesn't make it his own or alter it all. He leaves it as Freddie had it. He adopts Freddie's clothes, his business, his tie pin. He has no self. He doesn't appear to have lovers or family. He even lacks a name. He is Gangster. Not just *a* gangster, or even *the* gangster, but the whole gangster principle. He's the very concept of making money through organised, violent crime in one slim, cold, anthropomorphic package.

The picture is entirely centred on this oddly eponymous Gangster (only one scene lacks either McDowell or Bettany) and it chooses to be a thoroughly condemning portrait of him. By connection it therefore condemns the whole culture of the gangster movie, and the whole notion of 'Gangster'. The movie hates what it is, which leads to some very interesting scenes.

Bettany's glowering, mannered performance, backed up by camera angles, hair and make-up that do their damnedest to make him look as much like McDowell at the appropriate age, is a triumph and has deservedly brought the actor to much wider recognition.

Director Paul McGuigan talks at length on the DVD of his film about his desire to avoid 'this cartoony laddish lock, stock, aren't-we-funny *shite*' and dismissed that kind of portrayal of organised crime as 'just nonsense'. It's a compelling argument, but what *Gangster No. 1* achieves is beyond that. It's emphatically, spectacularly unpleasant, a genuine cold, heart-in-mouth wake-up call. There's no joy in the occasional black humour of the film and no humanity in either version of its protagonist.

Michael Corleone (the Godfather himself) may have mellowed as he aged, but not Gangster. No, he sinks deeper and deeper into his own psychosis, like a genre becoming slowly more debased.

Gangster No. 1 begins at a boxing match, which is virtually as clear an indication of needless brutality, created through machismo, as you could want in fiction. Early on, the violence in the film is essentially cartoonish. Mays's gang's attack on the cab driver is predominantly played for laughs, as is the beating the gang dish out on the crazy golf course, but after this the more comic aspects of the film's presentation of physicality begin to drain away, until they culminate in Gangster's murder of Lennie, a genuinely sickening act of violence, perhaps unprecedented in British film.

Like *Sexy Beast* this film is concerned with the difference between those who choose crime because they feel they have no other option, and those who thoroughly enjoy it. Also like *Sexy Beast*, it sees in a single romantic love a redemptive spirit that can replace, if not actually redeem, a life of violent crime. It's also responsible in its portrayal of sickening violence, McGuigan cutting the lengthy scene of Gangster torturing Maxie by putting electrodes on to his genitals, feeling that it achieved nothing not already achieved elsewhere in the picture. It's a measure of the control and restraint of the film, an illustration of the seriousness of its intentions.

The script is, with a few exceptional lines apart, largely functional and straightforward. Well dressed and well heeled these people may be, but they're not *The Italian Job*'s Charlie Croker, even though they palpably want to be. Not even Freddie, the most positive of the male characters, comes close. Neither does Old Gangster when viewers first encounter him in wise-cracking-into-the-camera mode.

The film is desperate for audiences not to like, not to identify with, Gangster, merely to observe his vileness. When at the end of the movie he lights a funeral pyre for his love for Freddie, standing near naked on the roof of the home he took from him, screaming of his own greatness ('I'm Superman, I'm King fucking Kong!'), it comes shortly after the funniest line, and the most compellingly human moment, in the movie. Naturally, it comes from the redeemed Freddie, released from prison and planning a marriage he's waited three decades for: 'I'm just an old man in a crap suit, and I like it that way . . .'

Just as Gangster rewrites his own past (for example, he claims he didn't want to kill Lennie Taylor, when the audience have just seen that he did; he claims that he didn't enjoy it, when the audience have just seen that he did), he's unable to create his future, even with all the money and power he could need. Freddie has made himself a future despite thirty years in a cell.

The Warner Bros gangster films of the 1930s sought to present, in shocking detail, a real social problem, presenting their characters in a manner that allowed them to be emblematic, without glorifying them. All of them, even *Little Caesar*, failed in this ambition. Instead of emblems of a society gone wrong, they created icons of a kind of wish fulfilment of antiestablishment dissonance. This is where *Gangster No. 1* succeeds most spectacularly. No one could enjoy the behaviour of the utterly repellent Gangster, and his actions do seem to colour those of many other on-screen mobsters moviegoers have seen. Post-*Gangster No. 1* it doesn't seem to be such fun, any more.

THE VERDICT: While it may be dishonest to present the 'Gangster' as a beast, as a force of nature, to attack the film for that in this context would be as misplaced as denigrating Oliver Stone for showing President Richard Nixon as a physical embodiment of a certain kind of Americana, or William Shakespeare for making his King Richard III a self-aware and literally Machiavellian beast as he embodies and invokes the forces of civil war. As an act of clear-eyed deconstruction, this picture can only be loudly applauded. *Gangster No. 1* is a very good film.

Brother (2000)

(108 minutes)

Recorded Picture Company and Office Kitano Present
In Association with Film Four and Bac Films
A Jeremy Thomas and Masayuki Mori Production
A Takeshi Kitano Film
Japan Casting by Takefumi Yoshikawa
US Casting by Rod Reed
Music by Joe Hisaishi
Costumes by Yohji Yamamoto
First Assistant Director: Hiroshi Shimizu
US First Assistant Director: Edward Licht
Cinematography by Katsumi Yanagijima
Production Design by Norihiro Isoda
Written, Edited and Directed by Takeshi Kitano

PRINCIPAL CAST: Beat Takeshi (Yamamoto), Omar Epps (Denny), Claude Maki (Ken), Masaya Kato (Shirase), Susumu Terajima (Kato), Royale Watkins (Jay), Lombardo Boyar (Mo), Ren Osugi (Harada), Ryo Ishibashi (Ishihara), James Shigeta (Sugimoto), Tatyana Ali (Latifa), Makolo Ohtake (Chief of Police), Kouen Okumura (Hanaoka), Naomasa Musaka (Hisamatsu), Rino Katase (Night Club Madame), Tetsuya Watari (Jinseikai Boss)

SUMMARY: After agreeing to what he feels is a 'dishonourable peace' (and the absorption of the 'family' he has served all his life into one of its rivals), Yamamoto, a hit man for the yakuza (a Japanese criminal organisation), fakes his own death and escapes to America, where he hopes to find his younger half-brother, Ken, who was sent there years before. Ken has become a street-corner drug dealer in Los Angeles, and has a small gang. Yamamoto rescues the gang from a local crime big shot who is about to hurt them, possibly kill them, and then takes over Ken's gang. His efficiency, ruthless methods and sheer skill mean that his crew rise inexorably through the LA underworld, gaining more and more territory and absorbing more 'families' of many different ethnicities into themselves.

Yamamoto adjusts to life in Los Angeles, slowly beginning to learn English. He romances a Japanese American woman of a similar age to his, and forms a close bond with Denny, an African American street hood in Ken's gang whom he first encounters when Denny tries to mug him, unaware that he's Ken's brother. The process of territorial expansion is speeded up by the arrival of Yamamoto's comrade Kato from Japan, who gives his life so that rival gangster Shirase will pledge allegiance to Yamamoto (he commits suicide in front of Shirase to demonstrate his faith in Yamamoto's total superiority).

Soon, Yamamoto's gang have a smart business apartment from which to operate their rackets, but their fortunes become unravelled when Shirase's instability and drug-fuelled ambition lead them into conflict with the Mafia – the one criminal gang Yamamoto knows his relatively small organisation will not be able to defeat. All of Yamamoto's gang are killed, apart from Denny, who arrives too late to save his mother and sister from being massacred by the Italians.

Denny and Yamamoto seize the Mafia leader, and imply that they will kill him, but then Yamamoto lets him go after having convinced him that he's killed Denny. He orders

Denny to flee, giving him only the small gym bag he brought
with him when he first came to LA. The Mafia hunt down
and kill Yamamoto, who dies outside an out-of-town diner
in a hail of bullets. On the run, Denny realises that the bag
Yamamoto gave him is full of money and that the old
yakuza has given him another chance at life by dying,
convincing their enemies that he is dead. Crying, Denny
recognises that Yamamoto was truly his sworn brother.

THE PLAYERS: Omar Epps, a New York stage-trained
actor, came to notice as Dr Dennis Gant in *ER*, a
semiregular character persecuted by surgeon Peter Benton
(Benton was convinced that Gant, like him, would suffer for
being an African American doctor, and that he had to be
twice as good as their Caucasian rivals). Gant committed
suicide after months of Benton's taunts. Since then Epps has
struggled to find material worthy of his talents, and has
forever seemed to be on the verge of breaking through into
the mainstream.

   The Wood (Rick Famuyiwa, 1999), a sparkling 'buddy
comedy' about three bright young men growing up in the
middle-class African American suburbs of California, was
not a hit, and neither was *Dracula 2000* (Patrick Lussier,
2000) or *The Mod Squad* (Scott Silver, 1999). Only *Love &
Basketball* (Gina Price-Bythwood, 2000) has seen him reach
the kind of audiences he deserves.

   Epps is a tremendously talented performer, and that's
never more obvious than it is in *Brother*, where he has to
carry scenes in which he's the only character speaking
English and deliver monologues (often interlarded with
obscenities) straight to camera.

   In the minor role of Denny's sister is Tatyana Ali,
instantly recognisable as the youngest daughter in the Will
Smith sitcom *The Fresh Prince of Bel-Air*.

THE DIRECTOR: Probably the currently working
non-western film director most recognisable in Britain,

Takeshi Kitano (born 1947) started out as a stand-up comedian (he'd previously trained as an engineer) before becoming an actor, screenwriter, director, producer, film editor, author of short stories, essays and poetry and an accomplished painter. His 'acting credit' as 'Beat' Takeshi comes from his time in The Two Beat, a popular Japanese television comedy duo of which he was one half. Charismatic and popular, he turned his hand to film acting and – when Kinji Fukasaku was taken ill – directing, standing in for Fukasaku on *Sono otoko, kyobo ni tsuki* (*Violent Cop*) (1989) and, once his abilities in this field had been proven, going on to make more and more films from behind the camera, while continuing to act in others' pictures as well.

Notable films with him as actor include *Merry Christmas, Mr Lawrence* (Nagisa Oshima, 1983) with David Bowie and Tom Conti, *Battle Royale* (Kinji Fukasaku, 2001) and *Tokyo Eyes* (Jean-Pierre Limson, 1998). Since 1990 Kitano has directed an average of one film a year (despite spending most of 1994 in hospital following a motorbike accident) and quickly established for himself a visual style using freeze-frames, high crane shots and sudden violent physical action, contrasted with a love of slapstick and a tendency to leave the camera lingering lovingly on bodies of water.

Notable Takeshi films from this period include *Sonatine* (1993), but it was 1997's *Hana-bi* (*Fireworks*) – about a policeman who wants to be a painter – that won the Golden Lion at the Venice Film Festival and established him as a major creative player. No longer could he be dismissed as a TV star with a flair for simple, violent gangster movies (his kids' TV game show series, *Takeshi's Castle*, a cable TV staple, is often used to deride him, rather than as an example of his astonishing productivity).

Kikujiro no Natsu (1999), about the relationship between Kitano and a boy who is searching for his mother, only enhanced his status as a mature filmmaker, though, and *Brother* (2000) was his first, although as yet only, American film as a director. *Dolls* (2002) was his first film as director in six years in which he did not also perform and, combined with the multi-award-winning *Zatoichi* (2003) – in which Takeshi played a blind, aged samurai, as well as orchestrating some fantastic song-and-dance sequences – may mark the beginning of a new phase in the career of this extraordinarily versatile talent.

VISUAL INTEREST: Takeshi uses two subtly different visual styles to differentiate the scenes set in LA and Japan. The Japanese scenes are shot with largely static cameras using uplighting (often with blue filters). The sets have a preponderance of strongly visible vertical lines and many scenes take place in near darkness. The cameras are kept down low and colours (mostly whites and browns) and set decoration are spare. The setups of the scenes emphasise the 'courtly' aspect of Japanese life, with Takeshi's camera lingering on formalised eating, the ritualistic consumption of food and drink and rituals of supplication performed almost without thinking.

The LA scenes are, conversely, floodlit from above. The camera roams and spins and there are a number of point-of-view shots to emphasise Yamamoto's isolation in a country where he cannot speak the language and knows only one other person. The structure of the Japan scenes is contrasted with the chaos and clutter of the guys' pad. Interestingly, they become more orderly through association with him just as he learns English. The effects of the mingling of cultures/styles works two ways.

Other great visual moments include a brilliant, near-silent car chase and some spectacular violence. Takeshi cleverly chooses to move slowly away from the graphic killing one would associate with his Japanese gangster films. Initially deaths in the movie are like this, but later they become more stylised, taking place off screen, played out with light and sound all leading to the moment of Yamamoto's own death, where he walks out through a door that is punctured by bullet holes moments later, light streaming through. The viewer never sees him fall and never sees his corpse. It's a spectacular piece of mythmaking.

Also worth noting is the moment in Japan when Yamamoto reaches for a samurai sword in his rage, a clear indication of the tradition that Takeshi is thinking of the character as operating in; indeed there are some story similarities to *Yojimbo* (Akira Kurosawa, 1961) here, with Takeshi as the stranger who walks into a situation with only his wits and leaves a trail of death behind him. Takeshi's performance deliberately echoes both Toshiro Mifune in that film and Clint Eastwood's stoic, Americanised impersonation of him from the likes of *A Fistful of Dollars* (Sergio Leone, 1964).

Perhaps the film's stand-out visual moment is a horribly effective shot where the corpses of Yamamoto's murdered gang are used to spell out the Japanese pictogram for death across the floor of his blood-splattered apartment.

There's a great scene where all of Yamamoto's gang indulge in a game of basketball – playing basketball being the second Grand American Sporting Metaphor in film (after, of course, the playing of baseball). In this game, the smaller Japanese characters are unable to get the ball and the others are dancing round them with glee, scoring hoops. It's a great visual indication of people being kept outside of a society.

QUOTES:
Yamamoto: 'If you kill him in one shot, I'll give you ten dollars.'

Kato: 'They say they'll kill us.'
Yamamoto (smiling): 'Let them try it.'

Yakuza: 'That's some [false] finger you had made. With that on you won't get thrown out of golf clubs.'

CONTEMPORARY REACTION: In the *New York Times* of 27 September 2000, Elvis Mitchell wrote of the film as a 'yakuza spectacular', praising Takeshi's multitasking and the 'tortured minimalism' of his performance. He disliked, however, the final scene, which he felt Omar Epps overplayed, and thought the director's own rigid personal morality had an unfortunate effect on the film's substance. The rise and fall of Yamamoto was, he felt, too obvious from the beginning of the film and the shape of the drama was 'too heavily worked out', while the characters' fates were 'a Post-it carved in stone'.

Roger Ebert of the *Chicago Sun-Times* praised Takeshi's love of 'doom-laden irony, with grand gestures in defeat' as expressed in a film clearly designed to fit in the tradition of '1930s Warner Bros gangsters'. On the whole, however, he found the movie 'typical Kitano' but not 'one of his best', being too 'casual, perfunctory' with 'lots of gunfire' ultimately more like 'a video game than a stylised crime parable'. Harsh.

Made for $12 million, easily the most money ever made available to Takeshi for a picture, *Brother* made less than $500,000 in America.

SEX/MONEY/DEATH: This is another rise-and fall story, one crossed with a 'lone man' subgenre, but one that works very well indeed thanks to the thoughtful visuals and exquisite attention to detail. From the casual racism of the taxi driver (who complains that Yamamoto can't speak English, but why *should* he be able to?) to Yamamoto's lack of understanding of American currency (he tips the bell boy and the maid too much because all the notes are the same size), it puts a lot of thought into what it must be like to emerge into the United States for the first time as an absolute stranger.

Of course, how Yamamoto copes is to behave as if he were still in Tokyo, applying the methods he was successful with over there to the LA underworld and discovering, in the process, that no one at a particular level of organised crime has a hope of standing against him. Takeshi's impassive, yet oddly warm, performance is effective at putting across a man out of place, who has passions but is unable to demonstrate. The viewer never sees how he meets the Japanese American woman whom he romances in the picture's middle third, but does see the effect her death has on him.

For Yamamoto, though, this yakuza business, this gangster habit, isn't about sex or money or even ultimately about death: it's just about doing all that he can do to the best of his ability. It's about honour and brotherhood and never being afraid. The most pleasurable scenes in the movie are in the middle, as the audience sees Yamamoto's pleasure in his craft. They can see he's enjoying this process of taking over LA – it's *easy*, that's what the others can't understand. It's, if you like, art for art's sake. It is this casual violence that makes Takeshi's own character unable to escape from Takeshi the director's own moral worldview, where violence corrupts and what is gained by violence never lasts, a world where the horrors that one visits on others will be visited on one in turn. What makes Yamamoto a little different is in his final sacrifice for Denny, and the elaborate way he ensures that the younger man has a future. It's another perfect selfless act (see, for example, **Angels With Dirty Faces**) and it's the perfect capstone to a film that has indulged in much subversion and playing with roles.

THE VERDICT: A collision of two aesthetics brought to startling, vivid life. *Brother* is unique in its genre, and a minor classic of fine acting and subtle, smart directorial technique, with less blood than you'd expect and an ending to provoke tears in even the battle-hardened.

Love, Honour & Obey (Dominic Anciano, Ray Burdis, 2000)

A largely improvised gangster comedy made by the writing/directing team responsible for British comedy documentary series *Operation Good Guys* (1997–2000) which followed the misadventures of a group of London policemen. Turning to the other side of the law, *Love, Honour & Obey* is a portrait of a North London crime family headed by Uncle Ray. Much of the dialogue and action is improvised and there is a video, pseudo-documentary look to proceedings. Dismissed by many, with some justice, as a self-indulgent piece, the picture's popularity was also not aided by the prominence in it of many of the then-fashionable 'Brit Pack' of young, hip British actors including (then) 'Golden Couple' Jude Law (*AI* (Steven Spielberg, 2001)) and Sadie Frost. The improvised nature of the film meant it was easier for all concerned for the characters to have the same names as the actors playing them. Occasionally the effect of this is that the audience seems to have strayed into a warm-up exercise for some star-studded theatrical review.

The plot of the picture concerns postman Jonny (Jonny Lee Miller of *Trainspotting* (Danny Boyle, 1995)) who wishes to become involved with the criminal gang run by his friend Jude (Jude Law) and Jude's Uncle Ray (Ray Winstone – see Sexy Beast). Though he is accepted into this fraternity, Jonny finds that it is not really to his taste; his image of how gangsters should behave and what they should be like has been shaped by films and television and he's distressed by these thuggish, bored, non-violent, karaoke singing people who – having been involved in violent crime for decades – do their best to avoid it if at all possible. Jonny therefore attempts to start a gang war with the South London equivalent of Ray's gang by winding up Matthew (Rhys Ifans who is, oddly, not using his real name).

Intelligent as well as smug, *Love, Honour & Obey* works as well as it does because it fits in with the other late 90s/early 00s deconstructionist gangster films and appreciates the difference between film and reality. Touched with hubris and occasionally shambolic as it is there is as much wrong with the film as there is right with it, but Sean Pertwee's (*Event Horizon* (Paul Anderson, 1997)) karaoke rendition of the theme tune to Gerry Anderson's puppet science fiction series *Fireball XL 5* renders the film, for some, above criticism.

Gangs of New York (2002)

(160 minutes)

Initial Entertainment Group and Miramax Films Present
An Alberto Grimaldi Production
A Martin Scorsese Picture
Directed by Martin Scorsese
Screenplay by Jay Cocks and Steven Zallian and
Kenneth Lonergan
Story by Jay Cocks
Produced by Alberto Grimaldi, Harvey Weinstein
Executive Producers: Michael Ovitz, Bob Weinstein,
Rick Yorn
Director of Photography: Michael Ballhaus, ASC
Production Design by Dante Ferretti
Editor: Thelma Schoonmaker, ACE
Costume Designer: Sandy Powell
Original Music by Howard Shore
'The Hands That Built America' written and performed by U2
Casting by Ellen Lewis

PRINCIPAL CAST: Leonardo DiCaprio (Amsterdam Vallon), Daniel Day-Lewis (William Cutting), Cameron Diaz (Jenny Everdeane), Jim Broadbent (Boss Tweed), John C Reilly (Happy Jack Mulraney), Henry Thomas (Johnny Sirocco), Liam Neeson (Priest Vallon), Brendan Gleeson (Walter 'Monk' McGinn), Gary Lewis (McGloin), Stephen Graham (Shang), Eddie Marsan (Killoran), Alec McCowen (Reverend Raleigh), David Hemmings (Mr Schermerhorn), Larry Gilliard Jr (Jimmy Spoils), Cara Seymour (Hell-Cat Maggie), Roger Ashton-Griffiths (P T Barnum), Peter-Hugo Daly (One-Armed Priest)

SUMMARY: In New York, 1846, a pitched battle between Irish Catholics and the forces of Bill 'The Butcher' leads to the death of 'Priest' Vallon – the head of the Irish gang the Dead Rabbits. Vallon's son, Amsterdam, flees and ends up in a correctional house/seminary. Sixteen years later he is released into an America troubled by civil war, and heads back to the centre of New York to find and kill The Butcher and revenge his father. Finding that Bill is now more powerful, with connections in politics and legitimate business (such as with the infamous William Tweed), Amsterdam joins Bill's gang, hoping to get close enough to kill him.

Amsterdam comes to know Bill, and the older man begins to look upon the younger as a substitute son. After a year in his employ, Amsterdam tries to murder Bill, but Bill has been warned about Amsterdam's plans by Johnny, a friend of Amsterdam's who feels that the Priest's son has betrayed him by sleeping with Jenny, a petty thief for whom Johnny has always carried a torch. Bill spares Amsterdam's life, but burns his face so that men will always know that Amsterdam is the man Bill spared.

Bill feels doubly betrayed because Jenny is someone he took in when she was destitute as a twelve-year-old. Jenny and Amsterdam form an alliance with Boss Tweed, who has given up on Bill, and try to work legitimately, electing their friend Monk to the position of sheriff in order to raise the profile of Irish Americans. Bill murders Monk in broad daylight and so Amsterdam challenges Bill to a stand-up battle between Bill's forces and all the Irish Americans that Amsterdam can rally. They fight an almighty battle, against the backdrop of riots against the draft into the Union Army to fight the Civil War, and Amsterdam kills Bill as the city burns. Amsterdam and Jenny flee to San Francisco to start another life.

THE PLAYERS: Born 1974 and named after Leonardo da Vinci by his Italian American mother, LA native Leonardo DiCaprio is one of the world's most bankable stars and commands up to $20 million a picture. His first film was *Critters 3* (Christine Peterson, 1991), although it was his role in Michael Caton-Jones's *This Boy's Life* (1993) that brought him to critical attention. A terrific performance as a mentally challenged young man in *What's Eating Gilbert Grape?* (Lasse Hallstrom, 1993) gained him a well-deserved Oscar nomination, but since then it's arguably been a case of increasing fees and declining performances (with the exception of *William Shakespeare's Romeo + Juliet* (Baz Luhrmann, 1996)) in films such as James Cameron's bloated ship melodrama *Titanic* (1997), Danny Boyle's unfortunate Alex Garland adaptation *The Beach* (2000) and a silly, pouting swashbuckling mess, *The Man in the Iron Mask* (Randall Wallace, 1998).

To do *Gangs of New York*, DiCaprio accepted a reduction in wages to $10 million plus a percentage of the profits. His performance, despite a wandering accent, is his best for nearly a decade and, combined with his turn in *Catch Me If You Can* (Steven Spielberg, 2002), will hopefully prefigure a move back towards 'acting' and away from 'stardom' from this once hugely promising young actor.

Born English (not Irish as many assume) in 1957, Daniel Day-Lewis is the son of Cecil Day-Lewis, one-time Poet Laureate. He spent much time on the stage as a young man, and his first film work was a small role in *Sunday, Blood Sunday* (John Schlesinger, 1971), but he didn't appear on cinema screens again until *Ghandi* (Richard Attenborough, 1984), again in a small role.

Exposure in Stephen Frears's *My Beautiful Laundrette* (1985) and James Ivory's *A Room with a View* (1986) brought him leading roles and he won an Oscar for his performance in *My Left Foot* (Jim Sheridan, 1989). An exponent of extensive research for roles, he spent weeks in a wheelchair for that part, and learned Czech for his (English-speaking) role as a Czechoslovakian in *The Unbearable Lightness of Being* (Philip Kaufman, 1988).

Following his Oscar triumph, Day-Lewis played Hamlet to great acclaim at the National Theatre in London, but eventually left the production citing exhaustion. He didn't work as an actor again until 1992, playing the leads in the insipid, but hugely profitable, *The Last of the Mohicans* for director Michael Mann and the superb *The Age of Innocence* for Martin Scorsese. He followed with *In The Name of the Father* (Jim Sheridan, 1996), a heavily fictionalised account of a miscarriage of justice relating to terrorism in Northern Ireland, which won him another Oscar nomination. In semiretirement since then, he has been tempted out only twice, to play John Proctor in the film of his father-in-law Arthur Miller's *The Crucible* (Nicholas Hytner, 1996) and by Scorsese to do this picture. His performance in this film is *phenomenal*, and won him a third Oscar nomination. He has commented since that nothing that happened to him during the production of *Gangs* has had any influence on him one way or the other with regard to his cheerful return to retirement.

The terrifyingly versatile Jim Broadbent, a familiar face from British television and film for decades, has seen a Hollywood career come upon him in late middle age. Appearances in the Brit-com *Bridget Jones's Diary* (Sharon Maguire, 2001) and a stellar turn in *Moulin Rouge!* (Baz Luhrmann, 2001) culminated in his Oscar for a heartbreaking performance as John Bayley in *Iris* (Richard Eyre, 2001), about the life of the novelist, Dame Iris Murdoch.

Cameron Diaz was a model before turning to acting with *The Mask* (Chuck Russell, 1994). She earned her Indie spurs in the awesome *The Last Supper* (Stacy Title, 1995) and has since mixed mainstream Hollywood product (including the *Charlie's Angels* films (McG, 2000, 2003), *Shrek* and *There's Something About Mary* (Bobby Farrelly, Peter Farrelly, 1998)) with projects for Oliver Stone (*Any Given Sunday*, 1999) and Spike Jones (*Being John Malkovich*, 1999). Diaz is effective in *Gangs of New York*, but has zero sexual chemistry with DiCaprio.

The Northern Irish actor Liam Neeson remains best known for his Oscar-nominated performance in *Schindler's List* (Steven Spielberg, 1993). Other roles of note include those in Woody Allen's *Husbands and Wives* (1992) and as Jedi Master Qui-Gon Jinn in *Star Wars: Episode One – The Phantom Menace* (George Lucas, 1999).

VISUAL INTEREST: Scorsese's camera bounces and scuttles through a world somehow entirely real. The opening scenes, as the audience are forced to slide through the harsh yellows and oranges of what looks likes some infernal pit (lit strongly from both sides so that the centre of the picture is the nearest thing on screen to real darkness), have a hallucinatory conviction to them. Later, with the blacksmiths and screaming children visible as Vallon leads his son through the crowds, it seems even more hellish. Sweaty, noisy, uncomfortably warm even, the pull-back to the rows and rows of families crowded on shelved, open 'apartments' like so many hundred battery hens is an exquisitely executed visual horror.

The kicking open of the door to reveal the frost-bitten, snow-drowned square outside is almost a physical shock. The audience can feel the icy wind force its way into the boiling interior and the cold, crisp whiteness and blueness of the open space of the outside. It is an astonishing contrast to the interior. Suddenly, instantly, the audience are absolutely certain of the freedom that Vallon and his followers are fighting for.

Initially, the battle at the Five Points that follows lacks blood, and every blow that Bill strikes with his machete or axe seems to score a fatality without the slightest hint of the wet stuff. The way his victims sequentially fall is also seemingly precisely, slowly choreographed – it looks like some form of brutalised ballet. Only later in the scene does the blood begin to fly, staining that once perfect white with the red of the den whence his victims have shortly come.

The pull-out, after this, up and into the air and away to a CGI model of the city over which the caption 'New York, 1846' is written, is another startling visual choice, pulling the audience away from the world they've been forced to become quickly accustomed to and forcing them to confront what this charnel house of poverty and slaughter is: one of the greatest cities on earth, little more than a hundred and fifty years ago. It's an entirely apposite opening for a film that is largely concerned (see **SEX/MONEY/DEATH**) with forcing its audience to witness, and confront, the uncomfortable.

Gangs of New York is an assured world-building exercise, a masterful creation of a lost world for the sake of Scorsese's own revising of America's myths; but it is a far less assured piece of storytelling. All the best moments in the picture are the powerfully visual. Bill The Butcher emerging into Amsterdam's line of sight for the first time in sixteen years, sitting atop a steaming fire engine blazing in red – the very image of the devil Amsterdam has been dreaming of – is a spectacular example, but there are many more. There's always inspired comic business going on among the scores of extras who populate the vast sets the production had built at Cinecittà studios in Rome and everywhere the ever-mobile camera strays seems to be in the midst of spontaneous real life. Consider the sudden, sliding close-up of a girl's eyes as she looks, impressed, on Bill The Butcher for the first time. See the transvestite prostitutes, who are never drawn attention to with dialogue, and the constant, equally unremarked-upon, mistreatment of black extras in the background of shots. Scorsese, perhaps by insisting on the construction of those vast sets, has created a real world wherein his camera can wander, an anterior presence like a documentary recorder. It's breathtaking.

There are clever, more contrived, shots in here, too. The queue of Irish immigrants who walk off a ship and are given citizenship papers to sign at one table and then drafted into the Union Army at the next has to be seen to be believed. The further detail, as the men put on their uniforms and board the next ship to fight the war while coffins are lifted off the deck of that ship by cranes, completes a visual 'factory line' – an almost entirely metaphorical visual statement that somehow sits entirely comfortably within the naturalism around it.

Only in the third quarter does *Gangs of New York* disappoint on a visual level. That Miramax requested a cut to less than three hours has been widely reported; and it's easy enough to see where the material was lost. The film's prologue flows beautifully, as does the story of Amsterdam's first attempted revenge. The romance with Jenny lacks conviction a little, due to the performers, but plenty of screen time is allocated to it. The story of Amsterdam's plotting and absorption into Bill's gang and the demonstration of the society in which it's taking place fit neatly together. The last quarter, incorporating the riots and the final battle between Amsterdam and Bill, works equally well. But the section from Bill's sparing Amsterdam's life to the murder of Monk (incorporating Johnny's estrangement from Amsterdam, his murder by Bill and Monk's election to the office of sheriff) passes too quickly. The events of months pass by in minutes. There's nothing wrong with this, per se, but after the events of nearly a year passing by over hours as they have done in the earlier part of the film, it's an uncomfortable change of pace. The picture feels 'chopped up' and scenes stop and start suddenly and quickly and sit awkwardly with one another.

The audience could easily be forgiven for not realising that Monk has actually been elected sheriff when Bill murders him, so speedily has his confirmation been passed over. The movie quickly recovers, and moves to a magnificently orchestrated climax, and the mere facts that these scenes make sense, that the picture merely stumbles and doesn't fall during them, is cause to venerate the editor Thelma Schoonmaker. Is there a four-hour version of *Gangs of New York* trapped in a Miramax vault somewhere? Even speaking as someone normally scornful of protestations about studios ruining movies by demanding cuts, I'm anxious to see it.

QUOTES:
Bill The Butcher encourages his men to mutilate the dead: 'The ears and noses shall be the trophies of the day!'

Amsterdam describes New York: 'A furnace where a city might one day be forged.'

Amsterdam: 'That was the Five Points all rights, hangings of a morning, dancing of an evening'.

Bill The Butcher: 'Didn't anyone pay off the police?'
Boss Tweed: 'We paid off the municipal police, this is the metropolitan police!'

Amsterdam describes becoming Bill The Butcher's protégé: 'It's a funny feeling being taken under the wing of a dragon.'

SOURCES TO SCREEN: Scorsese had been trying to make *Gangs of New York* in some form since the late 1970s (according to some, as a vehicle for the punk band the Clash, with Robert De Niro as Amsterdam) but the collapse of studios' interest in large-budget prestige pictures caused by the financial horrors of *Heaven's Gate* (Michael Cimino, 1980) and *Ishtar* (Paul Sylbert, 1987) caused him to rethink, and embark on smaller-scale pictures.

The former *Time* magazine critic Jay Cocks's screen story and first-draft screenplay date from this period. This story and screenplay is heavily indebted to Herbert Asbury's book of the same title. This charts the evolution of gang warfare in the city beginning before the Civil War, and is largely drawn from the lurid and sensational journalism of the period. It is also one of the few books of any kind to incorporate the events of the draft riots of 1863. In these riots, organised to protest at the drafting of all young men into the Union Army, thousands died, orphanages were pillaged and whole city blocks were burned to the ground. The feeling was that white Americans should not fight and die to free black slaves in the South, and the mob showed their fury at being ordered to do so. Black Americans were lynched, gibbeted and massacred in their hundreds; in the end the army, coming straight from the battlefield at Gettysburg, had to be called in to suppress the riots.

What the *Gangs* screenplay does is use these events as a backdrop to the struggle between two men, one fictional (Amsterdam Vallon – although the Dead Rabbits gang was real enough) and the other, Bill Cutting, merely fictionalised. Bill 'The Butcher' Pool (Scorsese decided on a more symbolic surname for his monstrous antihero) was a gang leader some decades before the draft riots. He died in a pitched battle with another gang, protesting that he died 'a true American'. The film accurately records his anti-Irish, anti-immigration views, his skill at knife throwing, his involvement in corrupt local politics and his reputation for brutality. The glass eye is the screenwriters' embellishment, however.

Also real was 'Boss' William Tweed, head of the Democratic Party in New York for decades in the nineteenth century and still a touchstone for any American political discussion that concerns 'corruption'. He was brought down by the cartoonist Thomas Nast over the building of the Tweed Courthouse, where he was overpaid by obscene sums for items used in the construction of the building. He died in prison, despised, but left to New York the magnificent legacy of the American Museum of Natural History and the Metropolitan Museum of Art, both of which were built with his (embezzled) money.

The Five Points, the setting for much of this picture, was in the intersection of Cross Street, Anthony Street, Little Water Street, Orange Street and Mulberry Street, an area called Paradise Square where some of the worst slums in world history could be found in the mid-nineteenth century. Charles Dickens visited there in 1861 and found the situation more appalling than those he had witnessed – and campaigned for the improvement of – in London. 'Debauchery has made the very houses prematurely old,' he wrote; '. . . all that is loathsome, drooping and decayed is here'.

CONTEMPORARY REACTION: Roger Ebert in the *Chicago Sun-Times* (20 December 2002) saw the film as ripping up 'the postcards of American history' and reassembling them into 'a violent, blood-soaked story of our bare-knuckled past' achieving in the process a 'Dickensian grotesquerie'. The difference between it and Scorsese's other films was, in Ebert's eyes, a simple one. This was a story Scorsese had not sufficiently 'interiorised'. The players of his nineteenth-century drama 'kill because they like to and want to' rather than in order to achieve an objective, something he saw as uniting the antiheroes of Scorsese's other crime pictures. 'I'm not sure he likes this crowd,' Ebert concluded, arguing that more identifiable-with characters would have held the movie together. In the same day's *New York Times*, A O Scott found the film a 'brutal, flawed and indelible epic' and 'a near-great movie', one 'unsparing and uncompromised' in its revisionist approach to history, and its assault on American mythmaking directors such as D W Griffith and John Ford. 'People who care about American history', he stated, 'will, I hope, revisit some of their own suppositions' in light of Scorsese's film.

Budgeted at $83 million by Miramax, this cost $97 million despite the fact that DiCaprio and Scorsese used their salaries to fund overruns. It took $77 million domestically, meaning it has easily turned a hefty profit already, including worldwide ticket, VHS and DVD sales.

The film was nominated for ten Academy Awards, including Best Picture, Best Actor (Daniel Day-Lewis) and Best Director. It was widely felt that *Gangs* would finally net Scorsese the Oscar that he had been so long denied. It was not to be. None of the film's nominations was converted into an actual statuette on the night. The other nominations were Best Achievement in Art Direction (Dante Ferretti, art director; Francesca LosSchiavo, set decorator), Best Achievement in Cinematography (Michael Ballhaus), Best Achievement in Costume Design (Sandy Powell), Best Achievement in Editing (Thelma Schoonmaker), Best

Achievement in Sound (Tom Fleischman, Eugene Gearty, Ivan Sharrock), Best Writing, Screenplay Written Directly for the Screen (Jay Cocks, Steven Zaillian, Kenneth Lonergan). Bizarrely, U2's appalling end-credits 'song' was also nominated.

Thelma Schoonmaker did, however, pick up the much-prized Eddie – the award given by film editors to film editors – in recognition of her heroic work in making the film function as well as it does at its reduced length.

TRIVIA: Prior to the street battle in 1846, Vallon says the Prayer to St Michael: 'St Michael the Archangel, defend us in battle! Be our protection against the wickedness and snares of the devil . . .' However, this had not yet then been written. It was the work of Leo XIII (pope from 1878 to 1903), and written some four decades later.

The 'Dead Rabbits' were, historically, so called because their actual name, the Irish Gaelic for 'big hulking galoots', was a homophone for the English phrase 'Dead rabbits'. The term stuck and the gang took to marching into battle holding aloft the body of a dead rabbit on a spike – as shown in the film.

It is to be assumed, given his strict Catholicism, that either Vallon is not an actual priest or that his son was born to a mother now dead and conceived as part of a marriage he undertook before entering the priesthood, given that Catholic clergymen are not allowed to marry (and, as a Catholic, Scorsese knows this).

SEX/MONEY/DEATH: With the exception of Woody Allen, whom he increasingly grows to resemble, physically, as he grows older, there is no director more associated with New York City than Martin Scorsese. This picture, which sees Scorsese digging through what is, in essence, the prehistory of his city, also sees him working within and subverting the conventions of the genre of the gangster film.

The revenge plot, the corrupt city man, the cackling heavy-cum-godfather, the girl who begs her gangster lover to leave his life of crime behind – audiences have seen all of these many times in more traditional gangster pictures. The plot of this film, although grounded in real events, is entirely generic. This is a revenge tale wrapped in the story of a gangster's rise, one that is capped with a cathartic killing and the hero's escape. The movie, of course, needs this generic storyline so that it can be managed alongside the elaborate world-building exercise also going on at the same time.

What the incomprehensible preponderance of gangs and allegiances, ties and blood feuds, codes of honour and loyalty in this movie does is make a mockery of them all. Gangs are bad, yes, but all unthinking allegiances are bad, and even thinking allegiances can be exploited. There are arguably no 'good' people in this film, and no 'right' actions. The terrifying inferno of 1863 New York seems to be designed by the production as a warning as well as an education.

That's because, as well as the visual excitements offered by Scorsese's presentation of a New York even most New Yorkers don't know ever existed, there's also the opportunity to create a sort of 'prequel' to the New York films Scorsese has already made. To show that the criminal gangs of *GoodFellas* are nothing new and to illustrate that, while many of Scorsese's films have demonstrated that twentieth-century life is about a number of cliques all of whom look down on one another, this aspect of existence predates postmodernism.

What an audience watching *Gangs of New York* witnesses is a clash of two world orders. One a sort of bastard feudalism, fed by class hatred, race hatred and personal hatred, and another, a corrupt 'democracy' with a veneer of civilisation, also fed by class hatred, race hatred and personal hatred. He seems to be showing his audience what is buried beneath their skins and their streets. For not even the public – who are reliably, in a gang-based picture at least, a moral force, no matter how distant – can be counted on here. When the riot explodes we can be in no doubt that the whole city is part of the problem. The rioters are oppressed and mistreated, but so are those who battle with and for Bill The Butcher. Everyone's a barbarian in the end.

Scorsese's picture also firmly places this barbarity in parallel with the Civil War, fought in the popular imagination for 'freedom' to no less an extent than the Revolutionary war was fought. The puncturing of 'progress' assuming foolishness and of righteousness-assuming smugness that the terrifyingly brutal, sickeningly racist riot scenes at the movie's bloody climax achieves is hugely impressive. By graphically portraying uncomfortable facts, Scorsese forces questions to be asked. This New York may disappear in purifying flames at the film's ending, but the final shot, which shows the graveyard in which Vallon and Bill are both buried as overlooking New York to this day, sends the clear message that these impulses and horrors are part of Western civilisation still, even if they've been buried beneath courtesy, concrete and steel.

What are those who behave like Bill The Butcher, or even Amsterdam Vallon in later years, but throwbacks? Rico Bandello, Tommy DeVito, Michael Corleone, the picture seems to say, are not aberrations at all, and nor are those who rage against immigrants and form cliques and gangs. They are all, in fact, the beneficiaries of a sick legacy. They're the inheritors of the gangs of New York.

THE VERDICT: Hobbled by not being as long as it should be, but comprehensible and engaging because of the superb editing job done within the time constraints, *Gangs of New York* is part foundation myth for its city and part 'origin story' for the gangster picture. The performances are inconsistent, but the visuals are stunning and the education value and contemporary relevance of the subject matter cannot be overrated.

Kill Bill – Volume One (2003)

(111 minutes)

A Band Apart Production
The 4th Film by Quentin Tarantino
Director of Photography: Robert Richardson, ACE
Editor: Sally Menke
Casting by Johanna Ray
Production Designers: Yohei Taneda, David Wasco
Produced by Laurence Bender
Written & Directed by Quentin Tarantino
Based on the character 'The Bride' created by Q and U

PRINCIPAL CAST: Uma Thurman (The Bride), Lucy Liu (O-Ren Ishi), David Carradine (Bill), Daryl Hannah (Elle Driver), Vivica A Fox (Vernita Green), Michael Madsen (Budd), Michael Parks (Sheriff), Sonny Chiba (Hattori Hanzo), Chiaki Kuriyama (Go Go Yubari), Julie Dreyfus (Sofie Fatale), Gordon Liu (Johnny Mo), Jun Kunimura (Boss Tanaka), Kazuki Kitamura (Boss Koji), Akaji Maro (Boss Ozawa), Larry Bishop (Larry), James Parks (Deputy McGraw)

SUMMARY: Brutalised and beaten into a coma by the Black Viper assassination gang on her wedding day four years ago, a nameless bride wakes up in hospital and sets about orchestrating her revenge on those who she believes nearly killed her, wrecked her wedding party and caused her to miscarry her child. She's going to kill the gang in order, ending with Bill, their leader, and the father of her lost child.

Travelling to Okinawa, she meets a revered sensei (teacher, mainly of the martial arts), Hattori Hanzo, who, once she has told him whom she plans to kill, breaks his vow of three decades and makes for her a sword. Bill was one of his pupils, and he feels he bears some responsibility for his actions against the Bride and others.

She attacks the Japanese mob, fighting and killing hundreds of followers, before besting O Ren in hand-to-hand combat. She sends O-Ren's right-hand woman, now crippled, back to Bill as a message that she is coming for him, before returning to America to kill Vernita Green, the second of Bill's henchwomen. As the end credits roll Bill wonders aloud if the Bride is aware that her child, *their* daughter, is still alive.

THE PLAYERS: The years since *Pulp Fiction* hadn't really seen Uma Thurman add significantly to her list of accomplished performances. She had appeared in the financially, critically and artistically disastrous *The Avengers* (Jeremiah Chechick, 1998) and the only slightly less so *Batman & Robin* (Joel Schumacher, 1997) with only her splendid turn in *Sweet & Lowdown* (Woody Allen, 1999) to remind viewers of what she was capable of. *Kill Bill* gives the actress her best on-screen role to date, and its hard not to feel that her prompting Tarantino to revive the project (see **SOURCES TO SCREEN**) was caused by a self-awareness at how little her career had advanced since she last worked with him.

That said, if Thurman affirms anything in *Kill Bill*, it's that in no way can her lack of on-screen form be put down to her talents or her commitment. It's impossible to imagine any other A-list Hollywood actress subjecting herself to the training and fitness regime required by the part of the Bride, or accepting quite so readily camera angles that, say, dwell on the hairs on her toes or a tired, bruised, bloodied countenance.

New Yorker Lucy Liu exploded into the consciousness of the American public via her role as Ling Woo in TV's *Ally McBeal* (1997–2002), a supporting character who became a recurring presence, then a regular character and then one of the series' biggest assets – so much so that the series didn't survive her departure to take on other roles. These roles included Alex in the *Charlie's Angels* films (McG, 2000, 2003), a hugely amusing performance in *Shanghai Noon* (Tom Dey, 2000) and a stellar turn that was one of the few redeeming features of the dire Best Picture winner *Chicago*

(Rob Marshall, 2002). There was also an unheralded, but stunning, cameo in *Sex and The City*.

David Carradine, star of the television series *Kung Fu*, 1972–75 (a childhood favourite of Tarantino's), was cast after both Warren Beatty and Kevin Costner were considered for the role of Bill. Tarantino had read Carradine's autobiography while working on the draft screenplay and adjudged the actor's memoirs to be 'beautifully written'.

Hong Kong's Yuen Woo Ping and Japan's Sonny Chiba were cast with the triple purpose of having them choreograph fight scenes, play supporting roles and train Thurman for the ordeal of making the film. 'I've written this character for Uma, and they [Woo Ping and Chiba] are going to put her through training, where she will have to learn the kung fu animal styles,' Tarantino said when announcing their involvement during preproduction. Chiba's performance is reminiscent of the great Toshiro Mifune, and there really is no higher compliment.

Chiaka Kuriyama had appeared in the explosively wonderful *Lord of the Flies*-a-like *Battle Royale* (Kinji Fukasaku, 2000) with Takeshi Kitano, and was cast by Tarantino on the strength of that performance.

The father-and-son actors Michael and James Parks play father-and-son characters Sheriff and Deputy McGraw in this movie. Michael also played Sheriff McGraw in *From Dusk Til Dawn*, where the character was killed off. James Parks appeared as Deputy McGraw in from *From Dusk Til Dawn 2: Texas Blood Money* (1999).

THE DIRECTOR: Since *Pulp Fiction*, Quentin Tarantino had directed one major feature – the grievously underrated *Jackie Brown* (1998), an adaptation of Elmore Leonard's *Rum Punch*, starring Pam Grier and Robert Forster – but had mostly dabbled in acting and producing. Projects as an executive producer included the sequel (*Texas Blood Money* (Scott Spiegel, 1999)) and prequel (*The Hangman's*

Daughter (P J Pesce, 2000)) to his own script for *From Dusk Til Dawn* (Robert Rodriguez, 1996). Both were projects designed to give friends a movie break that he lent his name to. Neither was a success, though *Texas Blood Money* at least boasts a decent central performance from Robert Patrick and some witty dialogue.

He'd also directed a segment ('The Man from Hollywood') of the truly appalling portmanteau film *Four Rooms* (1995). The sizeable presence of the title card, 'The 4th Film by Quentin Tarantino', at the beginning of *Kill Bill – Volume One* seems designed to eject *Four Rooms* from any serious consideration of his directorial 'canon' (which it could only do damage to).

VISUAL INTEREST: *Kill Bill* begins with the 'Shaw Scope' logo of the Shaw Brothers company, makers of many Hong Kong exploitation pictures. *Kill Bill* was largely shot at the Shaw Bros studio. The film then proceeds to a caption, which reads, 'Revenge is a dish best served cold', and then to labels, with 'old Klingon Proverb'. It's actually a line from the French novel *Les Liaisons Dangereuses* by Pierre Choderlos de Laclos, filmed many times in both English and French. What Tarantino is referring to is the moment in *Star Trek II: The Wrath of Khan* (Nicholas Meyer, 1982) where the vengeance-obsessed maniac of the title (Ricardo Montalban) quotes this and labels it an 'old Klingon proverb'. It's a clever thing for Tarantino to do, placing his film in metaphorical quotation marks from the very start. He then follows this with a bleached-out black-and-white shot of the Bride's bloodied face, a sudden intrusion of real emotion and real horror after a few moments of jokey, parodic, colour-filled messing around. The shock is profound; audiences inevitably collapse into utter silence in less than a moment.

The domino masks worn by O-Ren's bodyguards (massacred by the Bride) are clearly indebted to those worn by Bruce Lee as Kato in TV series *The Green Hornet*

(1966–67); the theme tune is also heard. Given that Uma Thurman's yellow tracksuit is, obviously and self-confessedly, a deliberate lookalike for that worn by Bruce Lee in the unfinished *Game of Death* (Robert Clouse, 1978), one is faced with the image of Bruce Lee massacring an army of Bruce Lees.

The sudden 'blink' into black and white for the massacre in the House of the Golden Leaves is a reference to the habit of US television stations of showing black-and-white copies (or merely black-and-white copies of some scenes) of violent Eastern films in order to disguise the gore content.

Tarantino's camera usually finds Uma Thurman's face in *extreme* close-up, its long, slowly curving lines dragged up and out; it gives her features enormous power. Equally, when his camera goes wide she seems to stretch towards the sky and become more and less than human.

Often a close-up of the Bride's eyes is shown and then immediately followed by flashback footage of a massacre in black and white. This is a conceit taken from the majestic yet violent Lee Van Cleef western *Da uomo a uomo* (*Death Rides a Horse*) (Giulio Petroni, 1968), which, if you haven't seen, you should.

The release of the film as two separate instalments was, although something discussed at an early stage in production, a late decision made after the initial trailer had already been sent out. Tarantino's initial cut came in at over three hours. The executive producer Bob Weinstein, perhaps aware that he had hobbled *Gangs of New York* by asking for it to be cut down to a more audience- and Academy-friendly length, was fully behind the decision to make one film two. This was partly, at least, because it would virtually double the potential revenue from the picture without coming close to doubling the costs of something already shot.

Tarantino's motive was purer: aware of what a vast and garish canvas he had painted, he opined that 'the average moviegoer would overdose' if forced to sit through over 180 minutes of Tarantino trash aesthetic.

There's a brilliant shot where, having killed Vernita Green, the Bride kneels to touch the body, revealing to the audience that Vernita's daughter (who is about five) is standing in the doorway and has seen her murder her mother. The audience members' jaws hit the floor.

QUOTES:
O-Ren: 'You didn't think it was going to be that easy, did you?'
The Bride: 'You know, just for minute there, I kinda did.'
O-Ren: 'Silly rabbit.'

O-Ren: 'Silly Caucasian girl, likes to play with Samurai swords.'

Hattori: 'Revenge is not a path: it is a forest.'

The Bride: 'Those of you lucky enough to have your lives, take them with you! However, leave the limbs you've lost. They belong to me now.'

SOURCES TO SCREEN: The final script for *Kill Bill* reportedly took Tarantino a year, writing virtually every day, but its origins go back much further in the director's life. While shooting *Pulp Fiction* and indulging in an (entirely platonic) 'major artist love affair' with Uma Thurman, Tarantino came up with the notion of a pastiche revenge gangster flick that would begin, as the film as released does, with a black-and-white shot of a woman being taunted by an off-screen voice insisting that there is no sadism in its owner's actions, before its owner shoots her through the head. The title came a little later as the director found himself explaining to the actress that he'd like her to 'kill Bill'. Thurman, though, went one better than Hollywood's wunderkind by throwing back at him the question 'What if [in that shot] I'm in a wedding dress?' Thurman's suggestion was quickly incorporated into the rapidly expanding outline for the film.

Later that year, while exhibiting *Pulp Fiction* at the Stockholm Film Festival, Tarantino had a burst of *Kill Bill* inspiration and wrote thirty pages, calling Harvey Weinstein excitedly and reading sections to him in the middle of the night. Weinstein compared, somewhat bizarrely perhaps, the scenes to the work of the Polish filmmaker Krzysztof Kieslowski.

Time was not on the writer/director's side, however: he needed to return to America shortly to begin work on *Four Rooms*, and was booked in to act in Robert Rodriguez's production of Tarantino's pre-fame vampire/road movie script, *From Dusk Til Dawn*. Returning to America, Tarantino put *Kill Bill* aside, not wanting to work on another 'full-on, lurid exploitation movie experience' (as he called *Kill Bill* in the film's own press pack) immediately after the Rodriguez film, which was intended to be entirely that.

Years later, a chance meeting with Uma Thurman led Tarantino to dig out, finish and rework his screenplay, setting aside his completed script for *Glorious Bastards /Inglorious Bastards* (the title varies; it's a projected World War Two epic in *Dirty Dozen* (Robert Aldrich, 1967) style) in order to make the picture.

Kill Bill is a riot of influences. Here are a few of them.

Sonny Chiba's character, Hattori Hanzo, is meant to be a member of the family of characters he played on TV in *Hattori Hanzô: Kage no Gundan* (1980), in which he played members of a lineage of heroes down through history.

The tune whistled by Darryl Hannah's character as she sets off to murder the Bride is part of the score used to signify Hywel Bennett's murderous character in *Twisted Nerve* (Roy Boulting, 1968). The score, by the maestro Bernard Hermann, is actually sampled and used elsewhere in the picture.

Buck the nurse's line, 'My name is Buck, and I came here to fuck', is a quote from Robert Englund's character (Buck, naturally) in *Eaten Alive* (Tobe Hooper, 1977).

Buck also has similar sunglasses to those of Clarence in the Tarantino-scripted *True Romance* (Tony Scott, 1993) and at one point asks, 'Are we absolutely clear on Rule Number One?' – a line also spoken by Seth (George Clooney) in Tarantino's script for *From Dusk Til Dawn* (Robert Rodriguez, 1996). The whole film is like this.

CONTEMPORARY REACTION: At the time of writing, this film has been in cinemas less than a month. It took $22.7 million at the US box office in its opening weekend, a hugely impressive hit for half of a movie that cost – according to most estimates – between $55 million and $65 million. Reviewers (and indeed viewers) are and were split on the picture. The essential dividing line seems to be between those who felt the picture was beautifully made, but essentially lacked humanity, emotion and real merit, and those who felt its aesthetic qualities marked it out as a great film because of the inspired combination of those qualities and the film's almost awe-inspiring lack of human content. Your author is firmly in the latter camp, by the way.

'It's a slasher flick, a revenge comedy and a work of frivolous art that establishes Tarantino as the most indiscriminate film cannibal of them all,' wrote James Christopher in *The Times* of 9 October 2003. He went on to comment, 'One puff of cold reality and this house of cards will fold. But Tarantino never allows us a decent interval to draw that fatal breath. At least not when we are watching.' This argues, in essence, that the film was a conjuring trick, only a distraction while being performed.

A fellow Miramax filmmaker, Kevin Smith (director of *Clerks* (1991) and *Chasing Amy* (1997)), posted excitedly to his own message board on 30 September 2003, saying it '. . . made me so insanely happy . . . [It] delivers in ways few movies ever do . . . proof positive that Quentin's a mad genius . . . the kinda flick that makes me remember why I got into filmmaking in the first place.'

A O Scott in the *New York Times* of 10 October called the film 'above all an exercise in style' and a glimpse into a 'looking-glass universe that reflects nothing beyond . . . cinematic obsessions'. It was overall, oddly, 'endearing', with the Bride's massacre of 88 foot-soldiers 'as insouciant and elegant as a show-stopping musical number'.

Roger Ebert of the *Chicago Sun-Times* called Tarantino a 'virtuoso violinist racing through Flight of the Bumble Bee'. The movie, he pointed out, 'is all storytelling and no story' with that nonstory taking place in a 'parallel universe in which all of this makes sense in the same way that a superhero's origin story makes sense'.

In the *Village Voice* of 15 October 2003 Matthew Wilder stated the obvious but in clearer terms than any other reviewer: 'I had no idea that Tarantino possessed the skills to sustain . . . near-unbearable emotional intensity . . . in its meticulous craftsmanship and jacked-up cinephilic energy [*Kill Bill*] might be the most viscerally and emotionally overwhelming B movie ever made.'

TRIVIA: Vivica A Fox has mentioned when interviewed that when called upon to say the Bride's real name during shooting (the word is obscured by a sound effect in the finished picture) she said 'Beatrice'.

The Bride draws a rectangle (not a square, oddly) with her fingers when saying the word 'square' – Mia did much the same thing in **Pulp Fiction**, although there the action was accompanied by an on-screen line; here it isn't.

The members of the Deadly Viper Assassination Squad are all named for snakes: Sidewinder, Black Mamba, Cottonmouth, Copperhead and California Mountain King.

Conceptually, the squad is clearly a take on the notion of *Fox Force Five*, the TV show that Mia has shot a pilot for in *Pulp Fiction*.

The sword Hattori makes for the Bride is the same one that Bruce Willis uses to rescue Marsellus Wallace from the Gimp in *Pulp Fiction*.

If you're really paying attention, you can glimpse Samuel L Jackson playing the organ in the wedding scene flashbacks.

SEX/MONEY/DEATH: *Kill Bill* is almost exactly like, and also nothing whatsoever like, Tarantino's earlier directorial efforts. Tarantino is known for two things, principally: the intrusion of reality on genre clichés and his smart, witty dialogue. *Kill Bill* features neither of these. The dialogue is functional, to the point and occasionally, languidly, randomly prosaic. While the progression of the plot is defiantly nonlinear, another Tarantino trademark, there are no attempts to confuse or befuddle the audience as to chronology (compare Travolta's character's death in **Pulp Fiction**), and everything is clearly and slowly explained. His beloved Red Apple cigarettes may turn up (Red Apple cigarettes are the fictional brand Tarantino invented for *Reservoir Dogs*. They've featured in all his films) but at no point does a realistic approach ever intrude. This is Quentin In Wonderland.

You may question the inclusion of the genre-busting *Kill Bill* as the final film in this collection. Well, the titular villain is a crime lord, the heroine is a former mob enforcer who tried to get out of her lifestyle (a common enough trope of the gangster movie) and over a third of the picture details the activities of a group of yakuza. The main plot strand isn't a million miles away from *Get Carter*, *The Limey* or even the central thrust of *Once Upon a Time in America*. All have their disassociated loner, broken off from his or her life of crime, searching for redemption in revenge and truth in action.

Kill Bill is a fitting bookend to the evolution of the gangster picture as we've been looking at it, and it does contain most of the fascinations of the genre within it albeit in self-consciously distorted forms. But it also has nothing to say about them. It has, essentially, nothing to say about crime (organised or otherwise), no comment to make on the morality of violence, no thoughts to share on the effects of either of these things on either their perpetrators or their perpetrators' victims. It doesn't bother to question whether crime is a social phenomenon or a result of aberrant psychology. It doesn't seek to examine a renegade, yet brilliant, mind or to document an aspect of society. It doesn't try to excuse a real criminal's life or portray a fictional man's slow corruption.

If *Gangs of New York* seemed to mark a new beginning for the gangster movie by creating a common yesterday, *Kill Bill* doesn't so much push forward into the future as dance around pulling silly faces and then inexplicably throw fruit pies at the audience while wearing an oddly shaped hat. It looks *fabulous*, it moves like a dream and it's utterly engrossing, engaging and oddly humane, but it doesn't *do* anything.

Entirely focused on its visually astonishing presentation of a simplistic plot, acted with *conviction* but with little embellishment of the kind audiences had become used to from Tarantino's casts, *Kill Bill* doesn't function in the real world at all. It just takes pieces of it and submerges them into itself. It's 'not about real life', he said during the movie's prerelease and referred to it as a 'movie-movie' – something that exists only in relation to other cinematic pieces. *Kill Bill* is all the secret, twisted pleasures of the gangster film (the ones that the Hays Code so hated) run wild. It's the violence, the freedom, the almost tangible glamour, the lack of responsibility, the deluded self-respecting and the sheer *power rush* of it rendered as pure, torrid intoxication. It's wrong, but it's right; it's bad but it's good. Somewhere, Andy Warhol is smiling. Conceptually speaking only, of course.

THE VERDICT: An epochal, masterful piece of filmmaking, a sort of Noah's Ark of clichés, rendered with an astonishing beauty. Only time – and, admittedly, the second half – will tell if *Kill Bill* really is the first truly great American movie of the twenty-first century. What is perhaps more important right here and right now, however, is that its combination of visual majesty, colossal violence, deliberate moral vacuity and that final moment of unexpected suspended enigma seem, to me at least, to be the perfect place to end this particular history.

Index of quotations

Authors of newspaper reviews are named when known. Often, especially when dealing with pre-World War Two writing, pieces are uncredited. Known pseudonyms, such as those used in *Variety* have been ignored.

Scarface – The Shame of the Nation

43 'powerful . . .' *Scarface*, *Variety*, 24 May 1932.

43 'strong for . . . children' *Scarface*, *Variety*, 24 May 1932.

43 'more blood . . .' *Scarface*, *Variety*, 24 May 1932.

43 'blaming of the . . .' *Scarface*, *Variety*, 24 May 1932

Angels With Dirty Faces

57 'A typical Dead End . . .' *Angels With Dirty Faces*, *Variety*, 26 October 1938.

57 'no bonfire' *Angels With Dirty Faces*, *Variety*, 26 October 1938.

57 'completely implausible . . . hokey' *Angels With Dirty Faces*, *Variety*, 26 October 1938.

57 'human story . . . savage melodrama' Frank S Nugent, *Angels With Dirty Faces*, *New York Times*, 28 November 1938.

58 'realistic point . . .' Frank S Nugent, *Angels With Dirty Faces*, *New York Times*, 28 November 1938.

58 'familiarity of . . . and character' Frank S Nugent, *Angels With Dirty Faces*, *New York Times*, 28 November 1938.

58 'picturesque . . . his best' Frank S Nugent, *Angels With Dirty Faces*, *New York Times*, 28 November 1938.

The Roaring Twenties

68 'dynamite' *The Roaring Twenties*, *Variety*, 11 November 1939.

68 'plenty of . . . overlong' *The Roaring Twenties*, *Variety*, 11 November 1939.

68 'egregiously sentimental' Bosley Crowther, *The Roaring Twenties*, *New York Times*, 11 November 1939.

68 'annoying . . . false dignity' Bosley Crowther, *The Roaring Twenties*, *New York Times*, 11 November 1939.

68   'epic handling' Bosley Crowther, *The Roaring Twenties, New York Times*, 11 November 1939.

68   'already the most . . .' Bosley Crowther, *The Roaring Twenties, New York Times*, 11 November 1939.

White Heat

85   'too long . . . guy's kisser' *White Heat, Variety*, 31 August 1949.

85   'red hot . . .' *White Heat, Variety*, 31 August 1949.

85   'thermal intensity . . .' Bosley Crowther, *White Heat, New York Times*, 3 September 1949.

85   'conviction, confidence . . .' Bosley Crowther, *White Heat, New York Times*, 3 September 1949.

85   'cruelly vicious' Bosley Crowther, *White Heat, New York Times*, 3 September 1949.

85   'one of the most . . .' Bosley Crowther, *White Heat, New York Times*, 3 September 1949.

85   'technical perfection . . . style' Bosley Crowther, *White Heat, New York Times*, 3 September 1949.

85   'not entirely . . .' Bosley Crowther, *White Heat, New York Times*, 3 September 1949.

The Blue Lamp

91   'solid . . . lavish . . . well knit' *The Blue Lamp, Variety*, 9 January 1951.

91   'action, drama . . .' *The Blue Lamp, Variety*, 9 January 1951.

91   'spectacular . . .' *The Blue Lamp, Variety*, 9 January 1951.

91   'a new generation . . .' *The Blue Lamp, Variety*, 9 January 1951.

92   'warm, affectionate . . .' Bosley Crowther, *The Blue Lamp, New York Times*, 9 January 1951.

92   'assumes the characteristics . . .' Bosley Crowther, *The Blue Lamp, New York Times*, 9 January 1951.

92   'benign . . . stunningly naturalistic . . .' Bosley Crowther, *The Blue Lamp, New York Times*, 9 January 1951.

92   'racing ... observer' Bosley Crowther, *The Blue Lamp*, *New York Times*, 9 January 1951.

92   'unhealthy and malevolent' Bosley Crowther, *The Blue Lamp*, *New York Times*, 9 January 1951.

Robin and the 7 Hoods

99   'solid money' *Robin and the 7 Hoods*, *Variety*, 6 August 1964.

100   'stacked up ...' *Robin and the 7 Hoods*, *Variety*, 6 August 1964.

100   'a let down ...' *Robin and the 7 Hoods*, *Variety*, 6 August 1964.

100   'a pure gem ... look at' *Robin and the 7 Hoods*, *Variety*, 6 August 1964.

100   'minor musical ... cunning title' Bosley Crowther, *Robin and the 7 Hoods*, *New York Times*, 6 August 1964.

100   'an artless ... mildly amusing ... arrogance' Bosley Crowther, *Robin and the 7 Hoods*, *New York Times*, 6 August 1964.

Get Carter

111   'excellent drama ...' *Get Carter*, *Variety*, 20 January 1971.

111   'genuinely artistic ... was handled' *Get Carter*, *Variety*, 20 January 1971.

111   'excellent ... spare score ... artistry' *Get Carter*, *Variety*, 20 January 1971.

111   'logical ... characters' *Get Carter*, *Variety*, 20 January 1971.

111   'persistently ...' Vincent Canby, *Get Carter*, *New York Times*, 4 March 1971.

111   'the facts of ... complex' Vincent Canby, *Get Carter*, *New York Times*, 4 March 1971.

111   'more like ...' Vincent Canby, *Get Carter*, *New York Times*, 4 March 1971.

112   'a kind of ... excitement' Roger Greenspan, 'Hit Man', *New York Times*, 21 December 1972.

The Godfather

128 'flashes of . . . overlong' *The Godfather*, *Variety*, 7 February 1972.

128 'never so placid . . . screen drama' *The Godfather*, *Variety*, 7 February 1972.

128 'one great . . . half the job' *The Godfather*, *Variety*, 7 February 1972.

128 'most moving . . .' Vincent Canby, *The Godfather*, *New York Times*, 16 March 1972.

128 'truly sorrowful . . . truly exciting' Vincent Canby, *The Godfather*, *New York Times*, 16 March 1972.

128 'more drive . . .' Vincent Canby, *The Godfather*, *New York Times*, 16 March 1972.

128 'magnificent . . . as his Father' Vincent Canby, *The Godfather*, *New York Times*, 16 March 1972.

128 'false piety' Vincent Canby, *The Godfather*, *New York Times*, 16 March 1972.

128 'disturbing . . . the emotions' Vincent Canby, *The Godfather*, *New York Times*, 16 March 1972.

128 'excellent, epochal . . . superbly directed' *The Godfather – Part II*, *Variety*, 11 December 1974.

129 'callous, selfish . . .' *The Godfather – Part II*, *Variety*, 11 December 1974.

129 'Pacino is . . .' *The Godfather – Part III*, *Variety*, 17 December 1990.

129 'a dramatic . . .' *The Godfather – Part III*, *Variety*, 17 December 1990.

129 'very close . . .' *The Godfather – Part III*, *Variety*, 17 December 1990.

129 'full equal . . . physical beauty' *The Godfather – Part III*, *Variety*, 17 December 1990.

Black Caesar

139 'fits patly . . . photography' *Black Caesar*, *Variety*, 7 February 1973.

139 'imposing, tough . . . bad guys' A H Weiler, *Black Caesar*, *New York Times*, 8 February 1973.

139 'contrivances that . . .' A H Weiler, *Black Caesar, New York Times*, 8 February 1973.

The Long Good Friday
148 'swift, sharp . . . 30s Chicago style . . . flair' Janet Maslin, *The Long Good Friday, New York Times*, 2 April 1982.
148 'no shortage . . . sounds like' Janet Maslin, *The Long Good Friday, New York Times*, 2 April 1982.
148 'satisfactory . . . topical underpinnings . . . surprise' Vincent Canby, *The Long Good Friday, New York Times,* 11 April 1982.
148 'too intelligent . . .' Vincent Canby, *The Long Good Friday, New York Times,* 11 April 1982.

Once Upon A Time In America
159 'made some . . . lazily hallucinatory' Vincent Canby, *Once Upon A Time In America, New York Times*, 1 June 1984.
159 'seems endless . . . unfathomable' Vincent Canby, *Once Upon A Time In America, New York Times*, 1 June 1984.
159 'Surprisingly deficient . . . potent enough' *Once Upon A Time In America, Variety*, 23 May 1984.
159 'brutal . . . unsympathetic . . . slow film . . . boring' *Once Upon A Time In America, Variety*, 23 May 1984.

GoodFellas
170 'Most films . . .' Roger Ebert, *GoodFellas, Chicago Sun-Times,* 9 February 1990.
170 'No finer film . . .' Roger Ebert, *GoodFellas, Chicago Sun-Times,* 9 February 1990.

Pulp Fiction
185 'suspect . . . on the screen' Janet Maslin, *Pulp Fiction, New York Times,* 23 September 1994.
185 'You don't . . .' Janet Maslin, *Pulp Fiction, New York Times,* 23 September 1994.

185 'stunning vision . . . surprisingly tender' Janet Maslin, *Pulp Fiction, New York Times,* 23 September 1994.

Casino
196 'Scorsese tries . . .' Peter Travers, *Casino, Rolling Stone,* 14 December 1995.
196 'Shakespearean tragedy . . . dream back' Peter Travers, *Casino, Rolling Stone,* 14 December 1995.
196 'makes us feel . . . and pacing' Roger Ebert, *Casino, Chicago Sun-Times,* 22 November 1995.
196 'wealth of . . . city just right' Roger Ebert, *Casino, Chicago Sun-Times,* 22 November 1995.
196 'shockingly impoverished . . .' Janet Maslin, *Casino, New York Times,* 22 November 1995.
196 'staunchly journalistic . . . America's playground' Janet Maslin, *Casino, New York Times,* 22 November 1995.
196 'overloads [our] . . .' Janet Maslin, *Casino, New York Times,* 22 November 1995.

The Limey
209 'walking Proustian . . . distracting' Janet Maslin, *The Limey, New York Times,* 8 October 1999.
209 'every possible . . . every possible perspective . . . distant tone' Janet Maslin, *The Limey, New York Times,* 8 October 1999.

Sexy Beast
217 'the movie . . .' A O Scott, *Sexy Beast, New York Times,* 13 June 2001.
217 'a sociopath . . .' A O Scott, *Sexy Beast, New York Times,* 13 June 2001.
217 'stylish, eye-popping . . . Pinter play' A O Scott, *Sexy Beast, New York Times,* 13 June 2001.
218 'not only sensation . . .' A O Scott, *Sexy Beast, New York Times,* 13 June 2001.
218 'Who would . . .' Roger Ebert, *Sexy Beast, Chicago Sun-Times,* 22 June 2001.

218 'These are hard . . .' Roger Ebert, *Sexy Beast*, *Chicago Sun-Times*, 22 June 2001.

218 'trafficking in . . . flashy brilliance . . . dynamite' Peter Travers, *Sexy Beast*, *Rolling Stone*, 15 June 2001.

Gangster No 1

226 'a man who . . .' Roger Ebert, *Gangster No. 1*, *Chicago Sun-Times*, 19 July 2003.

226 'one of the most . . .' Roger Ebert, *Gangster No. 1*, *Chicago Sun-Times*, 19 July 2003.

226 'too pat to be . . .' Roger Ebert, *Gangster No. 1*, *Chicago Sun-Times*, 19 July 2003.

226 'surprisingly discreet . . .' Mark Kermode, *Gangster No. 1*, *Sight and Sound*, July 2000.

226 'It's a handsomely . . .' Mark Kermode, *Gangster No. 1*, *Sight and Sound*, July 2000.

226 'crisp, tart . . . atmosphere' Elvis Mitchell, *Gangster No. 1*, *New York Times*, 19 July 2003.

226 'dizzying unspoken . . . comedy' Elvis Mitchell, *Gangster No. 1*, *New York Times*, 19 July 2003.

226 'a potently . . . depraved wit' Peter Travers, *Gangster No. 1*, *Rolling Stone*, 4 July 2000.

228 'this cartoony laddish . . . just nonsense' Paul McGuigan, speaking on the *Gangster No. 1* DVD commentary track.

Brother

236 'yakuza . . . minimalism' Elvis Mitchell, *Brother*, *New York Times*, 27 September 2000.

236 'too heavily . . . carved in stone' Elvis Mitchell, *Brother*, *New York Times*, 27 September 2000.

236 'doom-laden . . . Warner Bros gangsters' Roger Ebert, *Brother*, *Chicago Sun-Times*, 27 September 2000.

236 'typical Kitano . . . his best . . . casual, perfunctory . . . gunfire' Roger Ebert, *Brother*, *Chicago Sun-Times*, 27 September 2000.

236 'a video game . . .' Roger Ebert, *Brother*, *Chicago Sun-Times*, 27 September 2000.

Gangs of New York

248 'the postcards . . .' Roger Ebert, *Gangs of New York*, *Chicago Sun-Times*, 20 December 2002.

248 'a violent, blood-soaked . . . Dickensian grotesquerie' Roger Ebert, *Gangs of New York*, *Chicago Sun-Times*, 20 December 2002.

248 'interiorised . . . want to' Roger Ebert, *Gangs of New York*, *Chicago Sun-Times*, 20 December 2002.

248 'I'm not sure . . .' Roger Ebert, *Gangs of New York*, *Chicago Sun-Times*, 20 December 2002.

248 'brutal, flawed . . . a near-great movie . . . uncompromised' A O Scott, *Gangs of New York*, *New York Times*, 20 December 2002.

248 'People who care . . .' A O Scott, *Gangs of New York*, *New York Times*, 20 December 2002.

Kill Bill – Volume 1

259 'It's a slasher . . .' James Christopher, *Kill Bill*, *The Times*, 9 October 2003.

259 'One puff of . . .' James Christopher, *Kill Bill*, *The Times*, 9 October 2003.

259 'made me so insanely . . .' posted by Kevin Smith on www.viewaskew.com.

260 'above all an . . . cinematic obsessions' A O Scott, *Kill Bill*, *New York Times*, 10 October 2003.

260 'endearing . . . musical number' A O Scott, *Kill Bill*, *New York Times*, 10 October 2003.

260 'virtuoso violinist . . . no story' Roger Ebert, *Kill Bill*, *Chicago Sun-Times*, 10 October 2003.

260 'parallel universe . . .' Roger Ebert, *Kill Bill*, *Chicago Sun-Times*, 10 October 2003.

260 'I had no idea . . .' Matthew Wilder, *Kill Bill*, *Village Voice*, 15 October 2003.

Selected Bibliography

For the purposes of this book the year of release is assumed to be the year of a motion picture's manufacture. On-screen accreditation of cast and crew is, however, taken directly from on-screen captions from the relevant films. Acknowledgement is also given to *www.the-numbers.com*, as well as *www.shinyshelf.com* and *www.filmsite.org*. Acknowledgement is made to the collections of the British Library, the *New York Times* online archive, the *Chicago Sun-Times*'s only archive, the British Film Institute Library and the University of London Libraries and the private collection of Jason T Douglas.

Note: Reviews and articles not included here are singled out with date of publication and periodical in the main body of the text itself and listed in the **Index of Quotations**.

Books

Amis, Martin (2002), *Koba The Dread: Laughter and the Twenty Million* (London: Hodder).

Amis, Martin (2003), *Yellow Dog* (London: Hodder).

Biskind, Peter (1998), *Easy Riders, Raging Bulls* (London: Bloomsbury).

Black, Gregory D (1994), *Hollywood Censored: Morality Codes, Catholics and the Movies* (Cambridge: Cambridge University Press).

Cornell, Paul, with Martin Day and Keith Topping (1996), *The Guinness Book of Classic British Television* (2nd edn) (Bath: Guinness World Records Ltd).

Halliwell, Leslie, and John Walker (eds) (2003), *Halliwell's Film & Video Guide* (London: HarperCollins).

Halliwell, Leslie, and John Walker (eds) (2003), *Halliwell's Who's Who in the Movies?* (London: HarperCollins).

Katz, Ephraim (ed.) (1994), *The Film Encyclopaedia* (London: HarperCollins).

Langman, Larry, and David Finn (1995), *A Guide to American Crime Films of the Thirties* (Westport, Connecticut: Greenwood Press).

Lewis, Norman (1964), *The Honoured Society: The Sicilian Mafia Observed* (London: Collins).

Maltin, Leonard (2003), *Leonard Maltin's Movie Encyclopaedia* (New York, NY: Plume).

Puzo, Mario (1969), *The Godfather* (London: William Heinemann).

Roddick, Nick (1983), *A New Deal in Entertainment: Warner Brothers in the 1930s* (London: BFI Publishing).

Rosow, Eugene (1978), *Born to Lose: The Gangster Film in America* (Oxford: Oxford University Press).

Vincent, Andrew (1994), *Modern Political Ideologies* (2nd edn) (Oxford: Blackwell's).

Yaquinto, Marilyn (1998), *Pump 'Em Full of Lead: A Look at Gangsters on Film* (New York, NY: Twayne Publishers).

Articles

Skinner, Richard Dana, 'Movies and Morals', *Commonweal*, 27 July 1934, p. 329.

Brown, Lawrence, 'What to do till the censor comes', *New Republic*, 31 October 1934, p. 334.

'Mr. Robinson Steps Up and Out – More Music – Life in Al-Yemen', *New Yorker*, 17 January 1931, pp. 65–7.

Rorty, James, 'It ain't no sin', *Nation*, 1 August 1934, pp. 121–3.

Walker, Helen Louise, 'Hunting for a Hero', *Motion Picture Magazine*, July 1931.

Picture Credits

The following pictures are from the Ronald Grant Archive:
Page 1 (top left, top right and bottom right) Warner Bros;
Page 1 (bottom left) Universal Pictures; Page 2 (bottom)
Warner Bros; Page 3 (bottom) Warner Bros; Page 4 (top and
middle) Paramount Pictures Corp; Page 4 (bottom)
HandMade Films; Page 6 (top and bottom) Warner Bros;
Page 7 (top) A Band Apart/Miramax; Page 7 (bottom)
Universal Pictures; Page 8 (middle and bottom) FilmFour

The following pictures are from the Kobal Collection:
Page 2 (top left and top right) Warner Bros/First
National/The Kobal Collection; Page 3 (top) Warner
Bros/The Kobal Collection; Page 5 Ladd Company/Warner
Bros/The Kobal Collection; Page 8 (top) Artisan Pics/The
Kobal Collection/Bob Marshak

Index